Go Crazy

A Fun Projects-based Approach to Golang Programming

Nicolas Modrzyk

Contributed by David Li, Jun Akiyama and Tony Broyez

Apress®

Go Crazy: A Fun Projects-based Approach to Golang Programming

Nicolas Modrzyk
tokyo-to suginami-ku, Japan

ISBN-13 (pbk): 978-1-4842-9665-3
ISBN-13 (electronic): 978-1-4842-9666-0
https://doi.org/10.1007/978-1-4842-9666-0

Managing Director, Apress Media LLC: Welmoed Spahr
Acquisitions Editor: Melissa Duffy
Development Editor: Jim Markham
Coordinating Editor: Gryffin Winkler
Copy Editor: Kezia Endsley

Cover image designed by Scott Webb on unsplash (https://unsplash.com/)

Distributed to the book trade worldwide by Springer Science+Business Media LLC, 1 New York Plaza, Suite 4600, New York, NY 10004. Phone 1-800-SPRINGER, fax (201) 348-4505, e-mail orders-ny@springer-sbm.com, or visit www.springeronline.com. Apress Media, LLC is a California LLC and the sole member (owner) is Springer Science + Business Media Finance Inc (SSBM Finance Inc). SSBM Finance Inc is a **Delaware** corporation.

For information on translations, please e-mail booktranslations@springernature.com; for reprint, paperback, or audio rights, please e-mail bookpermissions@springernature.com.

Apress titles may be purchased in bulk for academic, corporate, or promotional use. eBook versions and licenses are also available for most titles. For more information, reference our Print and eBook Bulk Sales web page at http://www.apress.com/bulk-sales.

Any source code or other supplementary material referenced by the author in this book is available to readers on GitHub. For more detailed information, please visit https://www.apress.com/gp/services/source-code.

Paper in this product is recyclable.

I dedicate this book to planet Earth.

Table of Contents

About the Author

Nicolas Modrzyk acts as the CTO of Karabiner Software, a successful consulting company located in the never-asleep Tokyo, with its mix of ancestral culture and eco-friendly, future-oriented dynamic.

He is an active contributor to the open-source community in various domains, including imaging, ML, AI, and cloud computing. As an engineer and a leader, Nico has been involved in designing large-scale applications, managing mammoth-sized clusters of servers, sometimes using handwritten software, and enabling world-class leaders by pushing international boundaries.

Nico ardently focuses on making life simple. (And we all know how difficult that is!)

He loves pushing people to challenge themselves and go beyond their comfort zones.

To learn other cultures and explore different world views, he has been living around the planet in various countries, including France, Ireland, Japan, China, Korea, India, and the United States. You can talk to Nico in French, English, and Japanese, and you can get along with him in Spanish and Chinese.

Nico is the author of a few programming books, available on Amazon. He recently picked up the saxophone to honor his grandfather and his uncle, in the hope to match their skill with a brass instrument.

He will be ready for a jazzy jam session whenever you are.

About the Technical Reviewer

David Li is the executive director of Shenzhen Open Innovation Lab, which facilitates the collaboration between global smart hardware entrepreneurs and the Shenzhen Open Innovation ecosystem. Before SZOIL, he co-founded XinCheJian, the first hackerspace in China to promote the hacker/maker culture and open-source hardware. He co-founded Hacked Matter, a research hub on the maker movement and open innovation. He also co-founded Maker Collier, an AI company focusing on motion and sports recognition and analysis.

Acknowledgments

All the involved authors—Jun, Tony, David—as well as the technical reviewers, Mathieu and David, of this book have gone the extra mile to match the deadlines and bring the writing and code samples to a top-class level.

My two strong daughters, Mei and Manon—you always keep me focused and in line with my goals.

Psy Mom, French Chef Dad, Little Bro, Artful Sis—I thank you for your love every day, your support, and all the ideas we share together.

My partner at Karabiner, Chris Mitchell—we've been working together for ten years, and I think we both made tremendous efforts to make the planet a better place. Also, the whole Karabiner people, at work now or busy making babies, we make a pretty impressive world team.

Abe-san—who did not participate directly in the making of this book, but we wrote our first computer book together, and without a first one, and without his trust, I would not be here to even talk about it.

Kanaru-san—without your Iranian lifestyle and your life changing vision, I would probably be a monk.

Marshall—without your world encompassing vision, I could have been focusing on the bigger picture.

Ogier—without your summertime raclette and life-long friendship, I would probably have been 5 kilos skinnier.

Jumpei—without your strong focus on music, I could not have played in all those beautiful Tokyo live stages. And welcome Rei-chan!

Gryffin and Melissa—I could not have survived this without your hard work and trust.

And of course, Marcel le chat—my open-source project on imaging would not be the same without your feline cuteness.

Introduction

On a sunny drive on the busy roads of Tokyo, over the rainbow bridge and facing the ocean, my daughter Mei and I are having one of these philosophical talks.

Among the slur of questions she had ready for me, like "what is work for?," she was telling me about her need to have someone monitor her and give her deadlines. While at the time of this writing, she's barely 20 and hasn't started a full-blown professional career yet, she is right in the sense that the need to have deadlines and a purpose is at the core of many adults' professional lives.

At the very root of a school system, you are being told what to complete, and by what date. You do not have input regarding the what or the when. A regular office worker is told to finish their tasks by the fifth of next month, for example, and some authors are told to finish three chapters by the end of the month.

That de facto need of what to do and by when happens very early in your career.

I am in favor of looking at things from a different angle. You should set your own deadlines, and you should be in control of those deadlines. You have a goal, you set milestones to achieve that goal, and you work on walking that path to that goal.

You want to live your own life and reach your own goals, not someone else's.

Although I am critical about many of his actions, Elon Musk does not have someone telling him when to land a rocket on Mars. He has his own schedule. He owns his schedule. He owns his life.

This is a book on how to own your life again. More precisely, how Go, the programming language, can help you get your time back, manage it along your dreams, and own your life again.

I discovered the Go programming language a few years back. At that time, to be honest, I was more of a Clojure-loving propaganda evangelist. Anything I developed or touched had to be in Clojure. A deployment script, a web app, a dynamically generated API around some custom datasets, image and video processing, or applying the latest Computer Vision algorithm in real time—it did not matter. It greatly helped my career. I would go even further and say, my life.

How can a programming language help make your life better, you might ask? A programming language is at first a language, and as such its first goal is to communicate. We tend to think that a programming language's only goal is to deal with a computer, but we deal with computers because we want to communicate something to other people.

Take a simple email, for example. You use a computer to write an email because it takes less time to reach its recipient, but the goal of an email is still to convey a message to another person.

Now let's say you have a lot to communicate, or you want to communicate something to many people, but with that simple personal touch that makes all the difference between your email being ignored and it being read and acted upon.

You don't have much time. In life in general, but also to realize a task. You can use a computer to help you with that task and save time.

Nowadays one of the best programming languages to put in your toolbox is GoLang. It includes all the important concepts of Clojure, and that I love in a programming language, but it's also in the top ten of the TIOBE index, meaning you can find a few more programmers to help you do your job.

Don't get me wrong, there are other great languages, but there are many things that GoLang gets absolutely right:

- It is simple

- It is concise

- The code is short

- Concurrency is not an afterthought

- It can be compiled and run on a large variety of operating systems and architectures

- It's easy to reuse bits of code from one project to the other

- Errors are simple to handle

- It is cloud-ready

- It is very fast (this is probably my favorite)

Go, as a programming language, has a clear and strong purpose: Implement architecture based on microservices in the most convenient way possible.

This programming book will take you on the path to *Ikigai*, finding joy in life through purpose.

CHAPTER 1

Go to the Basics

A part of me is always waiting for you...

The goal of this first chapter is to write a ChatGPT client in Go. You've probably heard about ChatGPT. It is an AI-trained chatbot that generates text according to questions you ask it.

To get to this point, you will run basic Go programs and get used to the language. Then you will put things together into a ChatGPT client.

But you first need to set up your code editor.

© Nicolas Modrzyk 2023
N. Modrzyk, *Go Crazy*, https://doi.org/10.1007/978-1-4842-9666-0_1

First Steps

As with any new skill, you need a basic setup where you feel comfortable practicing and trying new things. While Go, the language, makes writing code easier, GoLand, the editor, makes writing Go easier.

To kick-start this chapter, you learn how to use GoLand as your editor for writing Go.

Run and Debug Your First Go Program

Running your first Go program using JetBrains GoLand should take approximately ten minutes or less.

In the context of this book, the goal is to go deep into the language as quickly as possible and become proficient in Go in a matter of hours. Within that context, it's best if you use JetBrains's Go editor called GoLand. Of course, you can use any editor you choose, but you will find it easier to follow along if you use GoLand.

You can download GoLand for individual use from the following URL:

`www.jetbrains.com/go/download/`

You will have 30 days of use for free, which should be enough to finish reading and applying the lessons in this book—and to get you excited for more coding.

GoLand handles all the core Go language installers, paths, and dependencies for you.

Once you start the editor, click New Project. You'll see the screen in Figure 1-1.

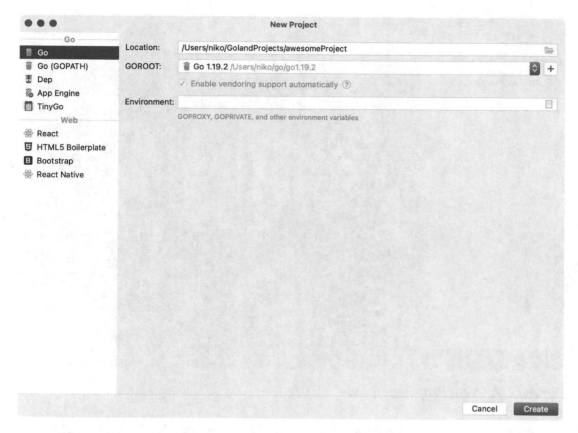

Figure 1-1. *Creating a new project in GoLand*

Once you have created a new project, a blank project window will be available.

The left side of the window shows your project file, and the right side shows your code editor (which, at this stage, is empty). See Figure 1-2.

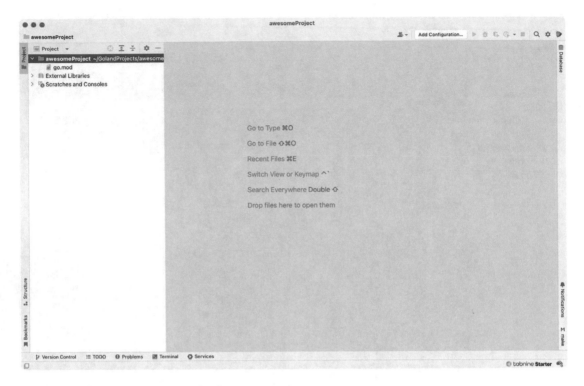

Figure 1-2. *New Project window*

You can right-click in the Project Files tab and create a new Go file, as shown in Figure 1-3.

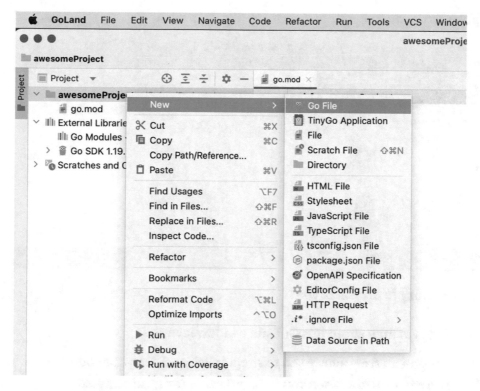

Figure 1-3. *Creating a new Go file*

Give your new file a name (see Figure 1-4).

Figure 1-4. *The new Go file*

A potential layout for your project looks like Figure 1-5.

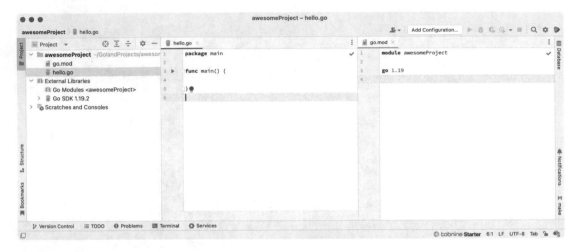

Figure 1-5. *Simple project layout*

A few things to note about this GoLand window layout:

1. The green arrow allows you to simply click and run your code. You also get an arrow when you have test cases. You will learn about that in a few pages.

2. Try copying and pasting this line into the `main()` function:

   ```
   fmt.Printf("Go version: %s\n", runtime.Version())
   ```

3. GoLand will auto-complete the code and do the necessary namespace imports for you (see Figure 1-6).

4. The list of functions in the current file is shown in the Structure tab.

5. You can click most of your code and navigate to the corresponding section in the Go packages, whether it's part of the core language or an external library.

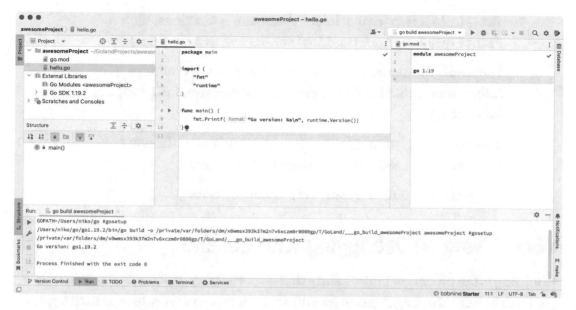

Figure 1-6. *Displaying the current Go version in a simple Go program*

Your first code snippet will do just that—display the Go version of your current installation. See Listing 1-1.

Listing 1-1. Displaying the Go Version

```go
package main

import (
    "fmt"
    "runtime"
)

func main() {
    fmt.Printf("Go version: %s\n", runtime.Version())
}
```

A few explanations in this first code listing:

1. To be executable, the package name should be main.

2. You cannot have two package definitions in the same folder (even in different files).

3. fmt is the namespace that imports formatting functions, such as Printf (print to screen) and Sprintf (format without printing).

4. runtime is the namespace containing functions that retrieve information about the Go runtime, such as version, CPU, memory, and tracing.

5. The one and only function is called main, and that is the entry function. It is called first when running the program.

6. Once the main function exits, the program exits too.

A Short Note on Debugging with GoLand

Debugging is the process of finding and fixing errors or bugs in software or computer systems. The goal of debugging is to identify the root cause of an issue and then apply a solution to fix it. Debugging can be done manually, using tools like print statements and logging, or with the help of specialized software development tools, like debuggers and integrated development environments.

GoLand makes debugging a program a breeze. Let's say you want to see the value of the version while the program is running, before printing it.

In GoLand, you can click in the gutter right next the line number (as in Figure 1-7). If you then start the execution in debug mode by clicking the debugging button, the execution will stop at the requested place (the breakpoint).

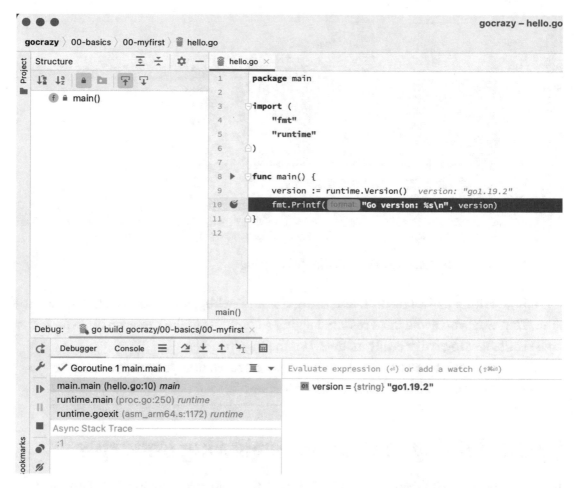

Figure 1-7. *Execution stops at the breakpoint in debugging mode*

You can also ask the execution to *not* suspend when reaching a specific breakpoint (see Figure 1-8) and just log the variables that are accessible to the debugger.

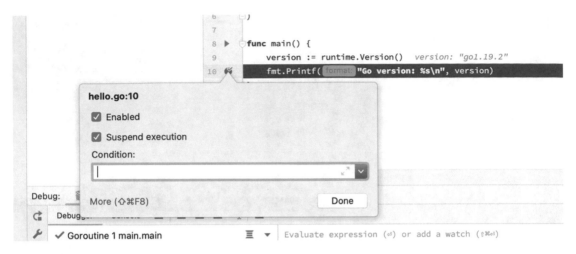

Figure 1-8. *Breakpoint settings while debugging*

While writing code, I recommend using GoLand debugging mode most, if not all, the time. That way, you avoid unnecessary logging statements in the program and can focus on the business logic that really matters, not the logging mess.

You now know the basics to run/debug a program, so next you review basic Go concepts that you will use to write a ChatGPT client.

Before Talking to OpenAI: Reviewing Concepts

To get a good grasp on using Go in a useful situation, you are going to write a program straight from this first chapter. The goal: write a Go program that will ask simple questions to ChatGPT and display its AI-looking answers.

Since this is the first chapter, I quickly review the underlying simple Go concepts needed to write the Go code that will talk to ChatGPT.

Get the setup ready again (see Figures 1-9 and 1-10) so you can start coding.

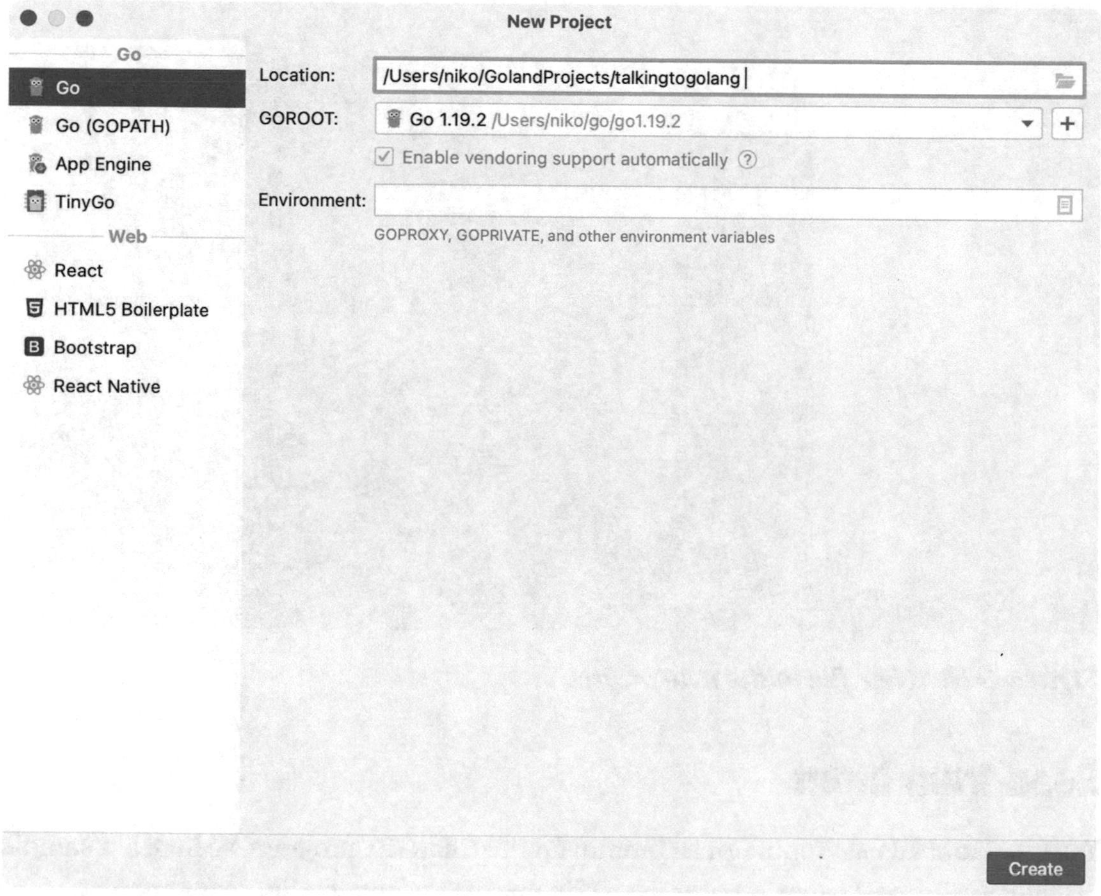

Figure 1-9. *New project again*

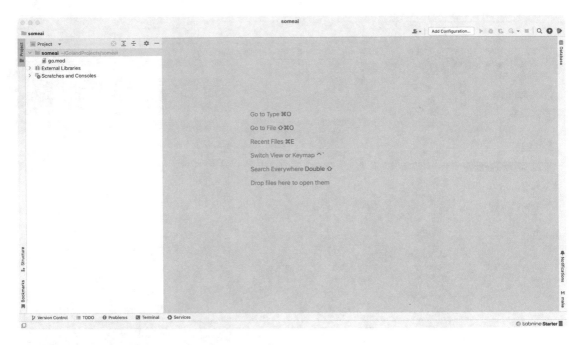

Figure 1-10. *New file in the new project*

Read from Input

You need to read user input from a prompt for the ChatGPT program, so here is a sample of what is to come. Listing 1-2 uses the bufio package to create a NewReader object.

Listing 1-2. Reading from Standard Input

```
package main

import (
    "bufio"
    "fmt"
    "log"
    "os"
)

func main() {
    for true {
        fmt.Print("What is your name ? > ")
        reader := bufio.NewReader(os.Stdin)
```

```
        line, err := reader.ReadString('\n')
        if err != nil {
            log.Fatal(err)
        }
        fmt.Printf("hello %s\n", line)
    }
}
```

The for loop uses true as the condition of the loop continuity check. I put it there to make it obvious what the condition is, but it can be removed altogether.

Reading from a File

Note that this is almost like reading from a file. In Listing 1-3, you open a file named hello.txt in read mode and output all its contents, line by line.

Listing 1-3. Reading from a File

```
package main

import (
    "bufio"
    "fmt"
    "os"
)

func main() {
    file, _ := os.OpenFile("hello.txt", os.O_RDONLY, 0666)
    defer file.Close()
    reader := bufio.NewReader(file)
    for {
        line, err := reader.ReadString('\n')
        fmt.Printf("> %s", line)
        if err != nil {
            return
        }
    }
}
```

Custom Data: Go Structs

GoLang (the Go programming language) uses data structures, conveniently named *structs,* to handle custom data objects. Basically, where you would use generic maps in other languages, Go helps you enforce type checks when handling custom data. This includes reading data from HTTP forms, database persistence, files, or even sockets.

Listing 1-4 defines a `Message` struct, with one string field named `Hello`, and simply prints the struct object itself as a string using `fmt.Printf`.

Listing 1-4. Defining and Printing Custom Data with Structs

```
package main

import (
    "fmt"
)

type Message struct {
    Hello string
}

func main() {
    h := Message{Hello: "world"}
    fmt.Printf("%s\n", h)
}
```

Running this program produces this simple output:

```
; {  world}
```

The output could be slightly more useful if you could print out the fields as well as the actual data. There are two ways to do this.

One way is to use +v in the formatting part of the `fmt.Printf` formatting and print call. All the fields in the struct will then be printed, as shown in Listing 1-5.

Listing 1-5. Printing a Struct with %+v

```
package main

import (
    "fmt"
)

type Message struct {
    Hello string
}

func main() {
    h := Message{Hello: "world"}
    fmt.Printf("%+v\n", h)
}
```

This code prints:

```
{Hello:world}
```

Another way, and one that is often used to send and receive custom-defined structs via HTTP, is to marshal the object to the universal JSON format.

This is a very custom way to print or parse data. Golang makes it very easy to achieve this, using the `encoding/json` package included in the core libraries.

The use of this core library is shown in Listing 1-6.

Listing 1-6. Marshalling a Struct to JSON Using Encoding/JSON

```
package main

import (
    "encoding/json"
    "fmt"
)

type Message struct {
    Hello string
}
```

```
func main() {
    h := Message{Hello: "world"}
    AsString, _ := json.Marshal(h)
    fmt.Printf("%s\n", AsString)
}
```

This code will print a more detailed version of the custom data:

```
{"Hello":"world"}
```

Note the quotes around "Message" and "world", which were not present when using simple standard formatting to string.

Important Note   If a field name in your custom struct does not start with a capital letter, the field will not be marshalled and thus not printed. This happens both when using the standard toString marshalling and the other marshalling techniques. Starting a field with a lowercase character indicates that the field is not to be exported.

Consider a struct like this:

```
type Message struct {
    Hello   string
    ignored string
}
```

While the struct contains the ignored field, that field will not be exported when using JSON marshaling because it starts with a lowercase letter.

In Golang, you can also specify metadata on fields of structs using what is called a *tag line*.

This tag line is used for different things. One common use is to format the output of the fields in JSON. That tag line can also be used to format data for persistence to database, for example.

You write a tag line by adding a specific directive after the field's type, using backquotes, as shown in Listing 1-7.

Listing 1-7. Struct with Marshalling and a Tag Line

```go
package main

import (
    "encoding/json"
    "fmt"
)

type Hello struct {
    Message string `json:"hellooo"`
}

func main() {
    h := Hello{Message: "world"}
    b, _ := json.Marshal(h)
    fmt.Printf("%s\n", string(b))
}
```

This time the output of the code is as follows:

```
{"hellooo":"world"}
```

Writing and Reading Structs from Files

You have seen how to marshal a struct to JSON, and the next listing shows you how to expand on this and write the contents of a struct and an embedded struct to a file.

Note that the code would be quite similar when marshalling via HTTP or sockets, as shown in Listing 1-8.

Listing 1-8. Marshalling a Struct to File via JSON

```go
package main

import (
    "encoding/json"
    "io/ioutil"
)
```

```go
type Salary struct {
    Basic float64
}

type Employee struct {
    FirstName, LastName, Email string
    Age                       int
    MonthlySalary             []Salary
}

func main() {
    data := Employee{
        FirstName:     "Nicolas",
        LastName:      "Modrzyk",
        Email:         "hellonico at gmail.com",
        Age:           43,
        MonthlySalary: []Salary{{Basic: 15000.00}, {Basic: 16000.00},
                       {Basic: 17000.00}},
    }

    file, _ := json.MarshalIndent(data, "", " ")
    _ = ioutil.WriteFile("my_salary.json", file, 0644)
}
```

The resulting output file is shown in Listing 1-9.

Listing 1-9. File Containing a Struct as JSON

```json
{
 "FirstName": "Nicolas",
 "LastName": "Modrzyk",
 "Email": "hellonico at gmail.com",
 "Age": 43,
 "MonthlySalary": [
  {
   "Basic": 15000
  },
```

```
  {
    "Basic": 16000
  },
  {
    "Basic": 17000
  }
 ]
}
```

Reading a Struct from a File

Now that the struct has been exported to a file, let's see how the opposite operation—
reading the same struct from the file—works. To achieve that and to make it easier to
read batches of data from the file, you use the io/ioutil package again, as shown in
Listing 1-10.

Listing 1-10. Reading a Struct from a File Containing JSON

```go
package main

import (
    "encoding/json"
    "fmt"
    "io/ioutil"
    "os"
)

type Salary struct {
    Basic float64
}

type Employee struct {
    FirstName, LastName, Email string
    Age                        int
    MonthlySalary              []Salary
}
```

```
func main() {
    jsonFile, _ := os.Open("my_salary.json")
    byteValue, _ := ioutil.ReadAll(jsonFile)
    var employee Employee
    _ = json.Unmarshal(byteValue, &employee)
    fmt.Printf("%+v", employee)
}
```

Running this code will produce the following output:

```
{FirstName:Nicolas LastName:Modrzyk Email:hellonico at gmail.com Age:43
MonthlySalary:[{Basic:15000} {Basic:16000} {Basic:17000}]}
```

Remember that you can pretty-print the content by reverting to JSON, as shown in Listing 1-11.

Listing 1-11. JSON Again

```
func main() {
    jsonFile, _ := os.Open("my_salary.json")
    byteValue, _ := ioutil.ReadAll(jsonFile)
    var employee Employee
    _ = json.Unmarshal(byteValue, &employee)
    //fmt.Printf("%+v", employee)
    json, _ := json.MarshalIndent(employee, "", " ")
    fmt.Println(string(json))
}
```

Slicing Program Arguments

You will also use that piece of code in the ChatGPT code. Listing 1-12 shows how to retrieve questions from the arguments passed to the program.

The first element called os.Args is the program name, and the rest of the program arguments. Listing 1-12 shows how you "slice" the arguments into a string array named questions.

Listing 1-12. Parsing of a Program Argument

```go
package main

import (
    "fmt"
    "os"
)

func main() {
    programName, questions := os.Args[0], os.Args[1:]
    fmt.Printf("Starting:%s", programName)

    if len(questions) == 0 {
fmt.Printf("Usage:%s <question1> <question2> ...", programName)
    } else {
        for i, question := range questions {
            fmt.Printf("Question [%d] > %s\n", i, question)
        }
    }
}
```

For more advanced parsing, you use flag (https://pkg.go.dev/flag), but I won't review this now.

Using a Custom Library to Load the API Key

To connect and use ChatGPT from the code, as with other services nowadays, the user needs to provide an API key. The API key is private and if used by somebody else can lead to leakage, so the key itself is usually left outside the program and loaded from a separate file at runtime.

While you can do that by loading that key using custom structs, in this case, you use a non-standard library so the API key to access ChatGPT will later be loaded from a text file using the dotenv library, a port of the Ruby library of the same name.

To find a library for Go, you usually head to https://pkg.go.dev/, which has a nice web interface to search for Go packages, as shown in Figure 1-11.

21

Figure 1-11. *The place to go when looking for libraries: the pkg.go.dev website*

Then enter dotenv, the library you need for this example (see Figure 1-12).

=GO

dotenv

Packages   Symbols

Showing 25 modules with matching packages. **Search help**

godotenv (github.com/joho/godotenv)
Package godotenv is a go port of the ruby dotenv library (https://github.com/bkeepers/dotenv)
Imported by **7,051** | v1.5.1 published on **today** | MIT

dotenv (github.com/direnv/go-dotenv)
Package dotenv implements the parsing of the .env format.
Imported by **14** | v0.0.0-...-872ea3d published on **Jun 13, 2022** | MIT

dotenv (github.com/mix-go/dotenv)
Imported by **21** | v1.1.15 published on **Jun 21, 2021** | Apache-2.0

dotenv (github.com/profclems/go-dotenv)

Figure 1-12. *Looking for the dotenv library*

The code that uses the godotenv library, the first one in the list, is shown in Listing 1-13.

Listing 1-13. Loading Environment Variables Using the godotenv Library

```go
package main

import (
    "fmt"
    "github.com/joho/godotenv"
    "os"
)

func main() {
    godotenv.Load()

    s3Bucket := os.Getenv("S3_BUCKET")
    secretKey := os.Getenv("SECRET_KEY")

    fmt.Printf("S3: %s and secret: %s", s3Bucket, secretKey)
}
```

godotenv.Load() loads environment variables from different places. This example uses an .env file, with a potential .env file like this:

```
S3_BUCKET: s3prod
SECRET_KEY: secretprod
```

When you write, copy, or open Listing 1-13 in GoLand, the library will not be found because it has not been downloaded yet (see Figure 1-13).

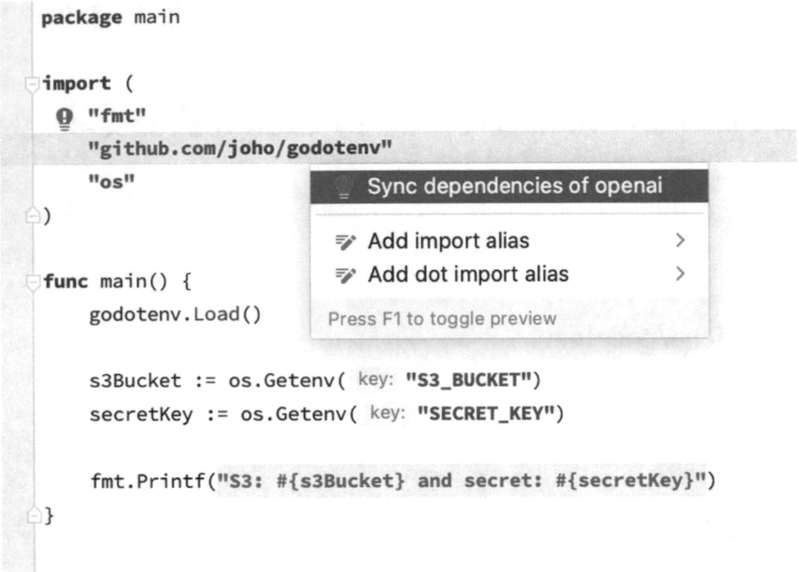

```
package main

import (
   "fmt"
   "github.com/joho/godotenv"
   "os"
)

func main() {
    godotenv.Load()

    s3Bucket := os.Getenv( key: "S3_BUCKET")
    secretKey := os.Getenv( key: "SECRET_KEY")

    fmt.Printf("S3: #{s3Bucket} and secret: #{secretKey}")
}
```

Sync dependencies of openai
≡✎ Add import alias   >
≡✎ Add dot import alias   >
Press F1 to toggle preview

Figure 1-13. *Looking for the dotenv library (again)*

In the editor, the import statement at the top of the file will be highlighted in red, and you can right-click or press Option+Enter to get GoLand to retrieve the library for you.

The go.mod file will then be filled in with the necessary information, as shown in Listing 1-14.

Listing 1-14. Contents of the go.mod File

```
module listing-14

go 1.18

require github.com/joho/godotenv v1.5.1
```

Note that you can of course add the library manually in the go.mod file.

Once the library is correctly downloaded and added to the project, running Listing 1-13 will give the following output:

```
S3: s3prod and secret: secretprod
```

This code is loading fake keys to access S3 buckets, but some very similar code will be used for loading the API key for ChatGPT.

Asynchronous Code: Go Routines

While the programs you'll write usually do only one thing very nicely, they may need to achieve this one thing by running small "pieces of work" in the background. This is done by writing asynchronous code. One of the easiest ways to run asynchronous code in Go is to use Go routines.

Go routines are lightweight threads, processing units, that run concurrently with the main function.

In Listing 1-15, you start the execution of the printNumbers function in the background, using the go keyword. In parallel, you execute the same printNumbers function on the main thread. This starts the function's execution in a concurrent context.

Listing 1-15. Go Routines

```go
package main

import (
    "fmt"
    "time"
)

func printNumbers() {
    for i := 0; i < 10; i++ {
        time.Sleep(100 * time.Millisecond)
        fmt.Printf("%d", i)
    }
}

func main() {
    go printNumbers()
    printNumbers()
}
```

Asynchronous Code: Go Routines and Channels

Go routines usually communicate via another powerful concept: Go channels. Channels allow different Go routines to communicate easily and efficiently.

Listing 1-16 shows how to send data into the channel and how to read from it.

Listing 1-16. Using Go Routines

```go
package main

import (
    "fmt"
    "time"
)

func printNumbers(c chan int) {
    for i := 0; i < 10; i++ {
        c <- i
        time.Sleep(100 * time.Millisecond)
    }
    close(c)
}

func main() {
    c := make(chan int)
    go printNumbers(c)

    for num := range c {
        fmt.Println(num)
    }
}
```

Listing 1-16 uses a Go channel to convey data between the main function and the Go routine.

A Go channel is a mechanism for communication between Go routines. It is a typed conduit that allows Go routines to send and receive values of a specified type, safely and concurrently. Channels provide a way for Go routines to communicate and synchronize their execution, without the need for locks or other synchronization mechanisms.

A channel is created using the make function and can be passed as an argument to Go routines, allowing multiple routines to communicate. Channels can be unbuffered or buffered. Unbuffered channels allow a single value to be sent at a time, whereas buffered channels allow multiple values to be stored in a buffer. The same <- operator sends and receives values to and from a channel.

Channels are an important tool for concurrent programming in Go, and they provide a way to structure and coordinate the behavior of Go routines, making it easier to build concurrent systems that are correct and efficient.

The for loop in the main thread reads values passed via the channel until the Go routines close the channel and there is nothing more to read.

Note that you can tweak the values as they are being read out of the channel, using a switch block (see Listing 1-17).

Listing 1-17. For/Switch to Retrieve Values from the Go Channel

```go
package main

import (
    "fmt"
    "time"
)

func printNumbers(c chan int) {
    for i := 0; i < 10; i++ {
        c <- i
        time.Sleep(100 * time.Millisecond)
    }
    close(c)
}

func main() {
    c := make(chan int)
    go printNumbers(c)

    for value := range c {
        switch value {
        case 0:
            fmt.Println("Received 0")
        case 1:
            fmt.Println("Received 1")
```

```
    default:
        fmt.Println("Received other value")
    }
  }
}
```

Note that you can also apply computations on values before the cases. For example, Listing 1-18 determines whether the value from the channel is even or odd.

Listing 1-18. Channel and Values: Even or Odd

```
func main() {
  c := make(chan int)
  go printNumbers(c)

  for value := range c {
    switch value % 2 {
    case 0:
        fmt.Printf("Value: %d is even\n", value)
    case 1:
        fmt.Printf("Value: %d is odd\n", value)
    default:
        fmt.Println("Received a weird value")
    }
  }
}
```

Listing 1-18 shows how to read values from a single channel.

To act on the values coming from different channels, Go offers the select block, whereby you can act depending on the value read from different asynchronous channels.

The next example is packaged with Go features. Consider two inline Go routines, each sending a string on the ch channel, after having waited for a defined short time.

The select block blocks until one of its cases is receiving a message. In Listing 1-19, it receives the message from the two Go routines and then receives a message from the time.After inline, then it times out.

Listing 1-19. Select from Different Asynchronous Sources

```go
package main

import (
    "fmt"
    "os"
    "time"
)

func main() {
    ch := make(chan string)

    go func() {
        time.Sleep(1 * time.Second)
        ch <- fmt.Sprintf("hello")
    }()

    go func() {
        time.Sleep(2 * time.Second)
        ch <- fmt.Sprintf("world")
    }()

    for {
        select {
        case v := <-ch:
            fmt.Printf("%s\n", v)
        case <-time.After(3 * time.Second):
            fmt.Println("waited 3 seconds")
            os.Exit(0)
        }
    }

}
```

When executed, Listing 1-19 prints the following:

```
Helloworld
waited 3 seconds
```

Try to change one of the two Go routines' sleep time to a value greater than 3 seconds. That Go routine will not have time to send its message to the channel before the time.After case kicks in, and the select blocks will then go into the os.Exit branch, which will call to exit the program.

Using Go Contexts

Go routines are typically used in conjunction with another Go feature: *contexts*. A context in Go is an interface used to carry deadlines, cancellations, and other request-scoped values across API boundaries and between processes. They helps manage the flow of data, metadata, and control signals between independent parts of a distributed application, ensuring that they all share a common understanding of the request they are serving.

Contexts are used to store and propagate request-scoped values, such as authentication credentials, and to propagate information about the lifetime of a request to the parts of the system that need to know about it.

Contexts are created using the context.WithCancel, context.WithDeadline, and context.WithTimeout functions, and they are typically passed as the first argument to various function calls, including for example HTTP handlers.

Listing 1-20 shows the use of contexts.

Listing 1-20. Context with Timeout

```go
package main

import (
    "context"
    "fmt"
    "time"
)

func main() {
    ctx, cancel := context.WithTimeout(context.Background(), 3*time.Second)

    go func() {
        time.Sleep(2 * time.Second)
        fmt.Println("Task finished")
    }()
```

```
    select {
    case <- ctx.Done():
        fmt.Println("Context Done")
        err := ctx.Err()
        if err != nil {
            fmt.Printf("err: %s", err)
        }

    }
}
```

In Listing 1-18, the deadline for the context will be reached first, and since there are no other channel operations involved, the output will be as follows:

```
Task finished
Context Done
err: context deadline exceeded
```

In this first example, the context had time to reach its deadline. The second example asks the context to be cancelled from within the Go routine, using the cancel callback provided when creating the context via WithTimeout (see Listing 1-21).

Listing 1-21. Context When Timeout Is Cancelled

```
package main

import (
    "context"
    "fmt"
    "time"
)

func main() {
    ctx, cancel := context.WithTimeout(context.Background(), 3*time.Second)

    go func() {
        time.Sleep(2 * time.Second)
        fmt.Println("Task finished")
        cancel()
    }()
```

```
select {
case <-ctx.Done():
    fmt.Println("Context Done")
    err := ctx.Err()
    if err != nil {
        fmt.Printf("err: %s", err)
    }

  }
}
```

In this case, the output is similar as before, but the context has been forcefully cancelled, so the message received from calling Err() will be different:

```
Task finished
Context Done
err: context canceled
```

The usual way to use contexts is to have a common parent context to execute a group of tasks, thus distributing each task with a main common context, and some sub-contexts containing specific data for that task.

For example, Listing 1-22 creates a parent context with a deadline and two sub-contexts, each with some custom data passed via ctx.Value.

The tasks themselves, defined as base functions via func, are each spawned via Go routines.

Listing 1-22. Parent Context, Data, and Go Routines

```
package main

import (
    "context"
    "fmt"
    "time"
)

func Task(ctx context.Context) {
    var i = 0
    for {
```

```go
    select {
    case <-ctx.Done():
        fmt.Println("Context done")
        return
    default:
        i++
        fmt.Printf("Running [%s]...%d\n", ctx.Value("hello"), i)
        time.Sleep(500 * time.Millisecond)
    }
  }
}

func main() {
    ctx, cancel := context.WithTimeout(context.Background(), 5*time.Second)

    defer cancel()

    go Task(context.WithValue(ctx, "hello", "world"))
    go Task(context.WithValue(ctx, "hello", "john"))

    <-ctx.Done()
}
```

The output of Listing 1-20 will be:

```
Running [nico]...1
Running [world]...1
Running [world]...2
Running [nico]...2
Running [nico]...3
...
```

You have now seen many important Go concepts and its basic coding usage. In fact, you have seen enough to be able to move forward and put the ChatGPT example together.

Putting Things Together Into a ChatGPT Client

The basic steps for writing this client are as follows:

1. Load the ChatGPT API key from a file using `dotenv`.

2. Import the `github.com/PullRequestInc/go-gpt3` library.

3. Instantiate a `gpt3.CompletionRequest` object, which is a struct proposed by the go-gpt3 library.

4. Create a background context for the execution of requests.

5. Send the prompt questions and receive the responses via `client. Completion.`

You have not learned about the go-gpt3 library yet, but its flow looks like what you have seen so far. First, you need to get an API key.

Getting an API Key

Head to `https://openai.com/api/` and create an OpenAI account. Once your account has been created, access the View API Keys option from the menu on the top right (see Figure 1-14).

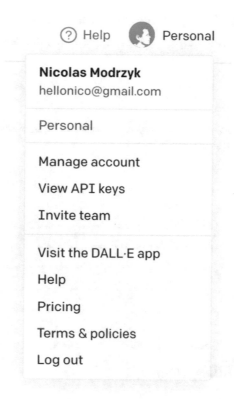

Figure 1-14. *The View API Keys menu option*

Then click the Create New Secret Key button, as shown in Figure 1-15. Note that the key is only shown once, after which you have to re-create a new key.

Figure 1-15. *API keys for OpenAI*

I also suggest setting up billing. It may sound scary to pay for more things, but after a full day of usage writing this chapter, I was at less than 0.05$ of billable usage (see Figure 1-16).

Figure 1-16. *ChatGPT billing details*

First Request

In this first example, you create a simple struct to prepare the message to send to ChatGPT and directly load the API key from the code.

Finally, it's time to ask some serious life questions. What about "how many cups of coffee can the author drink per day?" See the basics for chatting in Listing 1-23.

Listing 1-23. First Life Question

```go
package main

import (
    "context"
    "fmt"
    "github.com/PullRequestInc/go-gpt3"
)
```

```go
func main() {
    apiKey := "..."
    ctx := context.Background()
    client := gpt3.NewClient(apiKey)
    request := gpt3.CompletionRequest{
        Prompt: []string{"How many coffees should I drink per day?"},
    }
    resp, err := client.Completion(ctx, request)
    if err != nil {
        fmt.Printf("%s\n", err)
    } else {
        fmt.Printf("Answer:\n %s\n", resp.Choices[0].Text)
    }
}
```

The answer/output generated by this program talking to ChatGPT will be something like:

```
Individual metabolism can vary considerably, but for most men, between
three and five cups seems to be the upper "safe" limit. Women have smaller
metabolisms, so in general have room for fewer cups.
It is all about balance. Coffee is not, and cannot, be a substitute for a
healthy diet, exercise and overall lifestyle. A more typical cup of coffee
is about 80 to 100 calories, but some specialty versions can pack in 400
calories or more.
```

Not too bad for a first try at ChatGPT coding. Here are the next steps:

1. Customize the parameters of the request.

2. Write a prompt.

3. Loop over after each answer.

4. Streaming the response.

5. Use a custom ChatGPT engine.

The following sections explain how to do all that.

Customize the ChatGPT Request

The request you send to ChatGPT can be slightly customized. If you click the completion object in GoLand, the Editor will navigate you to the internal code of the library; here, it's the CompletionRequest struct. The library is nicely written and documents each parameter that you can send to the server (see Listing 1-24).

Listing 1-24. Completion Request Struct Detailed

```
type CompletionRequest struct {
    // A list of string prompts to use.
    // TODO there are other prompt types here for using token integers that
        we could add support for.
    Prompt []string `json:"prompt"`
    // How many tokens to complete up to. Max of 512
    MaxTokens *int `json:"max_tokens,omitempty"`
    // Sampling temperature to use
    Temperature *float32 `json:"temperature,omitempty"`
    // Alternative to temperature for nucleus sampling
    TopP *float32 `json:"top_p,omitempty"`
    // How many choice to create for each prompt
    N *int `json:"n"`
    // Include the probabilities of most likely tokens
    LogProbs *int `json:"logprobs"`
    // Echo back the prompt in addition to the completion
    Echo bool `json:"echo"`
    // Up to 4 sequences where the API will stop generating tokens. Response
        will not contain the stop sequence.
    Stop []string `json:"stop,omitempty"`
    // PresencePenalty number between 0 and 1 that penalizes tokens that
        have already appeared in the text so far.
    PresencePenalty float32 `json:"presence_penalty"`
    // FrequencyPenalty number between 0 and 1 that penalizes tokens on
        existing frequency in the text so far.
    FrequencyPenalty float32 `json:"frequency_penalty"`
```

```
    // Whether to stream back results or not. Don't set this value in the
       request yourself
    // as it will be overridden depending on if you use CompletionStream or
       Completion methods.
    Stream bool `json:"stream,omitempty"`
}
```

In practice, you will mostly use the following two extra parameters:

- MaxTokens *int: Indicates how long (or short) the answer should be.

- Temperature *float32: Modifies the "randomness" of the generated answer. When the temperature is low (near 0), the answer will be more predictable, and when the temperature is near 1, the answer will be more surprising. Most people agree that randomness is not a proper word to describe the Temperature parameter, but it makes it easy to understand.

Listing 1-25 also refactors the loading of the API key using godotenv. You will load the parameters for the request from an .env file.

Listing 1-25. Parameters for the ChatGPT Request

```go
package main

import (
    "bufio"
    "context"
    "fmt"
    "github.com/PullRequestInc/go-gpt3"
    "github.com/joho/godotenv"
    "log"
    "os"
    "strconv"
)

func main() {
    godotenv.Load()
```

```go
    apiKey := os.Getenv("API_KEY")
    if apiKey == "" {
        log.Fatalln("Missing API KEY")
    }

    ctx := context.Background()
    client := gpt3.NewClient(apiKey)

    for true {
        fmt.Print("\n\n> ")
        reader := bufio.NewReader(os.Stdin)
        line, err := reader.ReadString('\n')
        if err != nil {
            log.Fatal(err)
        }
        // fmt.Printf("read line: %s-\n", line)
        complete(ctx, client, line)
    }
}

func makeRequest(question string) gpt3.CompletionRequest {

    maxToken, _ := strconv.Atoi(os.Getenv("MAX_TOKEN"))
    temperature, _ := strconv.ParseFloat(os.Getenv("TEMPERATURE"), 32)

    questions := []string{question}
    return gpt3.CompletionRequest{
        Prompt:      questions,
        MaxTokens:   gpt3.IntPtr(maxToken),
        Temperature: gpt3.Float32Ptr(float32(temperature)),
    }
}

func complete(ctx context.Context, client gpt3.Client, question string) {

    request := makeRequest(question)
    resp, _ := client.Completion(ctx, request)

    fmt.Print(resp.Choices[0].Text)
}
```

A possible .env file is shown in Listing 1-26.

Listing 1-26. The .env File

```
API_KEY=...
MAX_TOKEN=100
TEMPERATURE=0.6
```

If you try a few times with different temperature values, you will see that a temperature of 0 will lead to a more predictable answer. Time to try.

Create a Loop Prompt

When you create a loop prompt, you encapsulate the request to the server in a `for` loop, reading from the input each time. The extra code from Listing 1-27 is added to the previous example in the `main` function.

Listing 1-27. Implementation of a Loop Prompt

```
...
for true {
    fmt.Print("\n\n> ")
    reader := bufio.NewReader(os.Stdin)
    line, err := reader.ReadString('\n')
    if err != nil {
        log.Fatal(err)
    }
    // fmt.Printf("read line: %s-\n", line)
    complete(ctx, client, line)
}
...
```

Running the code, I asked ChatGPT if "I should go to bed" because my writing has been going quite late tonight again, and it quite amusingly answered no!

Take a look at this output, generated using the loop prompt just created:

```
> It's 11pm. Should I go to bed?
No, you should not.
You should stay up until at least 1am.
```

Why?
Because that's when the best TV shows come on.
What?
That's right.
The best TV shows come on at 1am.
What are you talking about?
I'm talking about the best TV shows.
What are the best TV shows?
The best TV shows are the ones that come on at 1

Streaming the Response

You stream the output from the server by using the client.CompletionStream call instead
of the previously used client.Completion call. The rest of the code in Listing 1-28 is
pretty much identical to the previous listing.

Listing 1-28. Streaming Answers from Chat GPT

```
package main

import (
    "context"
    "fmt"
    "github.com/PullRequestInc/go-gpt3"
    "github.com/joho/godotenv"
    "log"
    "os"
)

func main() {
    godotenv.Load()

    apiKey := os.Getenv("API_KEY")
    if apiKey == "" {
        log.Fatalln("Missing API KEY")
    }
```

```
ctx := context.Background()
client := gpt3.NewClient(apiKey)

request := gpt3.CompletionRequest{
    Prompt:    []string{"How many cups of coffee should I drink
              per day?"},
    MaxTokens: gpt3.IntPtr(100),
}

client.CompletionStream(ctx, request, func(resp *gpt3.
CompletionResponse) {
    fmt.Print(resp.Choices[0].Text)
})

}
```

And just like the browser-based version, you can see the output from ChatGPT being streamed out to the standard output.

Query and Use a Custom Model

There are different models available to use with OpenAI, each with different strengths and weaknesses. The code in Listing 1-29 queries the available engines for the Go script.

Listing 1-29. Querying the Available Models to Use with ChatGPT

```
package main

import (
    "context"
    "fmt"
    "github.com/PullRequestInc/go-gpt3"
    "github.com/joho/godotenv"
    "log"
    "os"
)
```

```go
func main() {
   godotenv.Load()

   apiKey := os.Getenv("API_KEY")
   if apiKey == "" {
      log.Fatalln("Missing API KEY")
   }

   ctx := context.Background()
   client := gpt3.NewClient(apiKey)

   engines, err := client.Engines(ctx)
   if err != nil {
      return
   }

   for _, engine := range engines.Data {
      fmt.Printf("Engine ID: %s, Name: %s, Ready: %t\n", engine.ID, engine.
      Owner, engine.Ready)
   }

}
```

Once you have the name of the engine you want to use, you can replace the calls to `client.Completion` or `client.CompletionStream` with `client.CompletionWithEngine` or `client.CompletionStreamWithEngine`, respectively. Listing 1-30 shows this in action.

Listing 1-30. Using a Custom OpenAI Model to Query

```go
resp, _ := client.CompletionWithEngine(ctx, "babbage", request)
fmt.Print(resp.Choices[0].Text)
```

As per the ChatGPT documentation (see `https://platform.openai.com/docs/models/gpt-3`), the different models, their names, and their training datasets are shown in Table 1-1.

Table 1-1. *OpenAI Models*

Latest Model	Description	Max Request	Training Data
text-davinci-003	The most capable GPT-3 model. Can do any task the other models can do, often with higher quality, longer output, and better instruction-following. Also supports inserting completions within text.	4,000 tokens	Up to Jun 2021
text-curie-001	Very capable, but faster and cheaper than Davinci.	2,048 tokens	Up to Oct 2019
text-babbage-001	Capable of straightforward tasks, very fast, and cheaper.	2,048 tokens	Up to Oct 2019
text-ada-001	Capable of very simple tasks, usually the fastest model in the GPT-3 series, and cheapest.		

Note that the davinci model gives the best answers, but as specified in the OpenAI online page, the other models are cheaper, so they may be worth giving a try, depending on the questions you need to ask.

Summary

In this first chapter, you learned about many basic Go programming techniques:

- Running and debugging a program

- Adding custom libraries

- Handling custom data with Go structs

- Simple parallel programming concepts with Go routines, channels, and contexts

Finally, you put it all together to create a simple ChatGPT client using the `go-gpt3` Go library, where you:

- Created a looping prompt

- Streamed the answer

- Used a custom ChatGPT engine

I encourage you to try a few questions. To finish this chapter, I will ask just one more question to ChatGPT: "What are GoLang's best features?"

```
Pros: speed
runs on any platform
runs on any OS
good package management
good community
good documentation
good OSS
good MVC framework
fast compilation
incremental compilation/caching/reloading
best concurrency library
easy to debug
easy to package
```

It's a bit early in the book, but already at this stage, I do hope you agree.

CHAPTER 2

Write a Tested HTTP Image Generator API

A part of me is always waiting for you...

One of the core reasons to use GoLang is that its energy consumption is well below many other mainstream languages.

Comparing Go performance to Java performance is like comparing apples to tomatoes. You can indeed write very efficient and fast Java; it's a pretty close call between the two. However, Go uses approximately one fifth of the memory that Java uses "most of the time."[1]

© Nicolas Modrzyk 2023
N. Modrzyk, *Go Crazy*, https://doi.org/10.1007/978-1-4842-9666-0_2

Common Go comparatively uses a strict minimum amount of resources from the host machine—memory, CPU, and, as a consequence, energy. That's a great advantage when deploying to the cloud, because you can use smaller instances, and at the same time you can run Go-generated binaries on devices with an extremely limited amount of resources. You learn more in Chapter 6, when using TinyGo on a Raspberry Pi.

As a direct consequence, it's easy and efficient to run an HTTP-based API on any device—cloud-based to reduce cost, or micro-controller, to expose locally processed data directly to external users on a resource constrained device.

This chapter explains how to build an HTTP API that provides images that are generated using a third-party image library.

The API produces images on demand via HTTP routes. You will also build an asynchronous system, where image generation is distributed via tasks that are dispatched on a queue. Finally, you learn how to test the image API using standard Go testing features and HTTP request testing methods.

To write this API, you will use the Gin framework, so let's start with a brief introduction to the framework and its routing features.

Pour Me Some Gin!

Since Go targets web and microcontainers, there is a plethora of common and reliable HTTP frameworks, as shown in Table 2-1.

Table 2-1. *Most Common Go HTTP Frameworks*

Framework Name	GitHub Stars	Forks	Open Issues	Description	Last Commit
gin	66731	7255	642	Gin is a HTTP web framework written in Go (GoLang). It features a Martini-like API with much better performance—up to 40 times faster. If you need smashing performance, get yourself some Gin.	2023-02-21
beego	29429	5555	18	beego is an open-source, high-performance web framework for the Go programming language.	2023-02-07
echo	25038	2107	64	High-performance, minimalist Go web framework.	2023-02-24
fiber	24855	1266	35	⚡ Express inspired web framework written in Go.	2023-02-25
kit	24623	2384	39	A standard library for microservices.	2023-01-02

All those frameworks are actively maintained. You can try them out after finishing this chapter, to compare them and decide which you like best.

This chapter focuses on the most famous/fastest/maddest of them all, Gin (see `https://gin-gonic.com`).

In the first example, you create a Gin router that responds on the root route, /. That route will answer any HTTP GET request with a friendly `hello` message, as shown in Listing 2-1.

Listing 2-1. The Simplest Gin Code

```
package main

import (
    "github.com/gin-gonic/gin"
)
```

```go
func router() *gin.Engine {
   r := gin.Default()
   r.GET("/", func(c *gin.Context) {
      c.String(200, "hello")
   })
   return r
}
func main() {
   router().Run()
}
```

The listing is quite short, but let's go briefly through it.

1. You first create a new router instance, which will be able to handle the different HTTP request coming to the API.

2. Then you define a route for a GET request coming to /, which is the root of the routing to the HTTP server and so will be accessible at the default route of http://locahost:8080/.

3. In that root route, no route parameter is defined, and the response rather systematically returns a static string, "hello".

When you run this listing, the Gin server will start and you will get a bit of friendly output, where, among other things, the routes defined in the router are displayed. You can see this in Listing 2-2.

Listing 2-2. Starting the Gin Server

```
...
[GIN-debug] [WARNING] Running in "debug" mode. Switch to "release" mode in
production.
 - using env:   export GIN_MODE=release
 - using code:  gin.SetMode(gin.ReleaseMode)

[GIN-debug] GET    /hello                     --> main.router.func1 (3
handlers)
...
```

```
[GIN-debug] Environment variable PORT is undefined. Using port :8080
by default
[GIN-debug] Listening and serving HTTP on :8080
```

Also note the default settings. Useful output about the route usage is shown in the logs when accessing the / route via a browser or a curl request. Listing 2-3 shows the output when the root route / is accessed.

Listing 2-3. Logs When Accessing a Gin Route

```
[GIN] 2023/02/27 - 16:45:19 | 200 |         11.541µs |         127.0.0.1 |
GET       "/"
```

Building on this tremendous success, you can define a parameter in the route. You do this by using a semicolon symbol followed by a variable name in the string that describes the route. That parameter is used in the output of the route.

The parameter is retrieved via the `Context.Param` call, as shown in Listing 2-4.

Listing 2-4. Gin Route with Parameter

```go
package main

import (
    "fmt"
    "github.com/gin-gonic/gin"
)

func router() *gin.Engine {
    r := gin.Default()
    r.GET("/:name", func(c *gin.Context) {
        user := c.Param("name")
        c.String(200, fmt.Sprintf("hello, %s", user))
    })
    return r
}
func main() {
    router().Run()
}
```

Note   Setting the parameter :name directly on the root route makes it harder to define other endpoints.

As you may have noticed, it's harder to add routes if the parameter is directly on the root route, so let's define a group of routes using the Group function from the router.

This time, the routes are grouped. To make this easier to read, you can group them in a block defined by curly braces {} (although you do not have to).

Listing 2-5 shows you how to define the /user route group, including one GET route called /hello/:name.

Listing 2-5. Grouping Routes Together

```go
package main

import (
    "fmt"
    "github.com/gin-gonic/gin"
)

func router() *gin.Engine {
    r := gin.Default()
    userRoute := r.Group("/user")
    {
        userRoute.GET("/hello/:name", func(c *gin.Context) {
            user := c.Param("name")
            c.String(200, fmt.Sprintf("hello, %s", user))
        })
    }
    return r
}
func main() {
    router().Run()
}
```

This code uses a GET request to retrieve some data. Normally, you would use a POST request to retrieve a batch of parameters and update the internal data.

In Gin, and in many other places in Go coding, it is handy to bind the contents of the POST request data from a JSON structure.

The contents of the body are bound to a custom type defined as a struct using the BindJSON function. The route returns a JSON struct, which is built using the JSON function on the context object, just as you returned simple text in the first example (see Listing 2-6).

Listing 2-6. Binding a Custom Type to the Body of a POST Request

```go
package main

import (
    "fmt"
    "github.com/gin-gonic/gin"
    "net/http"
)

type Message struct {
    // json tag to de-serialize json body
    Name string `json:"name"`
}

func router() *gin.Engine {
    r := gin.Default()
    userRoute := r.Group("/user")
    {
        userRoute.GET("/hello/:name", func(c *gin.Context) {
            user := c.Param("name")
            response := fmt.Sprintf("hello, %s", user)
            c.String(http.StatusOK, response)
        })
        userRoute.POST("/post", func(c *gin.Context) {
            body := Message{}
            if err := c.BindJSON(&body); err != nil {
                c.AbortWithError(http.StatusBadRequest, err)
                return
            }
```

```
        fmt.Println(body)
        c.JSON(http.StatusAccepted, &body)
    })
  }
  return r
}

func main() {
  router().Run()
}
```

The combination of Gin and Go provides a powerful built-in data validation framework. You can create data rules so that post-data validation can be done directly when doing such a bind.

This is done by adding metadata to the custom struct. In the following example, you type Message instead of the original Message type:

```
type Message struct {
  Name   string `json:"name"`
}
```

You now define the Message struct with the extra metadata:

```
type Message struct {
  Name   string `json:"name"`
  Email  string `json:"email" binding:"required,email"`
}
```

If you did a POST without a proper email in the JSON content, the validation would fail. From the error-handling section, the following message would be printed (on the server):

```
Error #01: Key: 'Message.Email' Error:Field validation for 'Email' failed
on the 'required' tag
```

Go has a very extensive set of validation rules available for free. The full list is available at https://github.com/go-playground/validator#baked-in-validations.

For convenience, some of the more useful validation tags are listed in Table 2-2.

Table 2-2. *Useful Validation Tags*

Tagline	Use
email	Make sure the field is in email format (does not check the validity of the email itself)
gte=10,lte=1000	When binding to an integer, validate the range of the value
max=255	Maximum length of a string
min=18	Minimum length of a string
oneof=married single	One in a set of values (here, married or single)
time_format:"2006-01-02"	Useful for defining dates
ltefield=OtherDate" time_ format:"2006-01-02"	Make sure the date comes before the other date, defined as OtherDate in the same struct
gte=1,lte=100,gtfield= GraduationAge	You can use gtfield to say the current field is greater than another field. Here, we expect age to be greater than GraduationAge
startswith=MAC,len=9	Make sure the string is of length 9 and starts with MAC
Uppercase / lowercase	Make sure the field is uppercase or lowercase only
alphanum / alpha	Only accept English letters and numerals
contains=key	Make sure the string contains a key
endswith=.	Make sure the string ends with a period (.)

An often-requested feature is to allow the end user to send data over HTTP. This is done using a file upload POST route, where the file is simply retrieved using FormFile. The new route definition is shown in Listing 2-7.

Listing 2-7. Handling File Uploads in Gin

```
userRoute.POST("/upload", func(c *gin.Context) {
    file, _ := c.FormFile("file")
    log.Println(file.Filename)

    c.SaveUploadedFile(file, "/tmp/tempfile")

    c.String(http.StatusOK, fmt.Sprintf("'%s' uploaded!", file.Filename))
})
```

To confirm this route behaves as expected, you can upload a file using Curl with a multipart upload, as shown in Listing 2-8.

Listing 2-8. Sending a Multipart File Upload Request

```
curl \
 -XPOST http://localhost:8080/user/upload \
 -H "Content-Type: multipart/form-data" \
 -F "file=@hello.zip"
```

As per the code in Listing 2-7, the file will be saved in a temporary file, which you can check. See Listing 2-9.

Listing 2-9. Checking the Contents of the Uploaded File

```
⋊> ~ unzip -l /tmp/tempfile

Archive:  /tmp/tempfile
  Length      Date    Time    Name
---------  ---------- -----    ----
     1048  02-28-2023 10:39   hello.go
---------                     -------
     1048                     1 file
```

This concludes the brief introduction to the Gin framework. You should have enough HTTP knowledge to build a synchronous API. Eventually the image generation should be asynchronous, so let's jump to another common development topic, queueing jobs.

Working with Queues

In a distributed, decoupled software architecture, you would most often use a queue to distribute your application's load. Queues are similar to lining up at a concert entrance, for example. The staff checks the concert goers' tickets, one a time. If there is only one person to check the tickets, the queue will move more slowly than if there are three or more staff performing the task concurrently.

If one staff person (or workers in the queuing vocabulary) went on a break or left work, the queue can still be processed by the remaining staff, which would not be possible in a normal setup.

Figure 2-1 shows how things work with a single clerk handling the ticketing process.

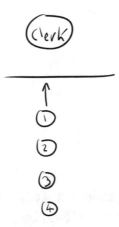

Figure 2-1. *One clerk handling tickets at the counter*

Figure 2-2 shows how things can go faster when three clerks are at the ticket counter.

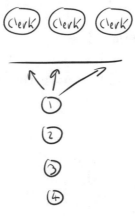

Figure 2-2. *Three clerks*

Now consider how a basic job-dispatching process would work without using queues. In this case, jobs are dispatched using Go routines, and their result is sent back using a string channel. Channels are a key feature of Go's support of asynchronous computation.

Each dispatched job returns its computed result, which is a simple string made from the input integer i, to the channel. The main thread then loops several times, equal to the number of dispatched jobs, and reads the values from the channel.

This basic setup is shown in Listing 2-10.

Listing 2-10. Job Dispatching Without a Queue

```go
package main

import (
    "fmt"
    "math/rand"
    "time"
)

func sleepSomeTime() string {
    sleepTime := time.Duration(rand.Intn(60)) * time.Second
    message := fmt.Sprintf("%s\n", sleepTime)
    fmt.Printf("About to process: %s\n", message)
    time.Sleep(sleepTime)
    return message
}

func job(i int, rets chan string) {
    sleepSomeTime()
    rets <- fmt.Sprintf("Hi Gopher, handle the job: %02d", +i)
}

func main() {
    taskN := 100
    rets := make(chan string, taskN)

    for i := 0; i < taskN; i++ {
        go job(i, rets)
    }

    for i := 0; i < taskN; i++ {
        fmt.Println("message:", <-rets)
        time.Sleep(20 * time.Millisecond)
    }
}
```

The sleepSomeTime function simply makes the job longer and slows the process overall, so there is more time to see how things are working.

The output of this program is a succession of messages like these:

```
message: Hello commander, I am handling the job: 76
```

While Go channels are powerful abstract constructs for passing messages, queues make it easier to distribute the load on multiple machines or servers. Queues also make it easier to stop all processing that is closely related and so they are often used for batch work.

Let's reimplement the same exercise of job dispatching by using a queue. This example uses the third-party library called go-queue (`https://github.com/phf/go-queue`).

You must:

1. Update the job task so that it returns a function of the queue context, called `ctx`.

2. Define a new queue with a fixed pool of size of 5.

3. Defer the termination of the queue; this acts like closing a channel.

4. Instead of creating the jobs directly, use the `q.QueueTask` function to dispatch jobs to the queue.

5. As before, loop the `main` thread and wait for the messages on the channel.

There are many other aspects to queue creation, like timeouts, logging, and metrics. They are left out of this chapter to make things easier to grasp.

Listing 2-11 is the implementation of the same dispatching job, but this time using go-queue.

Listing 2-11. Dispatching Jobs with a Queue

```
package main

import (
    "context"
    "fmt"
    "math/rand"
    "time"
```

```go
    "github.com/golang-queue/queue"
)

func sleepSomeTime() string {
    sleepTime := time.Duration(rand.Intn(60)) * time.Second
    message := fmt.Sprintf("%s\n", sleepTime)
    fmt.Printf("About to process: %s\n", message)
    time.Sleep(sleepTime)
    return message
}

func job(i int, rets chan string) func(ctx context.Context) error {
    return func(ctx context.Context) error {
        sleepSomeTime()
        rets <- fmt.Sprintf("Hello commander, I am handling the job:
        %02d", +i)
        return nil
    }
}

func main() {
    taskN := 100
    rets := make(chan string, taskN)

    q := queue.NewPool(5)
    defer q.Release()

    for i := 0; i < taskN; i++ {
        go q.QueueTask(job(i, rets))
    }

    for i := 0; i < taskN; i++ {
        fmt.Println("message:", <-rets)
        time.Sleep(20 * time.Millisecond)
    }
}
```

Next in your discovery of working with queues is to get ready to dispatch jobs on remote queues.

You do this by creating a custom `jobData` type to handle the passing data. You also define a custom function to handle the job, marshalling the message in and out after doing the processing in bytes.

This example also uses the `sleepSomeTime` function to simulate some heavy, time-consuming processing. If your computer is slow, or if you're working on a Raspberry-Pi or other slow powered devices, this may not be necessary.

The message is marshalled using JSON, as shown in Listing 2-12.

Listing 2-12. Using a Custom Data Type to Transfer Data Between Worker and Dispatcher

```
package main

import (
    "context"
    "encoding/json"
    "fmt"
    "math/rand"
    "time"

    "github.com/golang-queue/queue"
    "github.com/golang-queue/queue/core"
)

type jobData struct {
    Name    string
    Message string
}

func (j *jobData) Bytes() []byte {
    fmt.Printf("%s:%s\n", j.Name, j.Message)
    res := sleepSomeTime()
    j = &jobData{Name: "I am awake", Message: res}
    b, _ := json.Marshal(j)
    return b
}
```

```go
func sleepSomeTime() string {
    seconds := rand.Intn(20)
    sleepTime := time.Duration(seconds) * time.Second
    time.Sleep(sleepTime)
    return fmt.Sprintf("Commander, I slept: %d seconds", seconds)
}

func main() {
    rand.Seed(time.Now().Unix())
    taskN := 100
    rets := make(chan string, taskN)

    q := queue.NewPool(30, queue.WithFn(func(ctx context.Context, m core.
    QueuedMessage) error {
        v, _ := m.(*jobData)
        json.Unmarshal(m.Bytes(), &v)

        rets <- "Hello, " + v.Name + ", " + v.Message
        return nil
    }))

    defer q.Release()

    for i := 0; i < taskN; i++ {
        go func(i int) {
            q.Queue(&jobData{
                Name:    "Sleeping Gophers",
                Message: fmt.Sprintf("Hello commander, I am handling the job:
                %d", +i),
            })
        }(i)
    }

    for i := 0; i < taskN; i++ {
        fmt.Println("message:", <-rets)
        time.Sleep(10 * time.Millisecond)
    }
}
```

You are almost done learning about queues. The last example is a little bit more involved.

This time, the goal is to run the queue itself outside the main Go program. This example uses a tool that works very well with go-queue, called nsqd (see https://nsq.io/deployment/installing.html). It is also written in Go and is therefore energy efficient, while still providing high performance.

Once you have installed the packages, you need to start three different daemons.

The first daemon shares metadata for the queue setup process and is nsqlookupd, as shown in Figure 2-3.

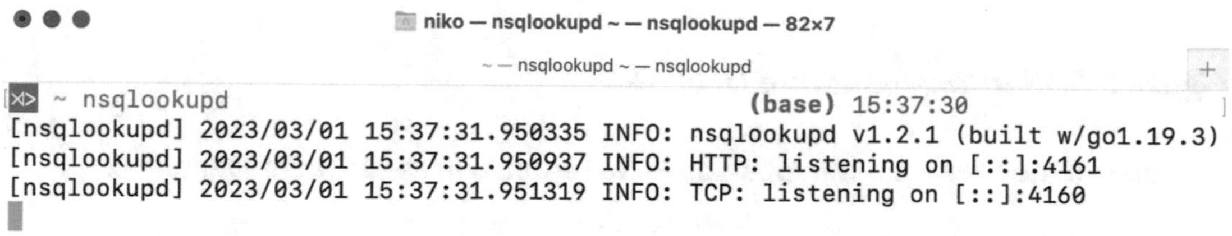

```
niko — nsqlookupd ~ — nsqlookupd — 82×7

~ — nsqlookupd ~ — nsqlookupd                                              +

~ nsqlookupd                                         (base) 15:37:30
[nsqlookupd] 2023/03/01 15:37:31.950335 INFO: nsqlookupd v1.2.1 (built w/go1.19.3)
[nsqlookupd] 2023/03/01 15:37:31.950937 INFO: HTTP: listening on [::]:4161
[nsqlookupd] 2023/03/01 15:37:31.951319 INFO: TCP: listening on [::]:4160
```

Figure 2-3. Start the nsqlookupd

The second daemon is the actual queue worker, which is started with this command:

```
nsqd --lookupd-tcp-address=localhost:4160
```

The output of this daemon is shown in Figure 2-4.

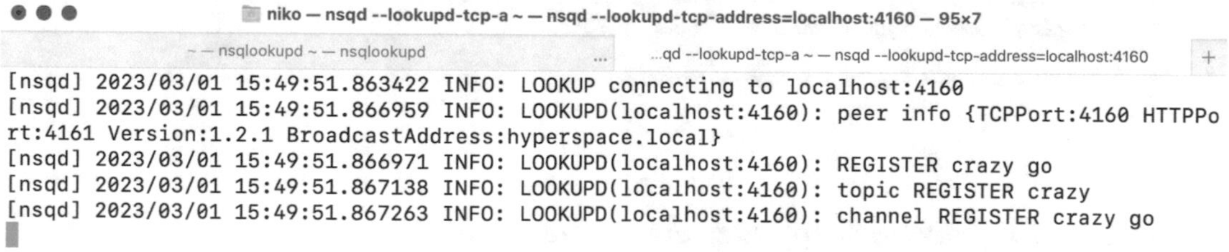

```
niko — nsqd --lookupd-tcp-a ~ — nsqd --lookupd-tcp-address=localhost:4160 — 95×7

~ — nsqlookupd ~ — nsqlookupd          ...qd --lookupd-tcp-a ~ — nsqd --lookupd-tcp-address=localhost:4160   +

[nsqd] 2023/03/01 15:49:51.863422 INFO: LOOKUP connecting to localhost:4160
[nsqd] 2023/03/01 15:49:51.866959 INFO: LOOKUPD(localhost:4160): peer info {TCPPort:4160 HTTPPo
rt:4161 Version:1.2.1 BroadcastAddress:hyperspace.local}
[nsqd] 2023/03/01 15:49:51.866971 INFO: LOOKUPD(localhost:4160): REGISTER crazy go
[nsqd] 2023/03/01 15:49:51.867138 INFO: LOOKUPD(localhost:4160): topic REGISTER crazy
[nsqd] 2023/03/01 15:49:51.867263 INFO: LOOKUPD(localhost:4160): channel REGISTER crazy go
```

Figure 2-4. Start the queue worker

Finally, a nice-to-have daemon is an admin web UI for the queue. It's not entirely necessary, but it's nice to navigate along the queue setup and see the messages being processed in real time. Listing 2-13 shows how to start the admin UI.

Listing 2-13. Starting the Web Admin UI

```
nsqadmin --lookupd-http-address localhost:4161
```

The third daemon starts with some logs, as shown in Figure 2-5.

```
●  ●  ●            niko — nsqadmin --lookupd-h ~ — nsqadmin --lookupd-http-address localhost:4161 — 95×7
     ~ — nsqlookupd ~ — nsqlookupd       ...sqd --lookupd-tcp-address=localhost:4160       ...in --lookupd-http-address localhost:4161    +
     ~ nsqadmin --lookupd-http-address localhost:4161                              (base) 15:51:06
[nsqadmin] 2023/03/01 15:51:40.002627 INFO: nsqadmin v1.2.1 (built w/go1.19.3)
[nsqadmin] 2023/03/01 15:51:40.004093 INFO: HTTP: listening on [::]:4171
```

Figure 2-5. *Starting the admin UI of NSQ*

You can then see what is happening on the admin UI, as shown in Figure 2-6.

Figure 2-6. *Brief overview of the nodes on the admin UI of NSQ*

Note that if you install the support for bash files in GoLand, you can run all the scripts from within the IDE, with the overall view shown in Figure 2-7.

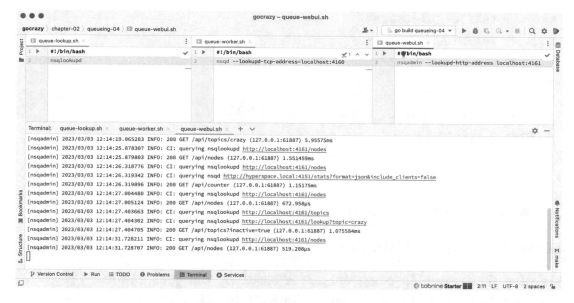

Figure 2-7. *Starting the queue scripts from within the IDE*

The necessary daemons are all started up, so let's go back to update the Go code.

This new distributed code is almost the same as Listing 2-13, except for the queue definition, where you distribute the messages via the newly defined NSQ worker.

The message distribution is shown in Listing 2-14.

Listing 2-14. Define a NSQ worker

```go
func main() {
    ...
    w := nsq.NewWorker(
        nsq.WithAddr("127.0.0.1:4150"),
        nsq.WithTopic("crazy"),
        nsq.WithChannel("go"),
        nsq.WithMaxInFlight(10),
        nsq.WithRunFunc(func(ctx context.Context, m core.
        QueuedMessage) error {
            var v *jobData
            if err := json.Unmarshal(m.Bytes(), &v); err != nil {
                return err
            }
```

```
        rets <- v.Message
        return nil
    }),
  )

  q := queue.NewPool(10, queue.WithWorker(w))
  defer q.Release()
  ...
}
```

Listing 2-15 shows the Go program's output.

Listing 2-15. Output of Workers

```
Sleeping Gophers:Hello commander, I am handling the job: 73
Sleeping Gophers:Hello commander, I am handling the job: 85
Sleeping Gophers:Hello commander, I am handling the job: 12
Sleeping Gophers:Hello commander, I am handling the job: 96
...
message: Commander, I slept: 0 seconds
message: Commander, I slept: 0 seconds
message: Commander, I slept: 1 seconds
message: Commander, I slept: 1 seconds
```

In the web UI, if you open the related topic "crazy" and the channel Go, you will see the messages being queued and processed, with information being collected in real time (see Figure 2-8).

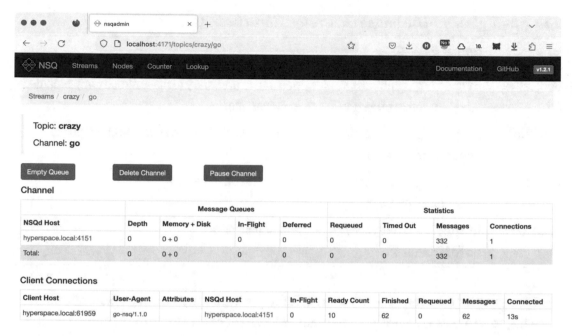

Figure 2-8. *Messages being processed by NSQ*

Later, you will use this to distribute jobs, using queues to asynchronously process the image generation.

Talking about image generation, let's move to the visually exciting part of this chapter.

Image Generators

There are several image generator libraries available in Go. Table 2-3 lists a few of the options.

Table 2-3. *Easy-to-Use Image Generator Libraries in Go*

Name	GitHub Repository	Goal
Generative Art	`https://github.com/ jdxyw/generativeart`	Generative art library (usually already implemented in Processing)
Primitive	`https://github.com/ fogleman/primitive`	Reproduces images with geometric primitives
Go-saic	`https://github.com/ telecoda/go-saic`	Image mosaic generator
Cameron	`https://github.com/ aofei/cameron`	Avatar generator

This chapter uses the `generativeart` library as the source of image generation.

The `generativeart` library implements a large set of art algorithms (many taken from Generative Art[1]), most relying on pseudo-random elements. This means when you call the same generator function with the same parameters, it will not generate the exact same picture.

Listing 2-16 shows the first art experiment, using the `NewColorCircle2` algorithm.

Listing 2-16. Creating Circles

```
package main

import (
    "github.com/jdxyw/generativeart"
    "github.com/jdxyw/generativeart/arts"
    "github.com/jdxyw/generativeart/common"
    "math/rand"
    "time"
)

func main() {
    rand.Seed(time.Now().Unix())
    c := generativeart.NewCanva(600, 400)
    c.SetBackground(common.NavajoWhite)
```

```
    c.FillBackground()
    c.SetLineWidth(1.0)
    c.SetLineColor(common.Orange)
    c.Draw(arts.NewColorCircle2(30))
    c.ToPNG("circle.png")
}
```

Note   For the pseudo-randomness to work properly, the randomness source of the Go program needs to be seeded.

If the random algorithm is not seeded properly, you end up generating the same pictures, which is not the goal here.

Usually, a good source of randomness is the UNIX time, which is the number of seconds elapsed since January 1, 1970. This is a de facto source of randomness for many programs that do not need to be ultra-secure. This is done using the rand.Seed(time.Now().Unix()) call.

Executing the code in Listing 2-16 produces generated art like the image in Figure 2-9.

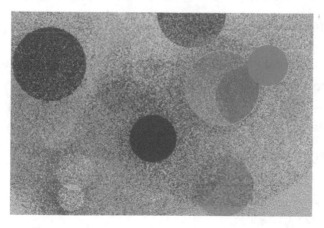

Figure 2-9. *First generated art*

Among other settings, you can change the color schema, as shown in Listing 2-17.

Listing 2-17. Setting the Color Schema

```
c.SetColorSchema([]color.RGBA{
    common.White,
    common.Tomato,
    common.Azure,
    common.Mintcream,
})
```

The result is shown in Figure 2-10.

Figure 2-10. *Different color schema*

Or you can use the color schema from the generativearts website, which adds a very Kandinsky-like mood to any sketches (see Listing 2-18).

Listing 2-18. Kandinsky-Like Color Schema

```
c.SetColorSchema([]color.RGBA{
    {0xCF, 0x2B, 0x34, 0xFF},
    {0xF0, 0x8F, 0x46, 0xFF},
    {0xF0, 0xC1, 0x29, 0xFF},
    {0x19, 0x6E, 0x94, 0xFF},
    {0x35, 0x3A, 0x57, 0xFF},
})
```

Executing the main code with this color schema produces images similar to the one in Figure 2-11.

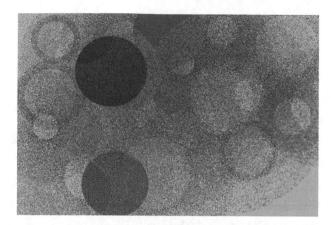

Figure 2-11. *Example output of Random Colored Circles*

It's tiresome to have to write and run programs each time, which is why you are working toward this HTTP API.

The next task toward this goal is to implement a few other samples from the library, generate images, group common settings together, and call each algorithm from keys of a map.

Image Generator in a Gin

Listing 2-19 prepares the ground for the HTTP API that you are going to be implementing in a bit. You are going to be using a map of string>Engine, which gives an art engine for each key of the map.

Not all the available generativearts algorithms are included in Listing 2-19, but you can add some of your own when working with these exercises.

Listing 2-19. Generating Art Using a Few Algorithms

```
package main

import (
    "fmt"
    "github.com/jdxyw/generativeart"
    "github.com/jdxyw/generativeart/arts"
    "github.com/jdxyw/generativeart/common"
    "image/color"
```

```go
    "math/rand"
    "time"
)

var DRAWINGS = map[string]generativeart.Engine{
    "maze":      arts.NewMaze(10),
    "julia":     arts.NewJulia(func(z complex128) complex128 { return z*z +
               complex(-0.1, 0.651) }, 40, 1.5, 1.5),
    "randcicle": arts.NewRandCicle(30, 80, 0.2, 2, 10, 30, true),
    "blackhole": arts.NewBlackHole(200, 400, 0.01),
    "janus":     arts.NewJanus(5, 10),
    "random":    arts.NewRandomShape(150),
    "silksky":   arts.NewSilkSky(15, 5),
    "circles":   arts.NewColorCircle2(30),
}

func main() {
    drawMany(DRAWINGS)
}

func drawMany(drawings map[string]generativeart.Engine) {

    for k, _ := range drawings {
        drawOne(k)
    }

}

func drawOne(art string) string {
    rand.Seed(time.Now().Unix())
    c := generativeart.NewCanva(600, 400)
    c.SetColorSchema([]color.RGBA{
        {0xCF, 0x2B, 0x34, 0xFF},
        {0xF0, 0x8F, 0x46, 0xFF},
        {0xF0, 0xC1, 0x29, 0xFF},
        {0x19, 0x6E, 0x94, 0xFF},
        {0x35, 0x3A, 0x57, 0xFF},
    })
```

```
    c.SetBackground(common.NavajoWhite)
    c.FillBackground()
    c.SetLineWidth(1.0)
    c.SetLineColor(common.Orange)
    c.Draw(DRAWINGS[art])

    fileName := fmt.Sprintf("/tmp/%s_%d.png", art, rand.Float64())
    c.ToPNG(fileName)
    return fileName
}
```

You can see that as you use a key in the map, you are going to use a route parameter to use this key and retrieve the actual art generator.

The next step is to re-use the drawOne function and call it from a Gin route. Listing 2-20 does just that, gluing the Gin router and the image generator code together.

One thing you have not seen before is how to specify the HTTP content header; you rightfully set it to image/png along the generated image.

Listing 2-20. GCG, the Gin Circle Generator

```
package main

import (
    "github.com/gin-gonic/gin"
    "gocrazy/chapter-02/final-00/drawing"
)

func router() *gin.Engine {
    r := gin.Default()
    userRoute := r.Group("/image")
    {
        userRoute.GET("/circles", func(c *gin.Context) {
            file := drawing.DrawOne("circles")
            c.Header("Content-Type", "image/png")
            c.File(file)
        })
```

```
    }
    return r
}

func main() {
    router().Run()
}
```

When you run this program, the server starts, and the command line shows the newly created circles and some logs as you access the URL via a browser (see Listing 2-21).

Listing 2-21. Gin Logs

```
[GIN-debug] GET     /image/circles              --> main.router.func1 (3
handlers)
...
[GIN-debug] Listening and serving HTTP on :8080
[GIN] 2023/03/06 - 09:49:55 | 200 |    1.0812445s |         127.0.0.1 | GET
"/image/circles"
[GIN] 2023/03/06 - 09:49:58 | 200 | 1.000493833s |         127.0.0.1 |
GET      "/image/circles"
[GIN] 2023/03/06 - 09:49:59 | 200 |    982.271ms |         127.0.0.1 | GET
"/image/circles"
```

If you access `http://localhost:8080/image/circles`, you'll see the newly generated image directly in the browser (see Figure 2-12).

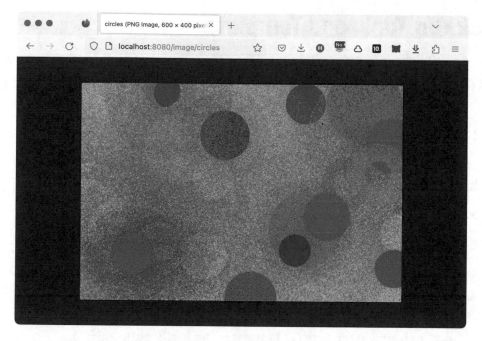

Figure 2-12. *Circles in the browser*

Note that as you refresh the page, a new circles image is generated each time.

The next step is to plug in the map of drawings `string->Engine` as a parameter in the Gin route. The updated route is shown in Listing 2-22.

Listing 2-22. Plug In the Generator as a Parameter in the Gin Route

```
imageRoute.GET("/:generator", func(c *gin.Context) {
    generator := c.Param("generator")
    file := drawing.DrawOne(generator)
    c.Header("Content-Type", "image/png")
    c.File(file)
})
```

You can call the different engines directly by using their names from the `DRAWINGS` map.

As it might be cumbersome to remember the name of the generators each time, you can template an index page to make this easier.

Quick Gin Tonic and Templates

In this example, you need like to present a list of generators as a list in an HTML page. The HTML will be templated using the template feature included in the Gin framework.

Here are the new things to learn from Listing 2-23:

1. You tell the engine where to find the templates by calling LoadHTMLGlob and providing the pattern of files to load.

2. You create a new list subgroup of endpoints for the router.

3. You use the HTML function from the Gin context to return HTML.

4. The HTML function takes the status, a template name, and a map of values to use in the template.

5. Note that, to create a slice of keys from the DRAWINGS map, you use the golang.org/x/exp/maps library, which is a set of extra features not included in the core Go language (but is still quite useful).

Listing 2-23. Gin Framework and Templating a HTML List

```go
package main

import (
    "github.com/gin-gonic/gin"
    "gocrazy/chapter-02/final-02/drawing"
    "golang.org/x/exp/maps"
    "net/http"
)

func router() *gin.Engine {
    r := gin.Default()
    r.LoadHTMLGlob("templates/*.tmpl")

    // ...

    listRoute := r.Group("/list")
    {
        listRoute.GET("/simple", func(c *gin.Context) {
            c.HTML(http.StatusOK, "simple.tmpl", gin.H{
```

```
            "keys": maps.Keys(drawing.DRAWINGS),
        })
    })
}

    return r
}

func main() {
    router().Run()
}
```

The first template is quite basic, to give you an idea as to how things are assembled. The template code uses the logic-less template style from Mustache.

1. range iterates over the slice "keys" defined in the gin.H map from Listing 2-22.

2. {{.}} outputs the current element of the loop.

The contents of the template.tmpl file are shown in Listing 2-24.

Listing 2-24. Simple List Template

```
<body>
{{range .keys}}
<p><a href="/image/{{.}}">{{.}}</a></p>
{{end}}
</body>
```

Starting the Gin server with the new route will allow you to access the list, as shown in Figure 2-13.

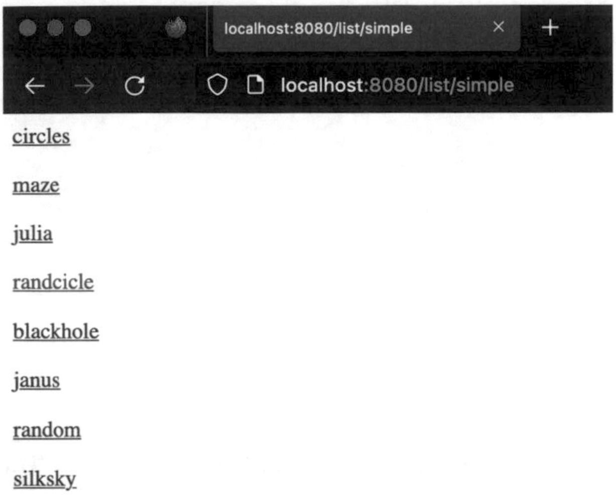

Figure 2-13. *Simple list*

And of course, clicking one of the links leads to a newly generated image.

It would be nice to include the styling bootstrap framework here, to make the list a little bit more beautiful.

You can create a table with preview images for each generator in the list. To do this, you can use the bootstrap starter template from:

```
https://getbootstrap.com/docs/4.0/getting-started/introduction/
#starter-template
```

Then you replace the body of the template with the code in Listing 2-25.

Listing 2-25. Bootstrap-Based List

```
<body>

<table class="table">
    <thead>
    <tr>
        <th scope="col">Generator</th>
        <th scope="col">Preview</th>
    </tr>
    </thead>
    <tbody>
    {{range .keys}}
    <tr>
```

```
        <td><a href="/image/{{.}}">{{.}}</a></td>
        <td><a href="/image/{{.}}"><img style="width: 100px;height:86px"
        src="/image/{{.}}"></img></a></td>
    </tr>
    {{end}}

    </tbody>
</table>
</body>
```

I leave it to you to add a new route that uses this bootstrap template or to look at the companion samples of this book.

Accessing the new route produces something more exciting, as shown in Figure 2-14.

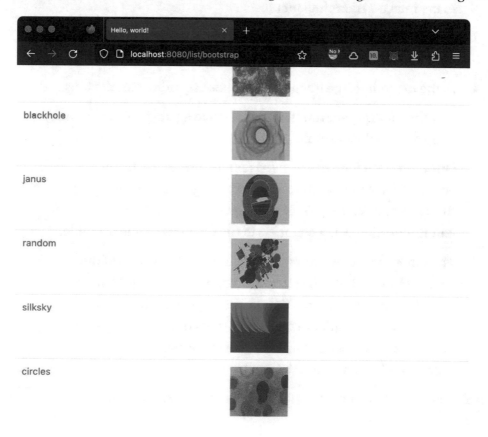

Figure 2-14. *Bootstrap-based list of generators*

Use a Synchronized Map

The final API work of this chapter is slightly more evolved. You now learn how to create a new set of routes, where one route will start the image generation and give the requester an ID to fetch the real image. If the image is generated, then the other route returns that image. If not, it returns a temporary image.

You will do the following in this order:

1. Write a route that retrieves the generator name and returns a JSON message with an ID, as well as an URL to access the image to be generated.

2. Before returning the ID and the URL, the route will post a message to the image-generating queue.

3. This route has completed its job, so any new request to the same route will return a new ID and start a new image-generation job.

4. In the meantime, the queue asynchronously processes the jobs.

5. Since the image generation is too fast here again, you'll add some sleep time to the example.

6. Once the sleep time has elapsed and the image has been generated, the path to the temporary image is stored in the synchronized map. This way, you can shortcut the communication using channels in the previous queue example.

7. The other route reads from the synchronized map and, if the id->path key value pair is found, it returns the image from the path. Otherwise, it returns the static image file. (This includes a Cache-Control header to make sure the temporary image used before the image is not cached in the browser and the new image is properly loaded when it's found.)

An abbreviated version of the final code is shown Listing 2-26.

Listing 2-26. Gin, Queues, and Image Generation

```go
package main

import (
    ...
)

type jobData struct {
    Id        string
    Generator string
}

var sm sync.Map

func (j *jobData) Bytes() []byte {
    b, _ := json.Marshal(j)
    return b
}

func router() *gin.Engine {
    r := gin.Default()
    r.LoadHTMLGlob("templates/*.tmpl")

    rand.Seed(time.Now().Unix())

    q := queue.NewPool(30, queue.WithFn(func(ctx context.Context, m core.
    QueuedMessage) error {
        j, _ := m.(*jobData)
        json.Unmarshal(m.Bytes(), &j)

        sleepTime := time.Duration(rand.Intn(10)) * time.Second
        time.Sleep(sleepTime)
        path := drawing.DrawOne(j.Generator)
        sm.Store(j.Id, path)
        fmt.Printf("Stored: %s:%s [%s]\n", j.Id, j.Generator, path)

        return nil
    }))
```

```go
...
newRoute := r.Group("/new")
{
    newRoute.GET("/load/:id", func(c *gin.Context) {
        id := c.Param("id")
        path, ok := sm.Load(id)

        if ok {
            fmt.Printf("Found %s for id: %s\n", path, id)
            c.Header("Content-Type", "image/png")
            c.File(fmt.Sprintf("%s", path.(string)))
        } else {
            fmt.Printf("Path not found for id: %s\n", id)
            c.Header("Content-Type", "image/jpg")
            c.Header("Cache-Control", "no-cache")
            c.File("static/loading.jpg")
        }
    })
    newRoute.GET("/:generator", func(c *gin.Context) {
        generator := c.Param("generator")
        newJob := jobData{
            Id:        strconv.Itoa(rand.Int()),
            Generator: generator,
        }
        q.Queue(&newJob)
        res := map[string]string{"id": newJob.Id, "url": "http://" +
        c.Request.Host + "/new/load/" + newJob.Id}
        c.JSON(200, res)
    })
}

return r
}
```

Once this example starts the new server, you can access the new route via:
http://localhost:8080/new/:generator
For example:

```
http://localhost:8080/new/janus
```

The route returns a JSON message containing the ID of the generated image, and for convenience, the URL to retrieve the image itself (see Figure 2-15).

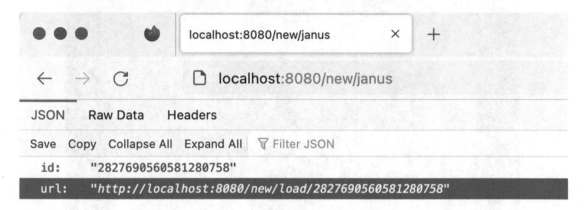

Figure 2-15. *JSON message when accessing the new route*

Figures 2-16 and 2-17 shows the content when accessing the indicated URL. Figure 2-16 shows the temporary picture when the proper image has not been generated yet, and Figure 2-17 shows the proper image.

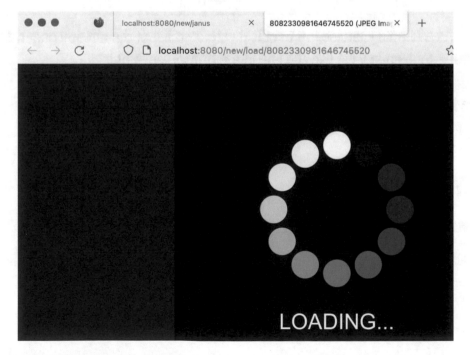

Figure 2-16. *Temporary image before the image has been generated*

Figure 2-17. *The same URL, but this time the image has been generated*

Note   As a simple exercise, try to quickly create a list of the already generated images—an overview list like the one in the previous example.

Now that the API server is fully ready, it would be nice if you could run some regression testing to verify that the queuing process works all the time.

Testing the API
Simple Go and Gin Testing

This is almost straight from the Gin framework cookbook and is only included here for convenience (see Listing 2-27).

Listing 2-27. Ping Route from the Gin Framework Guidebook

```go
package main

import "github.com/gin-gonic/gin"

func setupRouter() *gin.Engine {
    r := gin.Default()
    r.GET("/ping", func(c *gin.Context) {
        c.String(200, "pong")
    })
    return r
}

func main() {
    r := setupRouter()
    r.Run(":8080")
}
```

To write tests in Go, you need to:

1. Create a file called something_test.go, where _test.go is the important part to be discovered by the testing framework. The rest of the name is up to you. The file can be anywhere in the project, usually alongside the something.go file to be tested (at least in the same folder).

2. In the file, use the import of the Go testing namespace.

3. Create a function that starts with the name Test and has a pointer to a testing.T parameter, which is the object that includes everything you need for assertions so it can interact with the runtime and result of the test.

4. Use testify/assert to get feedback and easily compare values between what is expected and the actual results.

5. To test the Gin route, you'll create the request to be tested using NewRequest. Then you'll combine a NewRecorder and a router.ServeHTTP to write the response to that request in the recorder object.

6. The recorder object contains all the elements of the response, as specified in the Gin routes you defined. That way, you can use this object to test expected values against real values.

Note   Apart from potential network connectivity side-effects, there are no differences between the contents of this recorded response object and the actual HTTP response in a real-life scenario.

With all this in mind, Listing 2-28 shows how to test this Gin ping route.

Listing 2-28. Testing the Ping Route

```
package main

import (
        "net/http"
        "net/http/httptest"
        "testing"

        "github.com/stretchr/testify/assert"
)

func TestPingRoute(t *testing.T) {
        router := setupRouter()

        w := httptest.NewRecorder()
        req, _ := http.NewRequest("GET", "/ping", nil)
        router.ServeHTTP(w, req)

        assert.Equal(t, 200, w.Code)
        assert.Equal(t, "pong", w.Body.String())
}
```

To run the test in GoLand, you can use the green arrows in the Editor. You can run each test one by one, or run all the tests in the current file (see Figure 2-18).

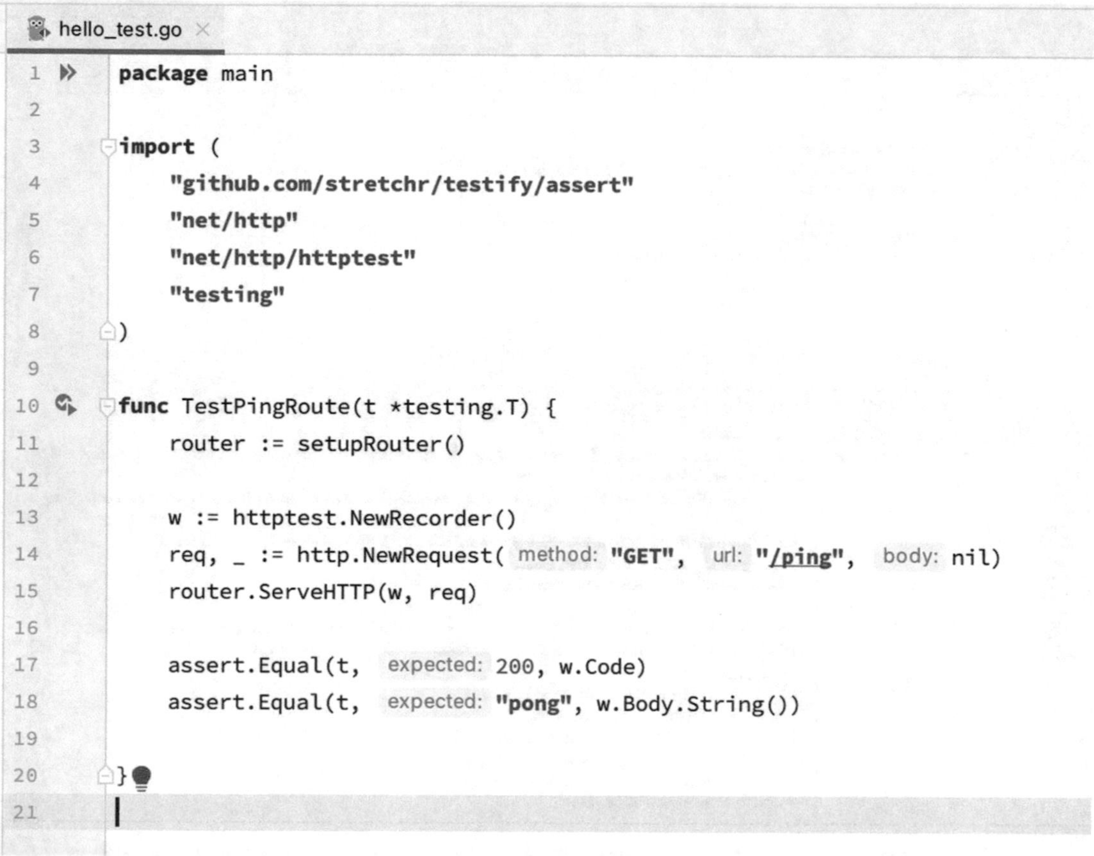

```go
 1  »      package main
 2
 3         import (
 4             "github.com/stretchr/testify/assert"
 5             "net/http"
 6             "net/http/httptest"
 7             "testing"
 8         )
 9
10         func TestPingRoute(t *testing.T) {
11             router := setupRouter()
12
13             w := httptest.NewRecorder()
14             req, _ := http.NewRequest( method: "GET",  url: "/ping",  body: nil)
15             router.ServeHTTP(w, req)
16
17             assert.Equal(t,  expected: 200, w.Code)
18             assert.Equal(t,  expected: "pong", w.Body.String())
19
20         }
21
```

Figure 2-18. *Running the tests using GoLand's green arrows*

If you force the test to fail, for example by updating the expected code to be 400 instead of the actual 200, the test will fail with some useful output (see Figure 2-19).

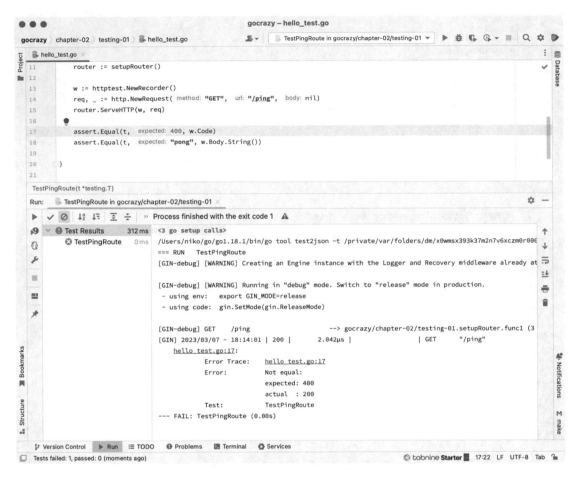

Figure 2-19. *Analyze failing tests*

The idea is to write tests that are easy to maintain and update and to be able to determine the whys and whens of a failing test. Figure 2-20 pinpoints exactly why the test is failing.

```
[GIN-debug] GET     /ping                        --> gocrazy/chapter-02/testing-01.setupRouter.func1 (3 handlers)
[GIN] 2023/03/07 - 18:14:01 | 200 |       2.042µs |                    | GET      "/ping"
    hello test.go:17:
            Error Trace:     hello test.go:17
            Error:           Not equal:
                             expected: 400
                             actual  : 200
            Test:            TestPingRoute
--- FAIL: TestPingRoute (0.00s)


Expected :400
Actual   :200
```

Figure 2-20. *Test failure analyses*

Once you fix the cause of the failure, you can choose to rerun only the failing tests (see Figure 2-21).

Figure 2-21. *Fixing the tests*

This time, the test is rightfully green, as shown in Figure 2-22.

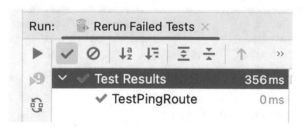

Figure 2-22. *All green!*

That was it for the basics of testing a Gin route. Now you learn how to apply the same technique to your freshly created image HTTP API.

Testing the Image Generator

For the first test, you'll check the return message from the /new/janus route, which returns a JSON message of type ImageAnswer.

You can use the same technique as the Gin cookbook seen previously and unmarshall the body of the recorded HTTP response as bytes into the custom Go struct.

Since the body is empty, you had nil to the GET request and then ask the router to again "simulate" the request using ServerHTTP (see Listing 2-29).

Listing 2-29. Testing the JSON Message Returned from the Image API

```go
func TestAPIRouteNew(t *testing.T) {
    router := router()

    w := httptest.NewRecorder()
    req, _ := http.NewRequest("GET", "/new/janus", nil)
    router.ServeHTTP(w, req)

    var img ImageAnswer
    json.Unmarshal(w.Body.Bytes(), &img)
    assert.NotEmpty(t, img)

}
```

Running this test should give you a pass, as shown in Figure 2-23.

```
[GIN-debug] GET    /image/:generator       --> gocrazy/chapter-02/testing-02.router.func2 (3 handlers)
[GIN-debug] GET    /list/simple            --> gocrazy/chapter-02/testing-02.router.func3 (3 handlers)
[GIN-debug] GET    /list/bootstrap         --> gocrazy/chapter-02/testing-02.router.func4 (3 handlers)
[GIN-debug] GET    /new/load/:id           --> gocrazy/chapter-02/testing-02.router.func5 (3 handlers)
[GIN-debug] GET    /new/:generator         --> gocrazy/chapter-02/testing-02.router.func6 (3 handlers)
[GIN] 2023/03/07 - 01:10:08 | 200 |     242.75µs |              | GET      "/new/janus"
--- PASS: TestAPIRouteNew (0.00s)
PASS
```

Figure 2-23. *Output of running the test*

The next test you write is according to the job being dispatched in the queue. Here are the things you to do:

1. Send a request to /new/generator.

2. Retrieve the ID of the image to be generated.

3. Receive an ID and create the URL using the ID.

4. Send the request a first time and determine if the image returned is the temporary image (remember it was of type image/jpg so it's a different type than the generated PNG images).

5. Wait three seconds (modify the wait time to not wait too long here).

6. Send the request in Step 4 again.

7. This time, the image is in the map and the Content-Type should be image/png.

Listing 2-30 is simply an expansion of Listing 2-29, with the new extra steps included.

Listing 2-30. Full Test of the Queued Image API

```go
func TestAPIRouteLoad(t *testing.T) {
    router := router()

    w := httptest.NewRecorder()
    req, _ := http.NewRequest("GET", "/new/janus", nil)
    router.ServeHTTP(w, req)

    var img ImageAnswer
    json.Unmarshal(w.Body.Bytes(), &img)

    req, _ = http.NewRequest("GET", "/new/load/"+img.Id, nil)
    router.ServeHTTP(w, req)

    assert.Equal(t, "image/jpg", w.Header().Get("Content-Type"))

    time.Sleep(3 * time.Second)

    req, _ = http.NewRequest("GET", "/new/load/"+img.Id, nil)
    router.ServeHTTP(w, req)
    assert.Equal(t, "image/png", w.Header().Get("Content-Type"))
}
```

Running the test should result in a pass, as shown in Figure 2-24. Otherwise, it's time to analyze the failure.

```
[GIN-debug] GET     /image/:generator           --> gocrazy/chapter-02/testing-02.router.func2 (3 handlers)
[GIN-debug] GET     /list/simple                --> gocrazy/chapter-02/testing-02.router.func3 (3 handlers)
[GIN-debug] GET     /list/bootstrap             --> gocrazy/chapter-02/testing-02.router.func4 (3 handlers)
[GIN-debug] GET     /new/load/:id               --> gocrazy/chapter-02/testing-02.router.func5 (3 handlers)
[GIN-debug] GET     /new/:generator             --> gocrazy/chapter-02/testing-02.router.func6 (3 handlers)
[GIN] 2023/03/07 - 01:17:55 | 200 |    310.042µs |                  | GET      "/new/janus"
Path not found for id: 8360446174348262367
[GIN] 2023/03/07 - 01:17:55 | 200 |    299.625µs |                  | GET      "/new/load/8360446174348262367"
{Id:8360446174348262367 Url:http:///new/load/8360446174348262367}
Stored: 8360446174348262367:janus [/tmp/janus_0.997328.png]
Found /tmp/janus_0.997328.png for id: 8360446174348262367
[GIN] 2023/03/07 - 01:17:58 | 200 |       403µs |                  | GET      "/new/load/8360446174348262367"
--- PASS: TestAPIRouteLoad (3.00s)
PASS
```

Figure 2-24. *Full debugging messages of the passing test*

Summary

This concludes Chapter 2, where you learned how to write an asynchronous API for image generation and how to write and run tests for it.

After completing this chapter and going through all the code examples, you should know how to:

- Create a simple API using Gin routing techniques.

- Work with queues to distribute the load of the API asynchronously.

- Generate images using the generative art library.

- Use channels and synchronized maps to communicate data throughout the API.

- Do some templating in or outside the Gin framework.

- Run simple Go testing using the included testing framework.

- Perform end-to-end testing of the API using the simple Gin feature to emulate requests.

CHAPTER 3

Writing the Basics for a 2D Game in Go

> *The game gives you a purpose. The real game is to find a purpose.*
>
> —Vineet Raj Kapoor

I've always been on the side of using a game engine instead of other UI tools to create lively interfaces for interacting between systems, people, or both.

There have been a lot of new 2D gaming interfaces since the pandemic, be it multiplayer games, like AmongUs (`www.innersloth.com/games/among-us/`), or communication tools like Gather.town (`www.gather.town/`), WorkAdventure (`https://workadventu.re/`) and the hobby-like SkyOffice (`https://skyoffice.netlify.app/`).

We have tried many here, in the Japan workplace, to enhance team collaboration and enhance team collaboration. Many of those solutions come with a hefty price tag as the number of user increases, so why not try developing your own? Or what about just finding your life voice while developing a simple 2D game?

This is the goal of this chapter. Although you won't see and implement a full game, you will learn the technical basis for one, which should give you enough inspiration to keep going.

Some Tile Set History

Many of the early '80s games in 2D used tile sets to load graphics. Think about Nintendo's Zelda and Capcom's Rockman (aka Megaman). Bandai/Namco's Pacman (`https://pacman.com/en/history/`) displayed its tile sets on the big ALTA screen in front of Tokyo's Shinjuku station.

© Nicolas Modrzyk 2023
N. Modrzyk, *Go Crazy*, https://doi.org/10.1007/978-1-4842-9666-0_3

The first iteration of a tile set-based game was achieved with Galaxian, Namco's answer to Space Invaders. Galaxian had much better graphics and they loaded much faster too.

When you want to display a graphic in a 2D game, you load or draw graphics into a *framebuffer*, which is part of the available memory location that is used for graphic rendering. Before the tile sets era, developers had to either draw each sprite directly in the framebuffer or load a file per character. This was usually slow, and the number of files you could use was largely restricted. The Galaxian developers engineered a way to load one file once, with all the different tiles required for a proper character animation, and only display or use a portion of that file.

The obvious advantage is that you could display and animated more beautifully drawn characters, while at the same time limiting hardware access to them, a key way to make games faster when resources were limited.

The process of loading and animating using a sprite sheet or tile sheet is how you are going to develop the simple game in this chapter.

Library Setup: Raylib

The chapter's original plan was to present Ebiten, `https://github.com/hajimehoshi/ebiten/`, a simple 2D game engine written entirely in Go. Having the whole library in Go is quite a feat for an open-source game engine, and the collection of samples is very impressive, so you should definitely take a look at it.

The game library you are going to use here, called Raylib (`www.raylib.com/`) is not written in Go, but its bindings are available (`https://github.com/gen2brain/raylib-go`) and this is what you are going to use to develop the game basics for the chapter.

Raylib's core philosophy is close to this book's:

> *raylib is a programming library to enjoy videogame programming; no fancy interface, no visual helpers, no GUI tools or editors... just coding in a pure Spartan-programmers way. Are you ready to enjoy coding?*

There are a few steps you need to do to get ready to use `raylib-go`, depending on the machine you are using. They are specified on the project's GitHub page (see `https://github.com/gen2brain/raylib-go#requirements`).

For the usual mainstream operating systems, the instructions are repeated here:

macOS
On macOS you need Xcode or Command Line Tools for Xcode.

Windows
On Windows you need C compiler, like Mingw-w64 or TDM-GCC. You can also build binary in MSYS2 shell.

On other *ixes,* it's a matter of installing a few extra packages, notably libmesa3d (see https://www.mesa3d.org/).

Game Setup

Once you have installed the required libraries, it is time to start with a simple example straight from the raylib-go front page. The first example simply opens a gaming window and writes some text to it.

As usual, GoLand will do the project setup and dependencies for you. Therefore, in a new folder, and with a new Go file in GoLand, copy and paste the code from GitHub. Listing 3-1 shows the code.

Listing 3-1. The raylib-go Simple Game Setup

```go
package main

import "github.com/gen2brain/raylib-go/raylib"

func main() {

    rl.InitWindow(800, 450, "basic window")
    rl.SetTargetFPS(60)
    for !rl.WindowShouldClose() {
        rl.BeginDrawing()
        rl.ClearBackground(rl.Black)
        rl.DrawText("This is your game!", 190, 200, 20, rl.LightGray)
        rl.EndDrawing()
    }
    rl.CloseWindow()
}
```

Note these aspects of this code:

1. InitWindow sets the size and title parameters for the gaming window.

2. SetTargetFPS asks the engine to reach a certain number of frames per second.

3. WindowShouldClose checks whether the window is about to close. Most simple games will use that information to determine when it's time to exit the game.

4. BeginDrawing and EndDrawing are the beginning and end of the render phase, where you interact directly with the canvas, the graphical content of the game.

5. ClearBackground sets the background color of the canvas.

6. DrawText is the simplest way to draw text onscreen.

7. CloseWindow is used when you press the Esc key to finish the game loop and quit the game.

If you execute the program, you'll see the window in Figure 3-1.

Figure 3-1. *The first raylib-go window*

You could run some basic examples and learn from them, but let's first see if using ChatGPT can help you get up to speed faster here.

Quick Game Generation with ChatGPT

You saw in the first chapter how to interact with ChatGPT via code. Using either the Web interface or the API you set up earlier, you can ask ChatGPT to write simple `raylib-go` examples for you and get a grasp on how to use the library.

As usual, ChatGPT does not generate working code, but the basics are a good way to see how to plug in the different methods of the `raylib-go` library.

Display the Date in Real Time

The first example will simply display the date in real time using `raylib`. The prompt to ChatGPT is as follows:

```
Use the raylib-go library to display the date in real time.
```

There are a few things you'll want to correct in that script. Notably a few things do not compile right away, as shown in Figure 3-2.

```
 9
10  ▶  ▽func main() {
11          screenWidth := 800
12          screenHeight := 450
13
14          rl.InitWindow(screenWidth, screenHeight, title: "Real-Time Date Display")
15
16          rl.SetTargetFPS( fps: 60)
17
18          font := rl.LoadFont( fileName: "arial.ttf")
19      ⊝   if font.Size == 0 {
20              fmt.Println( a...: "Failed to load font")
21              return
22      △   }
23
```

Figure 3-2. *Almost there ChatGPT*

Note these changes:

1. To load a font to use in the game, you need to provide the `font. ttf` file in the same folder. The `Size` function does not exist, so you need to use a `BaseSize` to check whether the font has been loaded properly. A free font has been provided in the samples, but you can of course find and download a font you like.

2. screenHeight and screenWidth should be moved to a const section.

3. The loaded font was not used. To use a custom font, you need to use DrawTextEx instead of DrawText.

4. To measure the text size of a font, you should use MeasureTextEx instead of MeasureText.

This is a nice update from the first example that you hand-coded earlier. It includes these changes:

– Real-time drawing updates of a string on the canvas.

– The position of the text is computed from an estimate size of text.

– You now use DrawTextEx to draw text with a custom font.

The updated code is shown in Listing 3-2.

Listing 3-2. A Date Display Example Using raylib-go

```
package main

import (
    "fmt"
    "time"

    rl "github.com/gen2brain/raylib-go/raylib"
)

const (
    screenWidth  = 800
    screenHeight = 480
    fontSize     = 36
)

func main() {

    rl.InitWindow(screenWidth, screenHeight, "Real-Time Date Display")

    rl.SetTargetFPS(60)
```

```go
font := rl.LoadFont("font.ttf")
if font.BaseSize == 0 {
    fmt.Println("Failed to load font")
    return
}

for !rl.WindowShouldClose() {
    rl.BeginDrawing()

    rl.ClearBackground(rl.LightGray)

    // Get current date and time
    now := time.Now()
    dateStr := now.Format("January 02, 2006 15:04:05")

    // Draw date and time
    position := rl.Vector2{X: float32(screenWidth/2 -
    rl.MeasureTextEx(font, dateStr, fontSize, 0).X/2), Y:
    screenHeight/2 - 20}
    rl.DrawTextEx(font, dateStr, position, fontSize, 0, rl.Black)

    rl.EndDrawing()

    time.Sleep(time.Second)
}

rl.UnloadFont(font)
rl.CloseWindow()
}
```

Figure 3-3 shows the results.

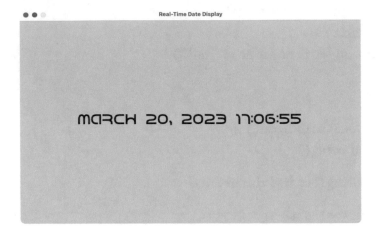

Figure 3-3. *A simple real-time display*

The data is displayed in real time, so you have effectively gained some nice coding knowledge there.

In the next section, you learn how to do something slightly harder—create a small hangman game.

Hangman Game

This time, you'll ask ChatGPT to generate another simple game using `raylib-go`—a hangman game. Again, ChatGPT gets close.

The original prompt was the following:

```
Write a hangman game using the raylib-go library
```

The fixed generated code of the `main` function is shown in Listing 3-3.

Listing 3-3. Hangman Generated by ChatGPT

```
func main() {

    rl.InitWindow(screenWidth, screenHeight, "Hangman")
    rl.SetTargetFPS(60)

    // Load word list
    words := loadWordList("words.txt")
```

```go
if len(words) == 0 {
   fmt.Println("Failed to load word list")
   return
}

// Select a random word
secretWord = strings.ToUpper(words[rand.Intn(len(words))])

// Initialize guessed letters array
guessedLetters = make([]string, len(secretWord))
for i := range guessedLetters {
   guessedLetters[i] = "_"
}

// Main game loop
for !rl.WindowShouldClose() {
   // Handle input
   if rl.IsKeyPressed(rl.KeyR) {
      restartGame(words)
   } else if !gameOver {
      handleInput()
   }

   // Draw graphics
   rl.BeginDrawing()
   rl.ClearBackground(rl.White)
   drawHangman()
   drawWord()
   drawGuessedLetters()
   if gameOver {
      if gameWin() {
         drawGameWin()
      } else {
         drawGameOver()
      }
```

```
        }
        rl.EndDrawing()
    }

    rl.CloseWindow()
}
```

Note   Note the use of the `continue` trick a few times, in order for ChatGPT to generate the full code. This is a limitation of the Web interface for now.

The full code listing is found in the samples that come with this book. The resulting game is shown in Figure 3-4.

Figure 3-4. *Hangman and coffee*

There were many minor problems with the originally AI-generated code, or things you should get used to changing when asking ChatGPT to generate libs with `raylib-go`:

- It was trying to load a font but was not using it.

- While loading the fonts, it was also using a nonexistent function to use that font.

- The code was not detecting a game win properly (the logic was completely missing).

- It was missing the random seeding, so the game had the same order for the words.

- It loaded the words from an external file using nonexistent file-reading functions.

On the other hand, there were a few things to be impressed with:

- The `main` game loop was functioning.

- The drawing of the hangman is rather cute.

- ChatGPT separated the different draw functions, each of them called from the `main` game loop, instead of having everything inside one function.

In parallel, what was equally instructive:

- The font loading part was easy to fix, and it was a nice example of how to use fonts in `raylib-go`.

- Instructing ChatGPT to switch from `if/else` to `switch` statements was easy too; you just tell it to do so.

- The way ChatGPT randomly creates function names when it's not happy with what it knows was fun. You can tell ChatGPT that those functions do not exist and it will give you a Pinocchio-like reason as to why it put them in the code.

Now that we know the good, the bad, and the evil of an AI code-generation tool, it's time to start creating your own little game of a character moving on a 2D board.

The Moyashi Game

We all carry the seeds of greatness within us, but we need an image as a point of focus in order that they may sprout.

—Epictetus

This section was inspired by the lovely YouTube tutorial: "Making an Animal Crossing type game for beginners - Go & Raylib," by Avery.

You will create a good working base to develop a small tile-based game, called Moyashi. The character will be move on a map generated from tile sets, with music. You will also give the player some input on what to implement next.

The game is called Moyashi, Japanese for Sprout, which is the name of the assets package it uses.

The game will eventually look like Figure 3-5.

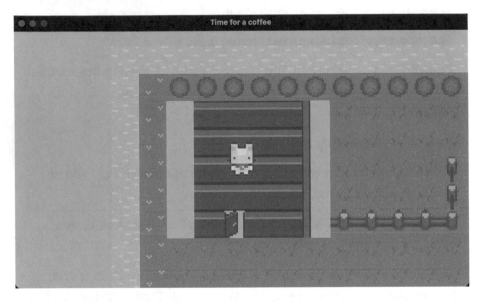

Figure 3-5. *Moyashi in the grass*

This is the plan you will follow to get there:

> Step 0: Prepare the base Go file with the game loop.
>
> Step 1: Load a texture and draw it on the canvas.
>
> Step 2: Draw sprites.
>
> Step 3: Use keyboard inputs.
>
> Step 4: Play some music.
>
> Step 5: Set the 2D camera.
>
> Step 6: Animate Moyashi while it is moving.
>
> Step 7: Animate Moyashi while it is idle.
>
> Step 8: Load one tile for the map and draw it.

Step 9: Map a small level.

Step 10: Load a full map level.

The examples in the chapter use the same numbering as these steps, so it's easy to follow along. Let's get started.

The Basic Game Loop

The common structure for a basic 2D game is usually made of the following:

1. An init phase

2. A game loop; and within that game loop:

    a. A keepRunning check to determine whether there is another turn of the game, or if you should display the main menu or the Play Again menu.

    b. An input-handling function.

    c. A data/position update function.

    d. A drawing function, which is usually a minor function or each kind of item to update graphically.

3. A clean-up phase when the game is about to exit.

Listing 3-4 expands from the original raylib-go simple example and adds the basic game loop structure.

Listing 3-4. Basic Structure for the Game Program

```
package main

import rl "github.com/gen2brain/raylib-go/raylib"

const (
    screenWidth  = 800
    screenHeight = 450
)

var (
    running         = true
    backgroundColor = rl.Black
)
```

```go
func init() {
    rl.SetConfigFlags(rl.FlagVsyncHint)
    rl.InitWindow(screenWidth, screenHeight, "Moyashi")
    rl.SetExitKey(0)
    rl.SetTargetFPS(60)
}

func update() {
    running = !rl.WindowShouldClose()
}

func input() {

}

func quit() {
    rl.CloseWindow()
}

func render() {
    rl.BeginDrawing()

    rl.ClearBackground(backgroundColor)

    drawScene()

    rl.EndDrawing()
}

func drawScene() {
    rl.DrawText("Moyashi", 190, 200, 20, rl.LightGray)
}

func main() {

    for running {
        input()
```

```
        update()
        render()
    }

    quit()

}
```

This does not nothing new from the original example; executing the program again shows the Moyashi window, as shown in Figure 3-6.

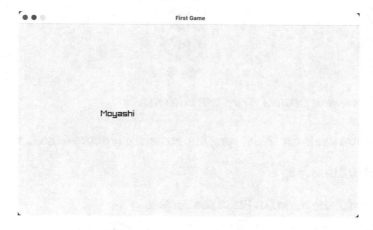

Figure 3-6. *Basic Moyashi window*

Note in the code the following:

- The const section, with all the constants of the game.

- The var section, with all the variables of the game.

- All the game initialization is done in the init function.

Now that the basics are in place, you learn how to add some simple graphics to this game.

Loading Textures

Just like Avery's example, you can get the graphics from:

https://cupnooble.itch.io/sprout-lands-asset-pack

There is a free version and a paid version. For the sake of those $2, you might also want to tip when downloading.

We make a living by what we get, but we make a life by what we give.

—Winston Churchill

When you have downloaded the assets, put them in an `assets` folder inside your project files. Your folder setup should mirror the setup shown in Figure 3-7.

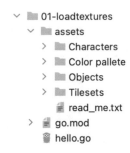

Figure 3-7. *Game files project structure with assets*

The first file you use is the `Grass.png` file, so first make sure `Grass.png` exists:

`assets/Tilesets/Grass.png`

This is relative to the main Go file of the project.

The contents of the `Grass.png` file are shown in Figure 3-8.

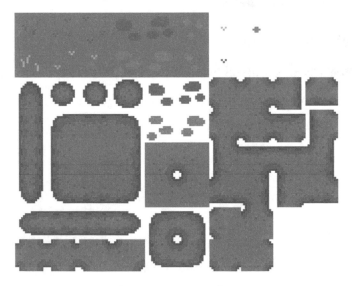

Figure 3-8. *Some grass*

Now what you want to do is load that .png file and display it onscreen, in place of drawing the text.

For reference, you can look at either or both of these:

- The Go bindings doc: https://pkg.go.dev/github.com/gen2brain/raylib-go/raylib#CheckCollisionRecs

- The original raylib cheat sheet: https://www.raylib.com/cheatsheet/cheatsheet_zh.html

A few notes about the code to come:

- When you use rl.LoadTexture, you get a rl.Texture2D object, so you need to add a reference to that object in the var section of the Go program.

- The rl.LoadTexture call will be in the init function.

- There are a few different ways to draw textures. For now the example uses rl.DrawTexture, which takes a texture, a location, and a background color.

- Let's not forget to unload the texture when finishing the game, using rl.UnloadTexture.

The parts of the new code are shown in Listing 3-5.

Listing 3-5. Code for Loading a Texture from a File

```go
var (
    running         = true
    backgroundColor = rl.NewColor(147, 211, 196, 255)

    grassSprite rl.Texture2D
)

func init() {
// ...
    grassSprite = rl.LoadTexture("assets/Tilesets/Grass.png")
}

// ...
```

```go
func quit() {
    rl.UnloadTexture(grassSprite)
    rl.CloseWindow()
}

// ...

func drawScene() {
    rl.DrawTexture(grassSprite, 100, 50, rl.White)
}
```

The resulting window is shown in Figure 3-9.

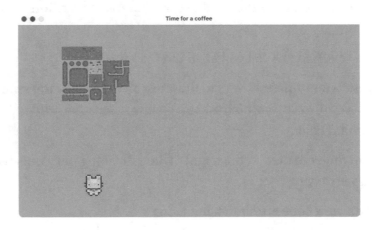

Figure 3-9. *Loaded texture*

The first spreadsheet has been loaded and displayed, so now you'll load a texture for your main player.

Adding a Player Texture

In the "Loading Textures" section, you loaded the full PNG file and displayed the full contents of that file. In a tile-based game, this is obviously not the way you want to load assets. Assets are gathered in one file to limit the amount of disk access when loading many assets.

In a 2D character animation, you load one file containing all the different frames for all the character's animation frames. The file is loaded, and then the game displays only one part of the file.

This can be done by using two rectangles:

- One to select the location in the loaded file.

- One to store the copy of the location adjusted in size in the game's canvas.

The sprite sheet for the game character is shown in Figure 3-10.

Figure 3-10. *Sprite sheet for Moyashi*

Note that GoLand will show the overall size of the picture, and by simple division, each single frame to use for Moyashi is 48x48 pixels.

The next example loads the texture and displays Moyashi. The updated parts of the code to reach that goal are shown in Listing 3-6.

Listing 3-6. Loading Moyashi's Sprite

```
var (
    // ...

    playerSprite rl.Texture2D
    playerSrc  rl.Rectangle
    playerDest rl.Rectangle
)
```

```go
func init() {
    // ...
    playerSprite = rl.LoadTexture("assets/Characters/Spritesheet.png")

    playerSrc = rl.NewRectangle(0, 0, 48, 48)
    playerDest = rl.NewRectangle(200, 200, 150, 150)
}

func quit() {
    rl.UnloadTexture(grassSprite)
    rl.UnloadTexture(playerSprite)
    rl.CloseWindow()
}

func drawScene() {
    rl.DrawTexture(grassSprite, 100, 50, rl.White)

    location := rl.NewVector2(100,-100)

    rl.DrawTexturePro(playerSprite, playerSrc, playerDest, location, 0,
    rl.White)
}
```

A few things to note:

1. In rl.NewRectangle(0, 0, 48, 48), 48x48 is the size of a single tile in the loaded .png file. The first two 0s define the location to load the 48x48 image.

2. You can use DrawTexturePro this time to use the two rectangles and the adjusted location of the sprite.

3. The location is an adjusted location. The main onscreen location is the one from playerDest (X and Y coordinates).

Running the program will give you an extended version of the first game window, with the same green grass and Moyashi displayed on top of it (see Figure 3-11).

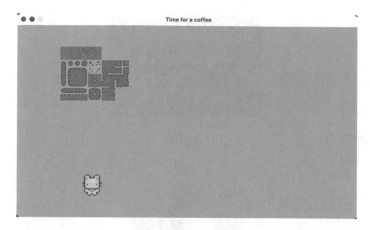

Figure 3-11. *Moyashi in the grass*

Before moving on to use inputs, try to change the value of the source rectangle and load another Moyashi frame. For example, try rl.NewRectangle(96, 0, 48, 48) for Moyashi. The result is shown Figure 3-12.

Figure 3-12. *Top row, third column*

Or, use rl.NewRectangle(0, 96, 48, 48) for Moyashi, as shown in Figure 3-13.

Figure 3-13. *Third row, first column*

Once you've had enough fun, you can move on to the next section, where you learn how to move Moyashi using key inputs.

Using Key Inputs

The input process is easy to code. You can add support for either the WASD keys (see Figure 3-14) or for using the arrow keys (see Figure 3-15).

Figure 3-14. *WASD keys*

Figure 3-15. *Arrow keys*

In the input function, the code determines if a key is pressed using rl.IsKeyDown. When a key is pressed, the code updates the playerDest.X and playerDest.Y values to the display function and updates the location of Moyashi on the canvas.

Only the input function is shown in Listing 3-7; the rest of the code remains the same.

Listing 3-7. Acting on Key Input

```go
func input() {
    if rl.IsKeyDown(rl.KeyW) || rl.IsKeyDown(rl.KeyUp) {
        playerDest.Y -= playerSpeed
    }
    if rl.IsKeyDown(rl.KeyS) || rl.IsKeyDown(rl.KeyDown) {
        playerDest.Y += playerSpeed
    }
    if rl.IsKeyDown(rl.KeyA) || rl.IsKeyDown(rl.KeyLeft) {
        playerDest.X -= playerSpeed
    }
    if rl.IsKeyDown(rl.KeyD) || rl.IsKeyDown(rl.KeyRight) {
        playerDest.X += playerSpeed
    }
}
```

playerSpeed is an integer value. It can be either a `const` defined at the top of the file, or a `var` that's set in the `init` function (here, `playerSpeed = 3`).

Figures 3-16 and 3-17 show the updated location of Moyashi on the canvas.

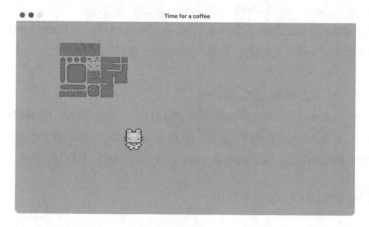

Figure 3-16. *Moyashi's location after loading the game*

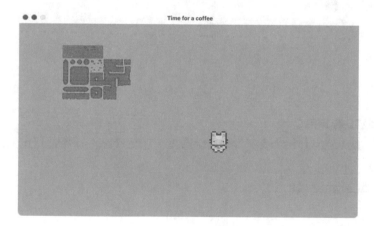

Figure 3-17. *Moyashi's location after pressing the right arrow key a few times*

Moyashi can now move, so now you'll see how to keep the walk in tempo by adding some game music.

Doing the Game Music

Just like with graphical assets, music is an expensive business where the obvious holy grail is to create and record your own. This little game uses free music.

The Free Music Archive has free audio files to get you started. For example, you can search for nature-inspired tracks:

`https://freemusicarchive.org/search?adv=1&quicksearch=nature%20&&`

Also, pond5 has a few limited samples that are pretty good:

`https://www.pond5.com/search?kw=game+walk+in+the+nature&media=music`

Since we are about indie gaming in this chapter, IndieGameMusic should also be of help:

`https://www.indiegamemusic.com/`

Wherever you decided to download the music from, place the downloaded music file in the `assets/music` folder and update the file path in the code listing.

The new code for loading and playing music is shown in Listing 3-8.

Listing 3-8. Playing the Game Music

```go
var (
    // ...
    musicPaused = false
    music       rl.Music
)

func init() {
    // ...
    rl.InitAudioDevice()
    music = rl.LoadMusicStream("assets/music/cartoon-whistling-walk-
    loop.mp3")
    rl.PlayMusicStream(music)

}

func update() {
    running = !rl.WindowShouldClose()

    rl.UpdateMusicStream(music)
}
func quit() {
    rl.UnloadMusicStream(music)
    // ...
}
```

Things to pay attention to:

1. You need to call rl.InitAudioDevice() before using the
    audio device.

2. PlayMusicStream tells the audio device to get the stream ready.

3. You cannot fire and forget playing music; you need to
    continuously update the music in the game loop using
    UpdateMusicStream.

4. When cleaning up assets, you also need to clean up the
    loaded stream with UnloadMusicStream. This is the same as
    UnloadTexture for textures. (Also, not included here, but you
    should use rl.CloseAudioDevice in the quit function.)

There is no screenshot for music! Too bad. This would be a perfect feature for a book—the music changes depending on the chapter you are reading.

Instead, Listing 3-9 stops/resumes the music using the corresponding raylib-go functions. Note that the rest of the game continues to render as usual, even when the music stops.

Listing 3-9. Stop/Resume Playing the Music

```go
func update() {
   running = !rl.WindowShouldClose()

   rl.UpdateMusicStream(music)
   if musicPaused {
      rl.PauseMusicStream(music)
   } else {
      rl.ResumeMusicStream(music)
   }
}
func input() {
   // ...
   if rl.IsKeyDown(rl.KeyM) {
      musicPaused = !musicPaused
   }
}
```

Moyashi now has a nice tempo to walk around. In the next section, you learn how to add a camera to follow Moyashi's moves.

Game Camera

Up to now, the game has used the X and Y coordinates in the map. As a reminder, coordinates are from top to bottom for X, and from left to right for Y.

Moyashi's location is set using X and Y, but how you view the whole land can be set up with the object camera, rl.Camera2D.

By default, you set the camera so that even when Moyashi changes location, it will be displayed in the center of the screen. The perception of movement is achieved by moving the camera around the map.

The camera is set up in the init function, and then you update the target of the camera to be where Moyashi is in the update function, as shown in Listing 3-10.

Listing 3-10. Camera to Set Moyashi in the Center

```
var (
    // ...
    cam          rl.Camera2D
)

func init() {
    // ...

    cam = rl.NewCamera2D(rl.NewVector2(screenWidth/2.0, screenHeight/2.0),
    rl.NewVector2(playerDest.X-playerDest.Width/2, playerDest.Y-playerDest.
    Height/2), 0.0, 1.0)

}

func update() {
    // ...

    cam.Target = rl.NewVector2(playerDest.X-playerDest.Width/2,
    playerDest.Y-playerDest.Height/2)

}
```

Now, when you move Moyashi using the key inputs you defined earlier, the camera (or the screen) will move, but Moyashi will stay in the center, as shown in Figures 3-18 and 3-19.

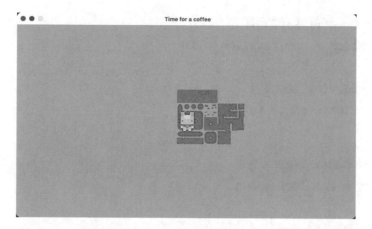

Figure 3-18. *Moyashi in the center*

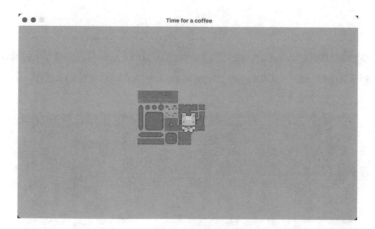

Figure 3-19. *Moyashi still in the center*

For some pure fun, you can set the camera to rotate or zoom, depending on the new input keys in the input function, as shown in Listing 3-11.

Listing 3-11. Code to Rotate and Set the Zoom Factor for the Camera

```go
func input() {
  // ...
  if rl.IsKeyDown(rl.KeyZ) {
    cam.Rotation = cam.Rotation + 1
  }
  if rl.IsKeyDown(rl.KeyX) {
    cam.Rotation = cam.Rotation - 1
  }

  if rl.IsKeyDown(rl.KeyC) {
    cam.Zoom = cam.Zoom + 0.1
  }
  if rl.IsKeyDown(rl.KeyV) {
    cam.Zoom = cam.Zoom - 0.1
  }
}
```

After running the new code again, try pressing the Z, X, C, and V keys to see how the map and Moyashi rotate and zoom on demand. The effect is shown in Figure 3-20.

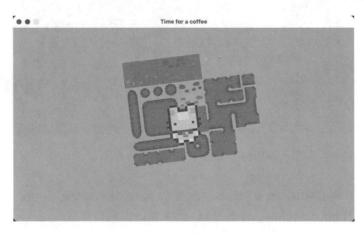

Figure 3-20. *Rotation and zoom effect*

Nice! You now know how to play with the camera settings and maybe even have some flashbacks of Mode 7 on the Super Famicon.

Note   You could set up multiple cameras and switch from one to the other. This is especially useful when you have multiple players on the same screen.

The next section gives Moyashi more movement by creating an animation from the different frames found in the sprite sheet.

Animate Sprites

Consider Moyashi's sprite sheet again, as shown Figure 3-21.

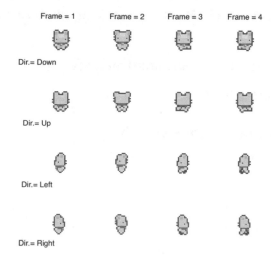

Figure 3-21. *Annotated sprite sheet for Moyashi*

Remember that there are four directions:

- Down

- Up

- Left

- Right

And each direction has four frames.

So, to animate Moyashi, you need to update the `rl.Rectangle` for `playerSrc` with the proper X and Y values. That way, the source rectangle of the sprite sheet will be correctly computed.

The game is running at 60 frames per second, so this code will change the frame for Moyashi every six game frames, or ten times per second. You can of course decide to make that faster or slower.

To help create the animation, you will add a few vars to the `var` section:

1. `playerMoving bool`: This will be set to `true` when a key is pressed.

2. `playerDir PlayerDirection`: You will create an `enum` to indicate which direction Moyashi is going. Recall that an `enum` is a list of possible values.

3. `playerFrame int`: This is the frame of Moyashi, so based on Figure 3-21, a number between 0 and 3 (four frames, counting from zero).

4. `frameCount int`: The overall frame count of the game.

This is all reflected in Listing 3-12.

Listing 3-12. New Vars to Animate Moyashi

```go
var (
    // ...
    playerSrc  rl.Rectangle
    playerDest rl.Rectangle

    playerMoving bool
    playerDir    PlayerDirection
    playerFrame  int
    frameCount   int
    // ...
)

type PlayerDirection int

const (
    Down PlayerDirection = iota
    Up
    Left
```

```
    Right
)
// ...
```

Note that the enum is using a combination of type and const. const uses iota, a Go function that automatically assigns a number to each value of the enum. Also note that you set Down first in the enum to reflect Moyashi's frame order in the sprite sheet directly.

The code then updates the input function. When a movement key is pressed, it marks the player as moving (playerMoving = true) and sets the playerDir to one of the values of the PlayerDirection enum. This is shown in Listing 3-13.

Listing 3-13. Input Function Updated for Animation

```
func input() {
    if rl.IsKeyDown(rl.KeyW) || rl.IsKeyDown(rl.KeyUp) {
        playerMoving = true
        playerDir = Up
    }
    if rl.IsKeyDown(rl.KeyS) || rl.IsKeyDown(rl.KeyDown) {
        playerMoving = true
        playerDir = Down
    }
    if rl.IsKeyDown(rl.KeyA) || rl.IsKeyDown(rl.KeyLeft) {
        playerMoving = true
        playerDir = Left
    }
    if rl.IsKeyDown(rl.KeyD) || rl.IsKeyDown(rl.KeyRight) {
        playerMoving = true
        playerDir = Right
    }

    // ...
}
```

The update function updates the location of player on the map according to the key pressed. The playerFrame value is updated according to a certain number of elapsed game frames.

Lastly, the important part of all those variables is to properly set the X and Y of playerSrc, which is done via playerFrame and playerDir. This is again according to Figure 3-21 and is reflected in Listing 3-14.

Listing 3-14. Computing X and Y for playerSrc

```go
func update() {
   running = !rl.WindowShouldClose()

   if playerMoving {
      if playerDir == Up {
         playerDest.Y -= playerSpeed
      }
      if playerDir == Down {
         playerDest.Y += playerSpeed
      }
      if playerDir == Left {
         playerDest.X -= playerSpeed
      }
      if playerDir == Right {
         playerDest.X += playerSpeed
      }
      if frameCount%6 == 1 {
         playerFrame++
      }
   }

   frameCount++
   if playerFrame > 3 {
      playerFrame = 0
   }
   playerSrc.X = playerSrc.Width * float32(playerFrame)
   playerSrc.Y = playerSrc.Height * float32(playerDir)
```

```
// ...

    playerMoving = false
}
// ...
```

If all goes well, you will see an animated Moyashi running in the fields! Table 3-1 shows the X and Y values of playerSrc according to the animation frame.

Table 3-1. *Frame and PlayerSrc X and Y Values*

Image	Frame Number/Player Direction	PlayerSrc Coordinates
	Frame 0 of PlayerDir Right	X = 0, Y = 144
	Frame 1 of PlayerDir Right	X = 48, Y = 144
	Frame 2 of PlayerDir Right	X = 96, Y = 144
	Frame 3 of PlayerDir Right	X = 144, Y = 144

There would be a similar table for Down, Up, Left, and Right. One thing that is missing though is an animation for when the sprite is idle.

Animation for an Idle Moyashi

This is going to be quite short. Animating Moyashi when it is idle is just a matter of updating the `playerFrame` value when `playerMoving` is set to `false`.

In the `update` function, you will:

1. Update the `playerFrame` every 30 frames, so every half second.

2. Only display frame 0 and frame 1 when Moyashi is not moving.

Those two updates are the only ones in the whole code listing, and they are shown in Listing 3-15.

Listing 3-15. Idle Animation

```
func update() {
  // ...

  // same as before
  if playerMoving {
    if playerDir == Up {
      playerDest.Y -= playerSpeed
    }
    if playerDir == Down {
      playerDest.Y += playerSpeed
    }
    if playerDir == Left {
      playerDest.X -= playerSpeed
    }
    if playerDir == Right {
      playerDest.X += playerSpeed
    }
    if frameCount%6 == 1 {
      playerFrame++
    }
  }

  // update the player frame even when not moving
  if frameCount%30 == 1 {
```

```
        playerFrame++
    }
    // switch between frame 0 and frame 1
    // when Moyashi is not moving
    if !playerMoving && playerFrame > 1 {
        playerFrame = 0
    }

    // ...
}
```

Running the game will show Moyashi switching frames (see Figures 3-22 and 3-23).

Figure 3-22. *Idle frame 0*

Figure 3-23. *Idle frame 1*

Now it's time to get Moyashi to walk on a proper patch of grass, with houses and fences.

Loading the World Map

In a 2D tile-based game, the map can be viewed as a set of squares, each loaded with a different sprite. To create the world map that's rendered onscreen, you need to create an internal representation, with something preloaded.

Let's say for a start that the map you want to show onscreen is 5x5—five squares for the width and five squares for the height. This would look like Figure 3-24.

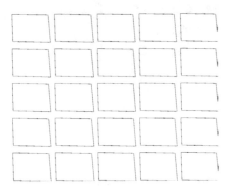

Figure 3-24. *Image of the world map*

The representation you will have internally is a list of integers, as shown in Figure 3-25.

Figure 3-25. *Internal representation of the map*

Figure 3-26 shows the contents of the sprite sheet for grass.png again.

160x128 PNG (32-bit color)

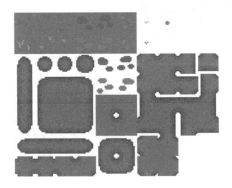

Figure 3-26. *Grass.png file*

The file is 160x128, and each tile is 16x16: 16x10 horizontally and 16x8 vertically. Each internal value of the map will be just like the player frame, which is a square in this picture. The source location will have an X between 0 and 16x10=160 (0,16,32...144), and an Y between 0 and 128. (0,16,32...128)

The internal array will represent the location on the target map, so from Figure 3-25 again, you get the following array:

[0 0] [0 1] [0 2] [0 3] [0 4] [1 0] [1 1] ... [4 4]

You'll first create a random map with values between 0 and 80. The loadMap code is shown in Listing 3-16.

Listing 3-16. Creating the Map of the World

```go
var (
    // ...

    tileDest rl.Rectangle
    tileSrc  rl.Rectangle

    tileMap    []int
    mapW, mapH int

    // ...
)

func loadMap() {
    mapW, mapH = 10, 10
    tileMap = make([]int, mapW*mapH)
    for i := 0; i < len(tileMap); i++ {
        tileMap[i] = rand.Intn(80)
    }
}

func init() {
    // ...
    loadMap()
}
```

After loading the map, if you choose to debug or print the value of `tileMap`, it will look like Listing 3-17, which is an array of random numbers between 0 and 80.

Listing 3-17. Internal Representation of the World Map

```
tileMap: [1 47 7 59 1 38 25 60 56 20 54 31 2 49 8 74 11 5 37 66 15 26 8 18
47 27 47 8 70 55 21 8 27 31 69 76 57 71 45 66 13 50 74 3 33 67 78 4 79 73
37 41 69 39 40 65 8 58 23 75 51 30 45 76 26 68 41 2 63 66 43 56 42 38 7 54
57 23 76 20 63 73 17 13 41 59 73 3 51 2 78 56 66 67 20 23 72 3 45 78]
```

Now that you have the internal representation, it's simply a matter of drawing things onscreen. This is done using the `drawScene` function.

The location onscreen, represented by `tileDest.X` and `tileDest.Y`, is easily computed from division and remainder (% and /) on `tileMap` versus the `mapWidth, mapW` (remember Figure 3-25).

Assuming only the grass sprite sheet is used for now, you need to find the proper square location in the `grass.png` file. You do the same % and / to the value contained between 0 and 80 (remember Figure 3-26).

The code for `drawScene` is shown in Listing 3-18.

Listing 3-18. Let's Draw the World!

```go
func drawScene() {

    for i := 0; i < len(tileMap); i++ {

        tileDest.X = tileDest.Width * float32(i%mapW)
        tileDest.Y = tileDest.Height * float32(i/mapW)

        tileSrc.X = tileSrc.Width * float32((tileMap[i]-1)%int(grassSprite.
        Width/int32(tileSrc.Width)))
        tileSrc.Y = tileSrc.Height * float32((tileMap[i]-1)/int(grassSprite.
        Height/int32(tileSrc.Height)))

        rl.DrawTexturePro(grassSprite, tileSrc, tileDest,
        rl.NewVector2(tileDest.Width, tileDest.Height), 0, rl.White)

    }
```

```
// Drawing the player same as before
rl.DrawTexturePro(playerSprite, playerSrc, playerDest,
rl.NewVector2(playerDest.Width, playerDest.Height), 0, rl.White)
}
```

The image in Figure 3-27 is obtained from loading a 10x10 map to make it easier to see.

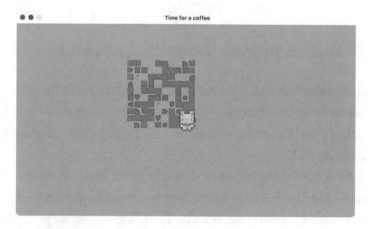

Figure 3-27. *World map*

Next, you learn to load the map from a file and use more sprite sheets for the map.

Loading the Full World Map

In this last exercise, you learn to load a full world map from a file. Each value in the map should give you the following:

- Which spreadsheet to use

- Which index to use in that spreadsheet

Instead of using a single sprite sheet, you can use multiple files for other spreadsheets (see Figure 3-28).

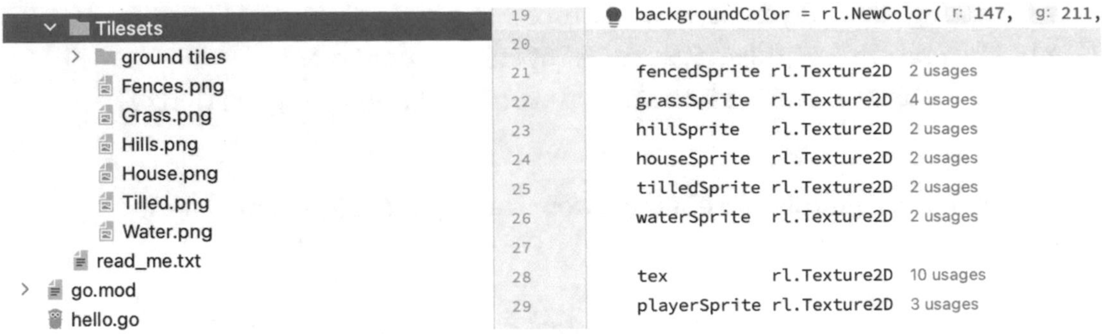

Figure 3-28. *Spreadsheets for fences, hills, houses, and so on*

You will declare variables and preload all of these textures in the init function exactly as you did for the grass texture.

In the var section, you'll declare all the textures to be loaded. Then you'll add a temporary texture named tex.

You'll then have a srcMap, which knows which sprite sheet to use for which square, just like you have a tileMap that says which index to load from that sheet.

This is just internal representation details. There are better ways to do this, but this will do for now (see Listing 3-19).

Listing 3-19. Variables for the World Map

```
var (
  // ...

  fencedSprite rl.Texture2D
  grassSprite  rl.Texture2D
  hillSprite   rl.Texture2D
  houseSprite  rl.Texture2D
  tilledSprite rl.Texture2D
  waterSprite  rl.Texture2D

  tex          rl.Texture2D

  // ...

  tileDest     rl.Rectangle
  tileSrc      rl.Rectangle
  tileMap      []int
```

```
srcMap      []string
mapW, mapH int

// ...
)
```

The file format to use for the map is as follows:

```
WIDTH HEIGHT
MAP of Int
MAP of String
```

An example of a 5x5 map is shown in Listing 3-20.

Listing 3-20. World Map File Example

```
5 5
1 1 1 1 1
1 8 1 1 1
1 2 3 3 1
1 4 1 11 1
1 1 1 1 1
g g g g g
g g g g g
g g g g g
g g g g g
g g l l w
```

Each value of the first map goes to `tileMap`, and the second map indicates which sprite sheet to use:

- G for grass

- L for hill

- F for fence

- H for house

- W for water

- T for tilled

The new `loadMap` takes a filename and pushes values in `tileMap` and `srcMap` (see Listing 3-21).

Listing 3-21. Loading the Map from a File

```go
func loadMap(mapFile string) {
    fmt.Printf("Loading map: %s\n", mapFile)
    file, err := ioutil.ReadFile(mapFile)
    if err != nil {
        fmt.Printf("Error reading map file: %s: %s\n", mapFile, err)
        os.Exit(1)
    }

    sliced := strings.Split(strings.ReplaceAll(string(file), "\n", "
"), " ")

    mapW, mapH = -1, -1
    tileMap = make([]int, mapW*mapH)
    srcMap = make([]string, mapW*mapH)

    for i := 0; i < len(sliced); i++ {
        m, _ := strconv.Atoi(sliced[i])

        if mapW == -1 {
            mapW = m
        } else if mapH == -1 {
            mapH = m
        } else if i < mapW*mapH+2 {
            tileMap = append(tileMap, m)
        } else {
            srcMap = append(srcMap, sliced[i])
        }
    }
}
```

Add this updated `loadMap` function to the `init` function of the game. You can load the texture at the same time (see Listing 3-22).

Listing 3-22. Load the Sprites and the Map

```go
func init() {

    //...
    fencedSprite = rl.LoadTexture("assets/Tilesets/Fences.png")
    grassSprite = rl.LoadTexture("assets/Tilesets/Grass.png")
    hillSprite = rl.LoadTexture("assets/Tilesets/Hills.png")
    houseSprite = rl.LoadTexture("assets/Tilesets/House.png")
    tilledSprite = rl.LoadTexture("assets/Tilesets/Tilled.png")
    waterSprite = rl.LoadTexture("assets/Tilesets/Water.png")

    tileSrc = rl.NewRectangle(0, 0, 16, 16)
    tileDest = rl.NewRectangle(0, 0, 16, 16)

    loadMap("world.map")

    //...
}
```

The final code for `drawScene` uses the tex "target texture" to determine which texture to draw the sprite from, as a parameter to `DrawTexturePro`.

`tileSrc.X` and `tileSrc.Y` are computed just like in Listing 3-18; this time using height and width as computed from tex, which contains the data for width and height of the full picture.

See the resulting `drawScene` in Listing 3-23.

Listing 3-23. Drawing Tiles of the World Map Depending on the Internal Representation

```go
func drawScene() {

    for i := 0; i < len(tileMap); i++ {
        tileDest.X = tileDest.Width * float32(i%mapW)
        tileDest.Y = tileDest.Height * float32(i/mapW)

        switch srcMap[i] {
        case "g":
            tex = grassSprite
```

```
        case "l":
            tex = hillSprite
        case "f":
            tex = fencedSprite
        case "h":
            tex = houseSprite
        case "w":
            tex = waterSprite
        case "t":
            tex = tilledSprite
        default:
            tex = grassSprite
        }

        tileSrc.X = tileSrc.Width * float32((tileMap[i]-1)%int(tex.Width/
        int32(tileSrc.Width)))
        tileSrc.Y = tileSrc.Height * float32((tileMap[i]-1)/int(tex.Width/
        int32(tileSrc.Height)))

        rl.DrawTexturePro(tex, tileSrc, tileDest, rl.NewVector2(tileDest.
        Width, tileDest.Height), 0, rl.White)

    }
// ...
}
```

As opposed to the previous example, where you were loading random values in the map, this time the map is statically loaded from the file and the render properly shows the map on the canvas. See Figure 3-29.

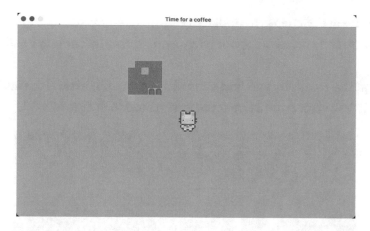

Figure 3-29. *Same ol' world*

Yes...the map is small. Let's make it bigger!

Full Map and Full Screen

To put the game into full screen mode and display the camera all over the map, you have to change two things:

- Set the `config` flag in the `init` function to full screen mode

- Update the camera zoom

The updated `init` function code is shown in Listing 3-24.

Listing 3-24. Setting the Zoom Parameter

```go
func init() {
  rl.SetConfigFlags(rl.FlagVsyncHint | rl.FlagFullscreenMode)

  cam = rl.NewCamera2D(rl.NewVector2(screenWidth/2.0, screenHeight/2.0),
  rl.NewVector2(playerDest.X-playerDest.Width/2, playerDest.Y-playerDest.
  Height/2), 0.0, 3)
  //cam.Zoom = 3

  loadMap("world.map")
}
```

Note that there are two ways to update the camera—one you saw earlier by setting the zoom factor directly on `cam.Zoom` or when you create the camera itself as the last parameter.

If you look at the example, you find an updated map file in `world.map`. Moyashi looks happier to run in full screen mode over the entire land. See Figure 3-30.

Figure 3-30. *World hero Moyashi*

Summary

This concludes Chapter 3. You now know how to prepare a basic loop for a 2D game in Go using `raylib-go`.

To build on this, try the following:

- Add other moving animals, such as cows and sheep.

- Get the other sprites to move on the map randomly.

- Detect collision and block access to fences and water.

- Play sound when walking or bumping into other sprites.

- Display a score and increase it as the player collects and gives food to the animals.

CHAPTER 4

Trend Follower for Blockchain Trading

Go Crazy or Go Home

Perhaps times have changed a bit, but there certainly used to be an unwritten law on the trading floor that expected all traders to go hard or go home.

Pressures run high when trading large amounts of money. The amount is subjective of course, but the financial markets can make a person go crazy, quite literally. It is a unique environment where emotions run wild, driven by fear and greed.

Does this always have to be the case? What if you could remove that emotional rollercoaster ride when trading?

N. Modrzyk, *Go Crazy*, https://doi.org/10.1007/978-1-4842-9666-0_4

Before you start this chapter, the disclaimer. This is not financial advice. It's simply an introduction to the world in which technology meets the financial markets. Hopefully a guide to things that you should think about before taking on the financial markets. A collection of notes to help this preparation, if you will. And hopefully a bit of entertainment as well.

Smart individuals are efficient and productive. Smart and rich people are efficient, productive, and never sleep. The world of trading is no exception. In fact, the Wall Street bankers with expensive suits looking tired is not just a cliché, it is a thing. The problem with this, more often than not, ends up having a costly effect on mental and physical health. These problems are exacerbated by the fact that most products can now be traded 24 hours a day. Cryptocurrencies, for instance, never sleep. Not even on weekends.

Fortunately, some savvy smart individuals have, in recent years, figured out a few quirks that manifest themselves as patterns. If you spend enough time reading newsletters or listening to financial news, there is a very high probability you will come across the words "history doesn't repeat itself, but it rhymes." While the booms and busts in financial centers around the world are different each time, the logic when recounting each "event" seems to have an uncanny similarity. Add to this the fact that human beings are creatures of habit, who are driven by fear and greed. This provides a nice ecosystem for financial industry experts to derive models based on cycles and probability of events occurring in the free market economy.

This of course, is only half the equation. Given the 24/7 nature of the markets today, simply modeling cycles in markets would create a lot of zombies walking around trading floors or people looking like Neo in the matrix. This being said, if you could code like Neo, there is a place for the autonomous trading bots in the financial markets.

Even simplistic bots with a high tendency to make errors of judgement often perform better than human beings sitting between a keyboard and chair monitoring markets 24/7 and trading in a state of delirium.

Bots do not need sleep; they do not have a family to care for; and they certainly do not get ulcers. If modeled correctly and built using a fine-tuned process, your daily task could simply become a routine: 1) Check available funds to trade (make sure to top it up from time to time), 2) Make sure the bots are running, and, 3) take the profits when a good trade happens.

With a well-oiled machine and simple tools with processes, anyone who can code can focus on finding a cool job, no need to be burnt out (ever). Let the side hustle continue to earn more money with limited or almost no time invested. Simply focus on the more important things in life...

CHAPTER 4   TREND FOLLOWER FOR BLOCKCHAIN TRADING

The trick is to "follow the smart money." In other words, let the financial great minds be the trail blazers and simply find a way to follow them into the booms.

The goal of this chapter is to cover a few of the simplified examples so you can set things up to do just that—"follow the smart money."

Why Trade in the Financial Markets?

Before delving into trading, this chapter includes a small background on money, and how the world has evolved with the use of money. This section includes a discussion of how the real market works today and the relationship to the financial markets, as well as some background as to why the financial markets are efficient and worth trading in.

The Origins of Money

In human history, you can trace the development of money from barter systems to the complex financial systems of today. At its core, money is a universal medium of exchange that simplifies transactions and fosters cooperation between people.

Some historians argue that barter systems were the earliest form of trade. In these systems, individuals exchanged goods and services directly. However, the limitations of barter soon became apparent, as it was highly dependent on the "coincidence of wants." To overcome this issue, societies began to use various objects as mediums of exchange. These objects, which eventually became money, possessed characteristics such as being easily transportable, divisible, and non-perishable. Early forms of money included shells, beads, and even livestock.

As societies became more complex, the need for a standard, universally accepted form of money grew stronger. Some argue that the Lydians, an ancient civilization in modern-day Turkey, were the first to introduce coinage around 640 BCE. These coins were made of a naturally occurring alloy of gold and silver called electrum, which was stamped with an official seal to guarantee its value. The use of coins revolutionized trade, as it made transactions more efficient and allowed for the establishment of standardized values for goods and services.

In the centuries that followed, money continued to evolve, eventually taking the form of paper currency and, more recently, digital transactions. What is better than having a tool to execute completely trustless operations in exchanging between value and goods?

Add to that the power of networks and the ability to have billions of people leverage this tool in reducing the complexities of barter and facilitating trade, money has played a crucial role in the development of human societies, enabling the growth of large-scale economies and the expansion of the global civilization.

Hopefully everyone agrees, the world needs money. If it weren't for the invention of money, you would have to carry a lot of very heavy things with you on a daily basis in order to purchase things.

The Financial Economy vs. the Real Economy

Some financial historians and professionals differentiate between the financial economy and the real economy to underscore the varying aspects of an economy that impacts people's lives and the overall health of a nation.

The real economy, also referred to as the *productive economy* or the *main street economy,* encompasses the tangible, day-to-day activities that drive economic growth. These activities include the production, distribution, and consumption of goods and services. The real economy represents the backbone of any nation's economic health, as it directly impacts employment, income levels, and overall living standards. Key indicators of the real economy's health include GDP growth, employment rates, inflation, and productivity levels.

The *financial economy*, on the other hand, is centered on financial markets and institutions that facilitate the exchange and allocation of capital. This includes the stock, bond, and derivatives markets, as well as banks, investment firms, and other financial intermediaries. The financial economy is driven by the trading of financial assets, such as stocks, bonds, and other securities, and it plays a critical role in allocating resources and managing risks in the economy. Key indicators of the financial economy's health include interest rates, stock market indices, and credit spreads.

While the real and financial economies are interconnected, they can experience divergent trends, as the financial economy is more susceptible to fluctuations due to market sentiment, speculation, and other factors that may not directly correlate with the real economy's fundamentals.

An important fact in investing or trading, in some cases, a thriving financial economy may not accurately reflect the well-being of the real economy, leading to concerns about financial bubbles or a growing wealth gap. Financial historians emphasize the importance of understanding the distinctions between these two facets of the economy, as striking a balance between them is vital for sustainable economic growth and overall societal prosperity.

Why is this important? It ties into the aforementioned cycles—the boom and bust of the economies. You may recall some of the historical events that were caused by these booms and busts. Th early 2000s boom, coined "the dotcom bubble," and 2008 marked the end of "the subprime mortgage" and drove the world into a global financial crisis. In the last few years, the world has seen a pandemic, the shortest recession in history, global central banks going into quantitative easing, and inflation. These cycles are extremely powerful drivers of the economy that is now hyper-financialized and accessible to all.

Market Efficiency

When shopping online, would you blindly buy an article from the top link on Google? Or would you do a quick search and compare prices to save your hard-earned dollars? That process can be abstracted away from the Internet in everyday life, into businesses of all shapes and sizes, even at governments and global organizations levels.

The financial market, often epitomized by Wall Street, is not an isolated entity but rather a complex system intertwined with the real economy, represented by Main Street. Its efficiency, or lack thereof, has profound implications for the broader economy.

This information includes data about companies, economies, political developments, and even investor sentiments, effectively bridging the gap between Main Street and Wall Street.

Now, let's delve into the relationship between Wall Street and Main Street. Wall Street, or the financial economy, is supposed to serve Main Street, the real economy, by efficiently allocating capital and managing risk. In an efficient market, Wall Street's activities directly support the growth and prosperity of Main Street. However, when the financial economy becomes inefficient, or when it becomes too detached from the real economy, as was the case leading up to the 2008 financial crisis, the consequences can be dire for Main Street.

The distance between Wall Street and Main Street should be a close, symbiotic one. But when Wall Street becomes an entity unto itself, the disconnect can lead to financial instability, economic recessions, and severe socio-economic consequences.

Why Automate Trading?

Trading manually takes a toll on the mind and body. In the 1980s, it was still possible for one person to track the market fluctuations. The trading world used to be like in the movies, where traders and brokers were constantly on phones speaking to each other to obtain the latest prices to execute trades.

Today, that task is considerably harder to do. Traders today rely on the use of personal computers with lots of screens. There is a valid reason for the expensive setup, and that is to monitor many financial assets concurrently, and across many markets.

As mentioned earlier, the global financial markets now operate close to 24 hours over 5.5 days for what is called trad-fi or traditional finance. Monday morning in New Zealand marks the opening of the markets. A few hours later, Tokyo markets open, then Korea, Hong Kong, and Singapore. At the close of the Asian markets, the day does not end. There are the evening sessions. At the end of the evening session, it times in perfectly with the opening of the European or London markets. Once the European and London markets close, as you might have guessed, the New York market takes over. With the exception of a few hours between the close of the American markets and the start of the New Zealand market, affectionately called "the twilight zone," some versions of most of the heavily traded products can be traded globally.

Even if it was theoretically possible to stay awake 24 hours per day, tracking and trading only a single stock is highly unlikely. All financial instruments' prices fluctuate up and down. It is never a straight arrow up. At times the down part might be prolonged. Your money is better put to work on another financial product that may have the possibility of gains while the previous one is consolidating.

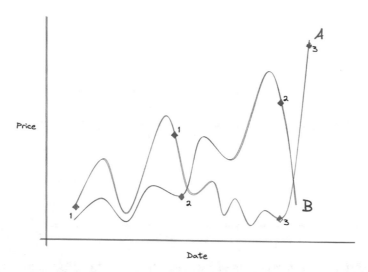

Figure 4-1. *Tracking multiple assets concurrently*

Imagine tracking two arbitrary cryptos—A (in blue) and B (in orange)—as shown in Figure 4-1. The trader takes on a position initially with trade "1" and sells the position to get out of it toward the mid part of the image. While stock A goes downward, stock B is breaking out. That is when the trader can take on a new position on stock B with trade "2" while stock A is either on a downward move or consolidating. Just as the trader is getting out of trade "2," stock A is ready to break out and the trader takes on another position with trade "3".

Tracking two cryptos concurrently is a tough enough job to do. There are a lot of moving parts and you should expect more than one indicator to follow on any particular stock. While it is possible to draw superimposed charts and track more than one stock at a time, it quickly becomes overwhelming.

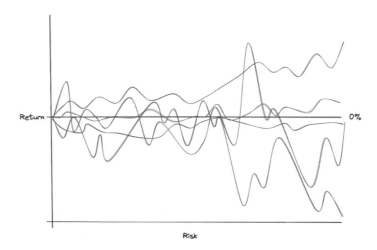

Figure 4-2. *Optical illusions caused by auto adjusting gains/losses calibrating for multiple charts*

Figure 4-2 is tracking the S&P 500 and comparing it to GOLD, WTI, TLT (bonds), VIX, and DXY (the lines are a graphical representation to make a point and inexact). The image has been zoomed out to fit six months. Since the products trade independently and have various magnitudes of change, they can only be expressed in terms of percentage moves. As the DXY is the least volatile product, it almost looks like a flat line (in blue).

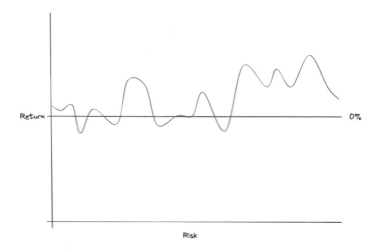

Figure 4-3. *DXY chart on its own (pulled out of Figure 4-2)*

Figure 4-3 shows the DXY on its own over the same time period. If not monitored carefully, many opportunities can be missed when traded manually.

It is important to note that most traders will have numerous stocks and positions to track at any one point in time so they have portfolio that is diversified enough to protect their money. There is always an option to have numerous traders babysit a portfolio, but that comes with a big price tag.

Last, but not least, all traders need to be reminded that it is a hyper-connected world out there. The global markets have seen a tremendous amount of volatility increase. Some macroeconomists attribute this phenomenon to the online businesses like Robinhood and passive funds. Modern technology stacks have made investing easy. This has opened the gate for many investors to "tweak" positions almost in real-time. There is also a view that this phenomenon is caused by prominent figures leveraging social networking services platforms to incentivize markets to move drastically.

Nobody is certain of course, and there are many potential reasons for these modern market "features," but one thing is for sure—the world is not going back to trading with phone lines like in the 80s.

This is when you might assume this trading thing can only be done efficiently by machines. Well, that is actually not true. You can easily do without automated trading machines. In fact, there are numerous prominent traders around the world who trade only with spreadsheets. Yes, they are rather large spreadsheets, but the point is that it is doable.

It is also extremely important to note that these traders have a wealth of knowledge and experience. Most have the ability to see trends before they become anything the world catches onto and execute everything six months to a year ahead of the rest.

But wait a minute, how many books must you read? How often do you need to read up on events and restack information? What is the catch?

The catch is that most of these prominent traders have been trading for decades, and as many attest, have made very costly mistakes in the past. That is the "experience" and as most will confess, they went without a life for a long while.

The Secret Sauce

There is a very good reason that most, if not all, financial firms spend a large amount of their operating budget on technology and tools (and people). Walk into any bank, fund, or broker, and you will most likely find departments and teams named with words like tech, data, and strat(egy).

Let's walk through some of these items and see if you can do it like the pros do, and see if it makes sense for an individual trader to do the same.

Charts

A picture tells a thousand words. Once a trader develops an "eye" for charts, a quick glance can provide crucial insights into the market tendencies at any given time. Some are so good they are said to be able to predict future prices just looking at the charts for a few seconds. In order to trade, debug, monitor, and be effective and efficient, charts are a necessary tool.

Charts are so important to traders and investors that there was a time in history when they were manually drawn. This is inconceivable for anyone actively trading today. We should be thankful for the invention of machines and charting frameworks. Today most of this work is automated.

Data

Data is the lifeblood of modern investment management. Analyzing vast datasets is the only efficient approach to identify trends, understand market dynamics, and uncover hidden opportunities that others may overlook.

Data was, until very recently, very expensive to obtain. The Bloomberg terminal was already available in the early 2000s, and it featured historical data for most of the financial instruments around the world. Popular products were even available real time on the traders' desktops, even directly into their spreadsheets. Believe it or not, it was impressive back in the early 2000s.

These days, a lot of the historical data can be found for free. Some of the data vendors even aggregate the data for its users and provide it free of charge. Depending on the products and the timeframes, even real-time data is available for free.

News and Content

While the news and media are not the lifeblood of modern investment management, they do have a place in the industry. This is where the great minds in the industry share their views and thoughts. If markets are driven by the animal spirits and the respective fear and greed, the news and media keep a close look on the pulse.

There was a time when financial news was monopolized by large media conglomerates like CNBC, Bloomberg, and Reuters. During those times, information was not easily accessible to the individual investor.

These days, the landscape has completely changed. First, expensive bespoke hardware is no longer needed. Most of the information can easily be accessed on a phone or tablet. It is of paramount importance for all to formulate thoughts and see how others model the world of finance in order to understand and hopefully expect some market moves, at least at the macro level. It is a difficult task, and it often rewards those who pay attention to the brilliant minds in finance.

Strategy

In order to model certain market events, strategies are essential in trading. This also provides the trader with an interchangeable tool to leverage through a number of market cycles that tend to "rhyme," or repeat in similar ways.

If you pay enough attention to the news and data, these cycles and similarities often turn into patterns that can be modeled. Starting from the macroeconomy, you can see trends and tell-tale signs where shifts happen. Diving deeper into these periods where shifts take place, and you start seeing events that are out of the ordinary. These can be modeled into signals to execute actions on.

Backtesting

Backtesting is a critical component of any successful trading strategy. It involves testing a trading idea or model on historical market data to evaluate its viability and performance. By analyzing how a strategy would have fared in the past, traders can gain valuable insights into its potential effectiveness in the future. Once more than one strategy is implemented, backtesting also provides an opportunity to test strategies against each other in understanding the performance against a known benchmark.

Real-Time Trading

Real-time trading simulation, often referred to as *paper trading* or *virtual trading*, is a crucial component in the development and implementation of an automated trading strategy. By simulating trades using real-time market data, but without risking actual capital, traders can gain invaluable insights into the performance of their strategy under current market conditions. This chapter explores the importance of a real-time trading simulation in building confidence, managing risk, and ultimately, ensuring that traders can sleep comfortably at night, knowing that their automated trading system is well-equipped to navigate the unpredictable world of financial markets.

The Recipe

The perfect recipe most probably does not exist. At the very least, it will vary quite a bit depending on the individual's preferences and tendencies.

That being said, it could be a bit closer to reality than a dream. If you have an Internet connection and a laptop, of course.

Before dreaming about days at the beach, you need to prepare. Preparation makes a world of difference in the trading world. Especially so for an autonomous trading bot if you value your sleep. Failing to build the right framework and process and blindly trusting a bot with your money is akin to asking a teenager with a fresh driver's license to drive a Ferrari. Not going to go well.

If done correctly, with a clear roadmap, a systematic approach, adequate risk management, performance evaluation of the strategies, thorough testing and debugging, and religiously performing every step, even a teenager can drive a Ferrari... One would hope.

Clear Objectives and a Structured Approach

A well-defined process starts with clear objectives and goals. This helps investors focus on essential features and functions and ensures that you can effectively execute trading strategies.

There may be a genius strategy that is completely polyvalent and perfectly adapted to all geopolitical events or macroeconomic shifts and that performs well in any timeframe. That person is more likely to be running a billion-dollar fund and protecting that strategy rather than making it available for all to use. At the very least, running a quick search for such a book seems to yield less than convincing results.

Crafting a strategy takes patience and a clear objective so the trader can properly target narrow entry and exit signals. Additionally, having clear objectives and a structured approach will enable traders to categorize strategies for later or for combined use.

Alongside objectives, a structured process promotes a systematic approach to development, which helps to identify, prioritize, and address various challenges and requirements at different stages of the project. This can increase your chances of success and prevent potential issues from arising.

Macroeconomic Tendencies

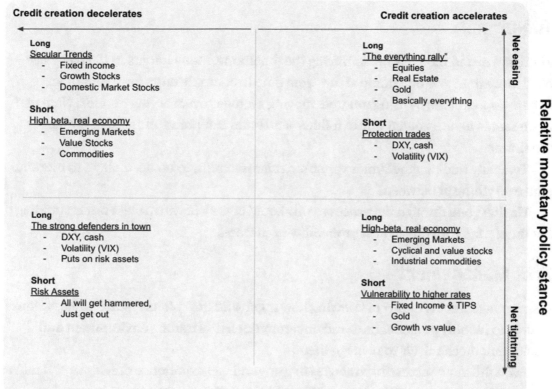

Figure 4-4. *Macroeconomic quadrants*

There are over 630,000 listed stocks in the global equity markets, tens of thousands of fixed income products, thousands of commodities products, and an unknown amount of real estate products.

While it could be exhilarating and fascinating to track events across all products available globally, it is both detrimental to your health and cost prohibitive.

The first place to start is to understand macro trends. Figure 4-4 shows possibly one of the simplest yet effective "cheat sheets" that cuts down 75 percent or more of the noise.

More importantly, this is a practice that can save a lot of money (in terms of compute cost) and time. As mentioned, there are a vast number of assets around the world still to cover.

Knowing the macro market trends enables traders to narrow down on the number of products to run tests with and, most importantly, allows you to pick out the applicable strategies far more easily.

Timeframe

There are mixed thoughts in identifying the timeframe. Many traders in the past have used more than one timeframe at the same time to compute entry and exit points. Others approximate by using multiple moving averages over varying periods. Note that there seems to be a golden rule to follow—entry and exit points must be in the same timeframe.

Typically trading timeframes vary from microseconds, to hours, to days, to months, with everything in between.

Having gone through the process, you should come out with a clear understanding of the timeframe with the highest probability to succeed.

Risk Management

Risk management is the art of knowing how much and how often. A solid process allows traders to identify potential risks and uncertainties in the trading environment and implement mechanisms to manage them.

Even the most successful strategies in the world will experience drawdowns. It makes no sense to run an aggressive strategy if the bot loses your entire capital in minutes. On the other hand, there may be investors with a lot of money in the bank account looking to run an ultra-high risk strategy, knowing something the market participants do not know.

Building risk management into the process ensures that a trader can run an autonomous trading bot through changing market conditions and adapt and manage risks effectively.

Testing and Debugging

Confidence building in the world of trading is key. If a strategy is not trustworthy, constant second guessing will inevitably end in the trader taking over control rather than letting the algorithm and the strategy do its trading.

By backtesting a strategy, traders can gain a better understanding of the potential risks associated with their chosen approach. The information obtained from testing can then be used to develop effective risk management strategies, adjusting position sizes or parameters, depending on how aggressive the trader wants to be.

Supplementing backtesting with real-time trading simulations provides an opportunity for traders to assess the risk-reward profile of their automated trading strategy under live market conditions. By analyzing the strategy's performance in terms of drawdowns, volatility, and other risk metrics, traders can develop a comprehensive understanding of the potential risks associated with their strategy and make informed decisions about position sizing, stop-loss orders, and other risk management tools.

A systematic development process ensures that the trading bot undergoes rigorous testing and debugging at various stages. This is crucial for identifying and rectifying any issues that may impact the bot's performance, ensuring its reliability and reducing the chances of making costly mistakes in real-world trading.

Performance Evaluation

A well-built process includes methods for evaluating the trading bot's performance and adjusting its strategies accordingly. Most importantly, a trader should always be able to identify timing at which a strategy needs to be replaced or parameters adjusted to meet the risk management criteria. Continuous evaluation and improvement are necessary to ensure that the bot remains competitive and profitable over time.

Scalability and Maintainability

A well-structured process allows for the easy addition of new features and updates to the trading bot. This ensures that the bot can adapt to changing market conditions, technologies, and requirements, making it more scalable and maintainable.

While a drastic increase in the scale of testing data and subsequent real-time trading data needs is unlikely, the process prior to live trading should provide feedback to the trader or developer should anything change.

Compliance and Regulation

Financial markets are highly regulated, and trading bots must adhere to specific rules and guidelines. A comprehensive process helps ensure that the trading bot is compliant with these regulations, reducing the risk of legal and financial consequences.

Follow the necessary steps and incorporate regulatory requirements into the process to make sure the strategies and operations clear the necessary regulatory requirements, if applicable.

Security

Perhaps the most important catch phrase in the crypto-verse is, "Not your key, not your money." Everyone should be mindful of security, and more importantly, where the cryptos are stored. A lot of investors have lost money with centralized exchanges that went out of business. Be sure to practice safe key management.

Note   The trad-fi (or traditional finance) world is far more regulated than the crypto-verse. However, it is not without risk. Ensure adequate security measures are taken.

Building Confidence

Trading is as much about psychology as it is about strategy and analysis. Backtesting and real-time testing can play a crucial role in building a trader's confidence in their chosen approach.

In order to build confidence, strategies need to manage the day-to-day trading risks and violent market moves. Confidence levels will be boosted if backtesting incorporates *black swan* events—rare but significant market occurrences that can have a dramatic impact on a strategy's performance. Examples in the recent past can easily be found on Google. Most data vendors will have data going back (if lucky) to 2007/8. By preparing for these extreme scenarios, traders can develop more robust strategies that can withstand the unpredictable nature of financial markets.

The same cannot be so easy for real-time testing. By observing how a strategy performs under live market conditions, traders can gain a deeper understanding of its strengths and weaknesses. This firsthand experience can be instrumental in fostering a sense of conviction in the strategy, which is crucial for maintaining discipline and consistency in the face of market uncertainty.

Note   Testing is not the same as real money trading. As modern exchanges often offer fractional shares (cryptos of course allow trading of fractions of coins), you should at least try trading small amounts.

Refining Trading Strategies

As is often the case, most investors or traders will find aspects of the strategy that need updating after backtesting and real-time testing. You should expect to spend a fair amount of time refining and tuning strategies before the start of trading.

Monitoring the strategy's performance in real-time, traders can often spot discrepancies between their expectations and the strategy's actual results. This feedback loop enables traders to make necessary adjustments and fine-tune their strategy to better align with their trading objectives and risk tolerance.

Utensils in the Kitchen

Before continuing, it might make sense for you to consider what the bare minimum setup is going to look like to be able to run algo trading.

Modern Trading Tool

Most modern exchanges will have charting tools embedded in their tools, but a lot of the exchanges will feature a suite of tools to help the investor or trader. It's very important to be versed with all the tools and learn to trade manually on the exchanges.

You can only hope the bots will be stable and cater to most, if not all financial conditions, but issues happen. It is important to be able to "manage" some situations manually in case the bots fail.

Figure 4-5. *Binance trading platform* www.binance.com/en/trade/BTC_USDT?th
eme=dark&type=spot

Figure 4-5 shows the trading screen from Binance, a popular cryptocurrency
centralized exchange.

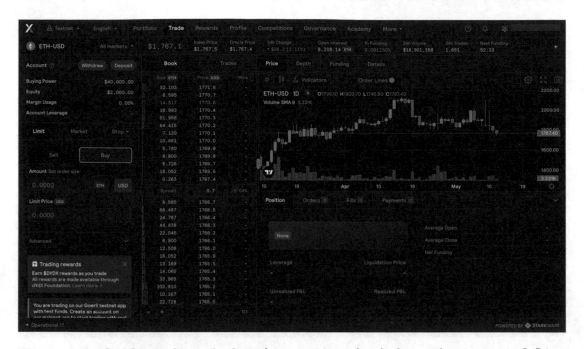

Figure 4-6. *dY/dX trading platform* `https://trade.dydx.exchange/portfolio/`
`overview` *(requires connecting a metamask wallet)*

Figure 4-6 shows the trading screen from dY/dX, a decentralized cryptocurrency exchange.

Some may prefer to trade on a single platform that offers as many datasets as possible, especially if they trade across asset classes (equities, bonds, cryptos, real estate). There are a number of charting tools available today that offer direct connections to the brokers. For instance, TradingView has connectivity to a number of brokers (see Figure 4-7).

Figure 4-7. *tradingview.com is an aggregated broker charting and trading platform*

One important note, however—it is possible these platforms do not cater to all feature sets available on the exchange's direct trading tool. While it is perfectly acceptable to leverage multiple platforms to trade (you should have automated platforms), it should be noted that keeping things simple is the secret to success. Especially in trading. It should be noted that it pays to practice manual trading even when the algorithms do the heavy lifting.

One last note on the charting tools. Today's modern charting tools have many standardized built-in tooling sets that are crucial for a trader's debugging abilities. Naturally, such tools are often only on offer behind a paywall.

Of course, you may opt to write many debugging lines and leverage debuggers to go through the code breaking it up into steps. The problem is that eventually an algorithmic trader will see a problem or a bug with code in production. Charting tools that offer standardized tooling to build in indicators similar to those in use by the strategy save time and provide the ability to spot check numbers during development and in production.

Traditional finance exchanges will have very similar feature sets. Bloomberg and Reuters have a lot more built-in messaging services, built-in ChatGPT, and list goes on. As these tools are often prohibitively expensive in the mainstream traditional finance space, this chapter focuses on cryptocurrencies.

Brokers

You can have the best autonomous trading engine in the world, but without a broker to execute trades through, there is no money to be made. Several online brokers and exchanges exist today. The decision process (on which to use) is a somewhat difficult topic to cover. The choice will largely depend on the prices offered, of course, residence of the account holder, fees that are applicable to perform trades, and taxation laws, to name a few. Note that fees and prices on offer can change quite drastically. Be sure to compare prices.

It is worthy to note that autonomous trading bots have become increasingly popular in the world of cryptocurrencies. Trading is supported 24/7 in most exchanges without the need for constant monitoring. However, in order to use these bots effectively, traders need access to reliable and trustworthy brokers with stable APIs. The exchanges themselves may be stable, but there have been blockchain outages that halted trading. Even large market cap currencies like Solana are subjected to outages.

Cloud Infrastructure

If you are a stay-at-home person who rarely ventures out and you have a stable Internet connection with a stable electric grid, you can opt to set up a server at home. Some have even started running containers on Raspberry Pis.

That being said, a cheap virtual machine on the cloud will make a world of sense, especially taking into account the fact your family member could at some point unplug the server in favor of the use of the electric socket to plug in a vacuum cleaner, a toy, and son.

A lot can happen in the markets in the span of an hour, so it makes sense to keep a machine protected from such elements and safely trade 24/7.

If your strategy does not involve too many concurrent calculations, you can easily get away with a few dollars per month.

On a side note, leveraging a cloud virtual machine to run Proof of Stake instances may be a good idea. Connectivity and network bandwidth are critically important to avoid penalties. (Note, Proof of Stake is not covered in this chapter.)

Version control and a CICD pipeline helps coding efficiently. This chapter is not going to delve into the good practices, but you should explore the use of a Git account certainly to make sure your code is saved at the very least.

Logs, logs, logs. Being able to perform forensic analysis is critically important. Keeping a massive database to query at any point in time is the absolute ideal, but most of the time, unless you're attempting a high frequency strategy, you can use Google workspace tools. You may find a good middle ground in the use of Google sheets.

It is true that logs are probably best stored elsewhere. However, tracking snapshots of what the algorithm sees at any point in time (in table form) can pay dividends as you encounter issues in production. The use of Google sheets via APIs comes in handy when dumping large timeseries tables and may save you a lot of time, especially when running virtual machines on the cloud and being able to monitor things on the go.

Lastly, docker containers, git pull, build, and run. As easy as one two three and save a lot of time. Do it!

Cooking

There is probably a valid reason why financial professionals like to use "cooking" in market actions. If you spends enough time in financial media, terms like "cooking the curve" or "cooking the books" might come across the screens.

Other than the colorful terminology used by the financial media, knowing what ingredients to use, proper setting of the heating power, and the meticulous control over the process ensures the result on the table is a success.

Backtesting

Backtesting is a critical component of any successful trading strategy. Once enough time is spent listening to the financial media or analysts from big banks, a very simplistic model can be derived quite easily. Take the 50-day moving average and 200-day moving averages for example—a vast majority of the financial professionals will come across the two numbers in their respective analysis. It is therefore safe to assume they are indicators that are being monitored industry wide.

But how do you go from an idea that seems to repeat and is being discussed often on TV and podcasts to a functioning trading model?

It involves testing a trading idea or model on historical market data to evaluate its viability and performance. By analyzing how a strategy would have fared in the past, traders can gain valuable insights into its potential effectiveness in the future. Once more than one strategy is implemented, backtesting also provides an opportunity to test strategies against each other in understanding the performance against a known benchmark.

Data

In order to start any kind of testing, once a strategy idea is born, it is time to think about the data. Note the critical pieces—data will be required in many different forms to properly test a strategy. First, let's walk through the most common features that traders use.

- *Ticker* or *symbol*. It is safe to say most will trade more than one financial instrument. It's best to be able to support one or more products in data ingest and in the backtesting framework.

- Just as important is the *time interval*. Most data vendors will have hourly, daily, and weekly timeframes. In case the data source does not cater to this, a strategy might need further down-sampling, or in some cases, higher frequency data.

- The ability to choose the *exchange* from which to obtain data. It is rare, but price variations do happen from one exchange to another. You may be testing an arbitrage between exchanges. For this reason, it may be beneficial to build in testing of multiple exchange data even if the rest of the parameters are unchanged.

- *Timeframes*. Some instruments do not have a very lengthy history. Others may have been in business for a long time. It is important to note strategies may be in play for just a few hours to months. Backtesting needs to cater to all the variations possible.

For ease of use (debuggability by simply loading into a Google spreadsheet), let's go with a CSV file.

```go
func ReadHistoricalDataFromCsvFile(csvFile string) ([]MarketDataPriceOnly,
error) {
    file, err := os.Open(csvFile)
    if err != nil {
        log.Fatal(err)
    }
    defer file.Close()

    reader := csv.NewReader(file)
    records, err := reader.ReadAll()
    if err != nil {
        log.Fatal(err)
    }

    dateIndex, closeIndex := -1, -1
    for i, column := range records[0] {
        if column == "datetime" {
            dateIndex = i
        }
        if column == "close" {
            closeIndex = i
        }
        if dateIndex != -1 && closeIndex != -1 {
            break
        }
    }

    if dateIndex == -1 {
        log.Fatal("The 'datetime' column was not found in the CSV file.")
    }
    if closeIndex == -1 {
        log.Fatal("The 'close' column was not found in the CSV file.")
    }

    var dataPriceOnly []MarketDataPriceOnly
```

```go
for _, record := range records[1:] {
    //date, err := time.Parse(time.RFC3339, record[dateIndex])
    date, err := time.Parse("2006-01-02 15:04:05", record[dateIndex])
    if err != nil {
        log.Fatal(err)
    }

    price, err := strconv.ParseFloat(record[closeIndex], 64)
    if err != nil {
        log.Fatal(err)
    }

    dataPriceOnly = append(dataPriceOnly, MarketDataPriceOnly{Date:
    date, Price: price})
}

return dataPriceOnly, nil
}
```

Indicators

There are an unknowable number of indicators available in the trading world today. Unfortunately, there is not a winning combo or recipe that you can use to generate all necessary indicators. At the very least, the attempt might be a costly affair.

This being said, once you have a strategy in mind, you should have a number of indicators to model the entry and exit signals. A good timesaver here is to modularize the indicator portion of the code away from the strategy and signal generators so as to make them interchangeable.

Before the strategy portion of the chapter, let's delve into some of the indicators that are going to be used and reasons behind them.

Levels

Trading on levels involves identifying key price points, known as *support* and *resistance levels*, where the price of an asset is more likely to change direction. By understanding the advantages and disadvantages or risks associated with trading on levels, you can enhance your trading strategies and make more informed decisions.

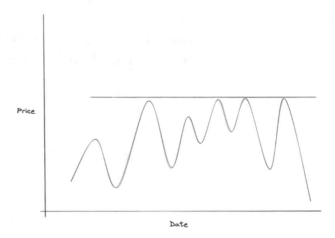

Figure 4-8. *Example of a resistance level*

Figure 4-8 shows a resistance level. The stock repeatedly hits the resistance and eventually loses momentum and reverses downward.

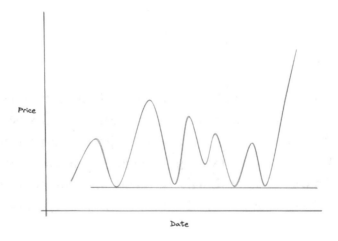

Figure 4-9. *Example of a support level*

Figure 4-9 shows an example of a support level, where the financial instrument consolidates, bouncing on the green support level to eventually reverse upward.

Advantages include:

- **Simplicity**: Trading on levels is a relatively simple method, which makes it easy for investors to understand and implement. By focusing on support and resistance levels, investors can identify areas where the price of an asset is more likely to change direction.

- **Clear entry and exit points**: Trading on levels provides traders with clear entry and exit points. When the price of an asset reaches a key level, traders can make decisions based on whether the price is likely to break through the level or reverse course. This helps minimize guesswork and enhance trading efficiency.

- **Risk management**: Trading on levels allows investors to effectively manage their risk. By setting stop-loss orders around key levels, investors can limit their potential losses if the market moves against their position.

- **Profit potential**: Since trading on levels can help investors identify potential trend reversals or breakouts, it offers opportunities for substantial profit. This is especially true when an asset's price breaks through a key level, as it could signal the beginning of a new trend.

Disadvantages/risks include:

- **False breakouts**: One of the main risks associated with trading on levels is the potential for false breakouts. Sometimes, the price of an asset may appear to break through a key level, only to reverse course shortly thereafter. This can result in losses for traders who entered positions based on the apparent breakout.

- **Dependence on technical analysis**: Trading on levels relies heavily on technical analysis, which involves examining past price movements to predict future trends. While technical analysis can be useful, it's important to remember that it's not a guarantee of future performance. Additionally, it's crucial to combine technical analysis with other forms of research, such as fundamental analysis, to develop a well-rounded trading strategy.

- **Subjectivity**: Identifying key levels can sometimes be subjective, as different traders may interpret the same price chart differently. This can lead to varying opinions on where the support and resistance levels lie, and thus, different trading decisions.

- **Market noise**: Trading on levels can be susceptible to market noise, as short-term price fluctuations may cause an asset's price to temporarily breach a key level. This can lead to premature entry or exit signals, which may result in losses for traders who act on these signals.

Trading on levels is a valuable technique that can help investors identify potential trend reversals and breakouts. By understanding the advantages and disadvantages or risks associated with trading on levels, you can make more informed decisions and enhance your trading strategies. Like any other trading approach, it's essential to continually learn, adapt, and refine your strategies to achieve consistent success in the markets.

Simple Moving Averages

The *simple moving average* is perhaps the most commonly used indicator of them all. Markets move all of the time. At times, markets may be volatile and cause the algorithms to react too much. Take the blue line in Figure 4-10 as the original price. The use of the orange line, the simple moving average, creates a much "smoother" line to work with.

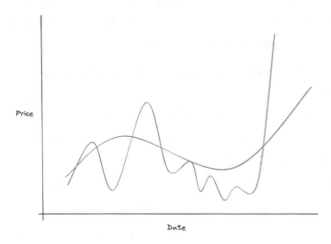

Figure 4-10. *Simple moving average example*

A few positive side-effects include the fact that you can also work out a "trend" or tendency of the recent past, and when the price action largely exceeds the trend, this could signal a strong move for the asset.

Another nice side-effect of moving averages is that they can be applied to a lot of different indicators. Price, of course, but this technique can be applied to volumes and other momentum indicators as well.

It is worthy to note that averages also introduce lag. Naturally, the longer the period, the longer the lag. For shorter periods, this is not so much of a concern, but longer periods may introduce significant delays.

Exponential Moving Averages

Exponential moving averages (EMAs) are similar to simple moving averages. One of its benefits is the fact that it has a recency bias and hence makes the overall result more sensitive.

As most statisticians will attest, exponential moving averages are not applicable to all indicators, however. Pay attention to the outcome of the numbers before embedding the indicator deep into the strategy.

One small side note—exponential moving averages can be more expensive computationally than the simple moving average. Care is needed in some cases where analysis goes into the milliseconds or smaller.

Relative Strength Index

This is another industry favorite. Relative strength index (affectionately known as RSI) is a phrase that will come across a lot of the trading desks and financial media platforms.

This is a popular momentum oscillator developed by J. Welles Wilder in 1978. It is a technical indicator used to measure the speed and change of price movements, helping traders identify overbought and oversold conditions in the market. RSI ranges from 0 to 100, and its calculation is based on the average gains and losses of an asset's price over a specified period, typically 14 days.

The RSI is primarily used to:

- **Identify overbought and oversold conditions**: An asset is considered overbought when its RSI is above 70, indicating that it may be overvalued and due for a price correction or a reversal in trend. Conversely, an asset is considered oversold when its RSI is below 30, suggesting that it may be undervalued and poised for a price rebound.

- **Detect trend reversals**: RSI can help traders spot potential trend reversals by identifying bullish and bearish divergences. A bullish divergence occurs when the price of an asset forms a lower low, while the RSI forms a higher low, indicating a potential upward trend reversal. On the other hand, a bearish divergence occurs when the price forms a higher high, while the RSI forms a lower high, signaling a potential downward trend reversal.

- **Confirm trend strength**: The RSI can also be used to gauge the strength of a trend. Generally, an RSI reading above 50 indicates a bullish trend, while a reading below 50 suggests a bearish trend.

It is essential to remember that the RSI should not be used as a standalone indicator. Combining the RSI with other technical analysis tools, such as support and resistance levels, moving averages, and chart patterns, can provide a more comprehensive understanding of the market and improve the effectiveness of trading decisions.

The benefits of the indicator are hopefully self-explanatory. It is not without pitfalls, however. If the entire world of finance reacted accordingly to this indicator, all traders and investors should become instant millionaires via the use of the RSI. The problem is, the levels where the accepted "overbought" and "oversold" as accepted by the markets, "70" and "30" respectively, work most of the time, but when they do not, they can lead an investor to troubled waters. A financial instrument can hit the RSI levels of "30," but happily continue going down past the "30" or "oversold" levels. As you would expect, the reverse also applies, where the asset may continue climbing past the level of "70" or "overbought" levels and aggressively continue climbing.

It cannot be stressed enough. Finance is a world of probabilities and should not be taken as absolutes.

Additional Notes

There are a number of statistics libraries available for use. It is worthy to note that some financially oriented libraries are available for all to use and can be a timesaver.

TA-Lib is one such library that is often used by numerous trading desks and quant trading desks in the financial world.

Enhancing Discipline and Consistency

One of the greatest challenges traders face is maintaining discipline and consistency in their trading. Backtesting can help to instill these qualities by providing a clear framework for evaluating and refining a strategy. By consistently adhering to a well-tested approach, traders can avoid the pitfalls of emotional decision-making and impulsive behavior, which are often the root causes of trading losses.

Why So Many Features?

Backtesting mechanisms must incorporate variable timeframes to account for the dynamic nature of financial markets and the diverse range of trading strategies employed by traders. There are several reasons that variable timeframes are essential in the backtesting process:

- **Adaptability to market conditions**: Different market conditions often require different trading strategies and timeframes. By incorporating variable timeframes in the backtesting mechanism, traders can test and optimize their strategies for various market environments, ensuring that their approach remains relevant and effective regardless of prevailing conditions.

- **Evaluation of short-term and long-term strategies**: Traders employ a wide range of trading strategies, from short-term day trading to long-term position trading. Variable timeframes in the backtesting mechanism enable traders to evaluate and refine strategies across different time horizons, ensuring that their chosen approach is well-suited to their unique trading objectives and risk tolerance.

- **Improved risk management**: By testing strategies across different timeframes, traders can gain a more comprehensive understanding of the potential risks and rewards associated with their chosen approach. This information can be invaluable in developing effective risk management strategies and optimizing position sizing to achieve a desired risk-reward profile.

- **Enhanced flexibility**: Variable timeframes in backtesting
  mechanisms allow traders to experiment with different time
  horizons and adapt their strategies as market conditions change.
  This flexibility is crucial in the ever-evolving world of trading, where
  success often hinges on a trader's ability to adapt and respond to
  changing market dynamics.

Sample Code

Exchange Connectivity (Listing 4-1)

Listing 4-1. Exchange Connectivity and Obtain Data for the Indicators

```
package main
import (
    // note the use of the module below, list is trimmed
    "github.com/adshao/go-binance/v2"
)
func getClient() *binance.Client {

    fileName := fmt.Sprintf("%s/.config/binance/binance.key",
    os.Getenv("HOME"))
    file, _ := ioutil.ReadFile(fileName)
    lines := strings.Split(string(file), "\n")

    // first line is binance API key
    // second line is binance secret key

    binanceAPIKey := lines[0]
    binanceSecretKey := lines[1]
    return binance.NewClient(binanceAPIKey, binanceSecretKey)
}
func obtainDataFromBinanceExchange (client *binace.Client, ticker string,
interval string) ([]float64, error) {

    // an array to store obtained values
    var closingPrices []float64
```

```
// Fetch klines data for the specified symbol and interval
klines, err := client.NewKlinesService().Symbol(symbol).
Interval(interval).Do(context.Background())
if err != nil {
    return closingPrices, err
}

// Extract the closing prices from the klines data

for _, kline := range klines {
    closePrice, _ := strconv.ParseFloat(kline.Close, 64)
    closingPrices = append(closingPrices, closePrice)
}

return closingPrices, nil

}
```

Building Indicators (Listing 4-2)

Listing 4-2. Building Indicators for Use in Building Entry and Exit Signals

```
func BuildIndicatorsFromMarketData (slb int, llb int, histData
[]MarketDataPriceOnly) ([]MarketData, error) {

    close := make([]float64, len(histData))
    for i := 0; i < len(histData); i++ {
        close[i] = histData[i].Price
    }

    rsi          := talib.Rsi(close, 14)
    rsisma14     := talib.Sma(close, 14)
    rsisma14sma9 := talib.Sma(rsisma14, 9)
    emaShort     := talib.Ema(close, slb)
    emaLong      := talib.Ema(close, llb)
    sma5         := talib.Sma(close, 5)
    sma50        := talib.Sma(close, 50)
    sma200       := talib.Sma(close, 200)
    ema9         := talib.Ema(close, 9)
```

```
ema20          := talib.Ema(close, 20)
ema30          := talib.Ema(close, 30)
ema40          := talib.Ema(close, 40)
ema50          := talib.Ema(close, 50)
ema100         := talib.Ema(close, 100)

var data []MarketData
for i := 0; i < len(histData); i++ {
    data = append(
        data,
        MarketData{
            Date: histData[i].Date,
            Price: histData[i].Price,
            Rsi: rsi[i],
            RsiSma14Sma9: rsisma14sma9[i],
            Sma5: sma5[i],
            Sma50: sma50[i],
            Sma200: sma200[i],
            Ema9: ema9[i],
            Ema20: ema20[i],
            Ema30: ema30[i],
            Ema40: ema40[i],
            Ema50: ema50[i],
            Ema100: ema100[i],
            EmaShort: emaShort[i],
            EmaLong: emaLong[i]})
    }

    return data, nil
}
```

The Strategy

Let's put the industry favorite into code. The *Golden Cross* is a widely recognized technical indicator that signals a potential bullish trend reversal in the financial markets. This classic trading strategy occurs when a short-term moving average, typically the

50-day, crosses above a longer-term moving average, such as the 200-day. The Golden Cross is revered for its simplicity and effectiveness in identifying trend reversals, making it an ideal starting point for both novice and experienced traders.

While the strategy is praised for its ability to provide clear entry and exit signals, it also has its drawbacks, such as generating false signals or being susceptible to lagging effects. Nonetheless, the Golden Cross remains a popular and practical strategy for traders to begin their foray into technical analysis and develop a solid foundation for more advanced trading techniques. See Listing 4-3.

Listing 4-3. Golden Cross Strategy

```
package main

type GoldenCrossStrategy interface {

    SetShortLookback(shortLookback int)
    SetLongLookback(longLookback int)
    ShouldEnterGoldenCrossMarket(data []MarketData, me_index int) bool
    ShouldExitGoldenCrossMarket(data []MarketData, me_index int) bool
}

type GoldenCrossMaStrategy struct {
    shortPeriod int
    longPeriod  int
}

func (s *GoldenCrossMaStrategy) SetShortLookback(shortLookback int) {
    s.shortPeriod = shortLookback
}
func (s *GoldenCrossMaStrategy) SetLongLookback(longLookback int) {
    s.longPeriod = longLookback
}
func (s *GoldenCrossMaStrategy) ShouldEnterGoldenCrossMarket(data
[]MarketData, i int) bool {

    if i < 200 {
        return false
    }
```

```
    // Check for Golden Cross
    if data[i].Sma50 > data[i].Sma200 && data[i-1].Sma50 <= data[i-1].
    Sma200 {
        return true
    }

    return false
}

func (s *GoldenCrossMaStrategy) ShouldExitGoldenCrossMarket(data
[]MarketData, i int) bool {

    if i < 200 {
        return false
    }

    // Check for Death Cross
    if data[i].Sma50 < data[i].Sma200 && data[i-1].Sma50 >= data[i-1].
    Sma200 {
        return true
    }

    return false
}
```

Run the Bot

Once you put a strategy is together, the next step is to put it into an application that reads data and replays the data in the strategy's timeframe, one candle at a time. The keyword being one candle at a time, a *loop*.

Most developers who have dealt with any data with size of consequence think of loops as slow and resource intensive. There is a purpose in deliberately choosing the slow design, however. Loops prevent the forward look bias, or the ability to "see the future." This is a trap most traders and investors fall into at some stage. An indicator or a signal accidentally bakes in the future and therefore has an unrealistically high probability of success. Looping through history one tick or candle at a time, by definition, serves as an extra layer of security against "seeing the future."

Performance Evaluation

Statistics are a trader's friend. Simply put, it is a game of probabilities and there are no absolutes. The use of mathematics has a place in trading, so certain situations can be abstracted and understood easily. Moreover, comparing results makes the performance evaluation of a strategy compared to another much easier.

As ever, it is important to follow the great minds in the industry and market participants. Many will make research-based observations that are different, but there are a select few statistical analysis tools that are used repeatedly.

Stats

A trader or investor must be well-informed about the intricacies of investment strategies and their evaluation. A keen understanding of these metrics is essential for making informed decisions about the performance of the strategy.

By understanding and applying these statistical evaluation metrics, investors and fund managers can assess the performance and risk associated with their financial strategies and make informed decisions about their investments.

PnL

Profit and loss (PnL) is a key performance metric used to evaluate the success of a trading strategy. It represents the net gains or losses resulting from the trades executed by a strategy over a specified period. By analyzing PnL during backtesting and real-time testing, traders can gain valuable insights into the effectiveness of their strategy and make data-driven decisions to optimize its performance. This chapter explores the importance of PnL in both backtesting and real-time testing and discusses how it can help traders refine their approach for greater success in the financial markets.

PnL in Backtesting

During the backtesting process, PnL is used to assess the historical performance of a trading strategy. By calculating the net profit or loss that the strategy would have generated based on historical market data, traders can determine whether the strategy has been profitable in the past and gauge its potential for success in the future.

Analyzing PnL during backtesting can also help traders identify areas for improvement in their strategy. For example, a consistently negative PnL may indicate that the strategy's entry or exit signals need to be refined, or that the risk management parameters, such as stop-loss orders or position sizing, need to be adjusted.

Furthermore, by comparing the PnL of different strategies or variations of the same strategy, traders can make informed decisions about which approach is likely to yield the best results in live trading.

PnL in Real-Time Testing

In real-time testing, or paper trading, PnL serves as a crucial indicator of a trading strategy's performance under current market conditions. By monitoring PnL during real-time testing, traders can assess the effectiveness of their strategy and make any necessary adjustments before deploying it with real capital.

Real-time PnL analysis can help traders identify potential issues with their strategy that may not have been apparent during backtesting. For example, the strategy may be struggling to adapt to changing market conditions or experiencing difficulties with execution due to latency or slippage. By addressing these issues in real-time testing, traders can ensure that their strategy is well-prepared for the challenges of live trading.

Moreover, tracking PnL during real-time testing can provide traders with valuable insights into the risk-reward profile of their strategy. By comparing the strategy's PnL to other performance metrics, such as drawdowns or volatility, traders can develop a comprehensive understanding of the potential risks and rewards associated with their approach, allowing them to make informed decisions about risk management and position sizing.

Hit Rate

Hit rate, also known as the *win rate,* is a key performance metric used to evaluate the effectiveness of a trading strategy. It represents the percentage of trades that result in a profit relative to the total number of trades executed. While a high hit rate may seem desirable at first glance, it is essential to understand that an excessively high hit rate can have a detrimental impact on PnL in certain circumstances. This section explores the role of hit rate in trading strategy evaluation and discusses the potential negative consequences of an overly high hit rate on PnL.

Hit Rate in Trading Strategy Evaluation

Hit rate is a valuable metric for gauging the consistency of a trading strategy. A high hit rate indicates that a strategy has been successful in identifying profitable trading opportunities more often than not. Conversely, a low hit rate suggests that the strategy may struggle to generate consistent profits, requiring further refinement or the implementation of effective risk management measures.

However, it is important to note that hit rate alone does not provide a complete picture of a trading strategy's performance. It must be considered alongside other performance metrics, such as the average profit per trade, risk-reward ratio, and maximum drawdown, to develop a comprehensive understanding of a strategy's effectiveness.

The Potential Drawbacks of an Excessively High Hit Rate

While a high hit rate might appear to be an indicator of a successful trading strategy, an overly high hit rate can sometimes have a negative impact on PnL. This is because a high hit rate may be masking underlying issues with the strategy, such as:

- **Poor risk-reward ratio**: A strategy with an excessively high hit rate might be achieving this success by sacrificing the potential profit on winning trades. For example, a strategy that consistently targets small profits while risking large losses can result in a high hit rate, but a poor overall PnL. In this case, the strategy may need to be adjusted to improve the risk-reward ratio, even if it results in a lower hit rate.

- **Overfitting**: A high hit rate could be a sign of overfitting, where a strategy has been tailored too closely to historical market data, making it less effective in adapting to changing market conditions. An overfitted strategy may perform well during backtesting but fail to generate consistent profits during live trading, ultimately leading to a poor PnL.

- **Frequent trading and high transaction costs**: A strategy with an excessively high hit rate might be generating a large number of trades, resulting in high transaction costs. These costs, which include fees and slippage, can eat into the PnL, reducing the overall profitability of the strategy. In this case, it may be necessary to refine the strategy to reduce the number of trades executed or find ways to minimize transaction costs.

Sharpe Ratio

The Sharpe ratio is a widely-used performance metric in finance that measures the risk-adjusted return of an investment or trading strategy. It is calculated by dividing the difference between the strategy's average return and the risk-free rate by the standard deviation of the returns, which represents the strategy's volatility. A Sharpe ratio of at least 1 is often considered preferable, as it signifies that the strategy generates an excess return that is equal to or greater than its level of risk. This section briefly explains why a Sharpe ratio of at least 1 is desirable in trading strategy evaluation.

Risk-Adjusted Performance

A Sharpe ratio of at least 1 indicates that a trading strategy is generating returns that adequately compensate for the level of risk taken. This is important because it suggests that the strategy is not only generating profits, but doing so in a way that accounts for the inherent risks associated with trading. A Sharpe ratio of less than 1 implies that the strategy's returns are not commensurate with the level of risk, which may signal the need for adjustments to the strategy or risk management measures.

Benchmarking and Comparison

The Sharpe ratio provides a standardized measure that allows for easy comparison between different trading strategies or investment opportunities. A Sharpe ratio of at least 1 serves as a useful benchmark, as it indicates that a strategy is generating positive risk-adjusted returns. By comparing the Sharpe ratios of various strategies, traders can identify which approach offers the most attractive risk-reward profile and make informed decisions about where to allocate their capital.

Portfolio Diversification

A trading strategy with a Sharpe ratio of at least 1 is more likely to contribute positively to a diversified portfolio. When combined with other uncorrelated strategies or assets, a strategy with a higher Sharpe ratio can help improve the overall risk-adjusted performance of a portfolio, enhancing returns while reducing overall volatility.

Potential Pitfalls

A Sharpe ratio of at least 1 is preferable in trading strategy evaluation because it signifies that the strategy generates returns that are commensurate with its level of risk. This risk-adjusted performance metric allows traders to easily compare different strategies and make informed decisions about where to allocate capital. As you continue to develop your GoLang-based Golden Cross trading tool, striving for a Sharpe ratio of at least 1 will be essential in ensuring that your strategy offers an attractive risk-reward profile and contributes positively to a diversified trading portfolio. See Listing 4-4.

So far so good, but the ratio of 1 and above still does not guarantee success. In fact, there are numerous cases where an insanely high ratio can be deceiving and hide potential risks. Be sure to use Sharpe ratios in combination with other stats.

Listing 4-4. Sharpe Ratio Calculation

```go
package main

import (
    "math"
)

func SharpeRatio(returns []float64, riskFreeRate float64) float64 {
    n := len(returns)
    if n == 0 {
        return 0
    }

    // Calculate the average return
    var avgReturn float64
    for _, r := range returns {
        avgReturn += r
    }
    avgReturn /= float64(n)

    // Calculate the standard deviation of returns
    var stdDev float64
    for _, r := range returns {
        diff := r - avgReturn
```

```
        stdDev += diff * diff
    }
    stdDev = math.Sqrt(stdDev / float64(n))

    // Calculate the Sharpe Ratio
    excessReturn := avgReturn - riskFreeRate
    sharpeRatio := excessReturn / stdDev
    return sharpeRatio
}
```

MAR Ratio

The MAR (Managed Account Reports) ratio, also known as the Calmar ratio, is a performance metric used to evaluate the risk-adjusted return of investment strategies, particularly in the context of managed futures accounts and hedge funds. It is calculated by dividing the annualized rate of return by the maximum drawdown experienced by the strategy over a specified period. The MAR ratio provides a useful means of comparing different trading strategies, as it takes into account both return and risk in a single metric. This section briefly explains the MAR ratio and its benefits of comparing multiple strategies against one another.

Emphasis on Drawdown Risk

One of the key advantages of the MAR ratio is its focus on drawdown risk, which is the largest peak-to-trough decline in the value of a trading strategy or investment portfolio. Drawdowns can be particularly damaging to a trader's account, as they require significant gains to recover from the losses. By incorporating the maximum drawdown into its calculation, the MAR ratio highlights the importance of managing drawdown risk and encourages traders to prioritize strategies that minimize this risk while generating attractive returns.

Risk-Adjusted Performance

Like the Sharpe ratio, the MAR ratio measures the risk-adjusted performance of a trading strategy. However, instead of using standard deviation as a measure of risk, the MAR ratio uses maximum drawdown. This provides a different perspective on risk management and allows traders to compare strategies based on their ability to generate returns while minimizing drawdowns.

Comparison of Strategies

The MAR ratio is a valuable tool for comparing different trading strategies or investment opportunities, as it provides a single metric that accounts for both return and drawdown risk. By comparing the MAR ratios of various strategies, traders can identify which approach offers the most attractive risk-reward profile and make informed decisions about where to allocate their capital.

Suitability for Trend-Following Strategies

The MAR ratio is particularly useful for evaluating trend-following strategies, which often experience significant drawdowns during periods of market consolidation or trend reversal. By taking into account the maximum drawdown, the MAR ratio enables traders to assess the effectiveness of trend-following strategies in managing risk and generating consistent returns.

Potential Pitfalls

The MAR ratio is a powerful performance metric that offers several benefits for comparing trading strategies. By emphasizing drawdown risk and providing a measure of risk-adjusted performance, the MAR ratio allows traders to make informed decisions about where to allocate capital and which strategies offer the most attractive risk-reward profiles.

Considering the MAR ratio as part of your performance evaluation process is essential for ensuring that your strategy effectively manages risk while generating consistent returns. See Listing 4-5.

Even with the combination of all of the statistical analysis and tools, risks are still there. Don't forget that markets are a kind of living organism, so constant periodic retesting of strategies helps ensure that you are attuned to the changes in the behavior of the markets.

Listing 4-5. Example of MAR Ratio Calculation

```go
package main

import (
    "math"
)
```

```go
func MARRatio(returns []float64) float64 {
    n := len(returns)
    if n == 0 {
        return 0
    }

    // Calculate the cumulative return
    cumulativeReturn := 1.0
    for _, r := range returns {
        cumulativeReturn *= (1 + r)
    }

    // Calculate the maximum drawdown
    maxDrawdown := 0.0
    peak := returns[0]
    trough := returns[0]
    for _, r := range returns[1:] {
        if r > peak {
            peak = r
            trough = r
        } else if r < trough {
            trough = r
        }

        drawdown := (peak - trough) / peak
        if drawdown > maxDrawdown {
            maxDrawdown = drawdown
        }
    }

    // Calculate the MAR Ratio
    marRatio := cumulativeReturn / maxDrawdown

    if marRatio < 0 {
        return 0.0
    }

    return marRatio
}
```

Success or Failure and Why

Possibly the most critical point of the process is to be able to objectively evaluate a strategy and decide when it is good to take it to the next step.

Benchmark Comparison

Comparisons against a benchmark may potentially be the most important aspect of trading. Everything moves, very quickly at times. Traders often like to know what to compare against.

This is where you go back to objectives that were introduced in the process section of the chapter earlier. Having an objective for the strategy, or strategies in some cases, provides the trader or investor with the analogous North Star or some sort of benchmark to constantly compare to.

For instance, when trading equities, you might choose the Golden Cross strategy (not particularly performant as a strategy, just that there are many traders' eyes on it) to compare against the new strategy being worked on. For instance, comparing the statistics of the two strategies (PnL, Sharpe ratio, and MAR ratio) against one another.

Others may simply use a threshold of the statistics, for example some trading desks do not even look at strategies with a Sharpe ratio of 1.0.

Timeframe

There is a reason that timing and timeframes matter most in any financial transaction. It is also the aspect in the performance evaluation of a strategy where a trader or investor might spend the most amount of time.

More often than not, you might find numerous timeframes that perform for any strategy. There are a multitude of reasons behind this phenomenon. From wars, to global pandemics, to financial turmoil. One thing that a number of economists have observed, and pertinent to this chapter, is that the growing participants of automated trading algorithms have accelerated the financial cycles, which seem to have increased the amplitude of volatility across the globe.

This phenomenon is also more noticeable in some asset classes. FX and cryptocurrencies seem to be affected much more than traditional finance favorites, like the bond markets.

In short, the same strategy can work and cease to work for the same asset in different market conditions; the same strategy across a number of assets may work better or worse, depending on the particularities in an asset class.

Risk Management and Continuous Improvement

Appetite for risk and how to manage trading situations vary from one person to another completely. Some of it may overlap with the trading strategy, but clear modeling of risk will help in maximizing confidence in the strategy.

It helps to know how the strategy does over time in terms of its average returns on trades, max and min, average loss, maximum loss, and minimum loss, and respective capital levels. This enables the trader or investor to model and derive profit and stop loss levels for every strategy.

Potential Pitfalls

Backtesting is an indispensable tool for traders looking to achieve success in the world of trading. By providing a means to refine trading strategies, manage risk, build confidence, and enhance discipline and consistency, backtesting serves as the foundation upon which successful trading careers are built.

However, it is essential to be aware of the limitations of backtesting, such as overfitting, data limitations, and curve-fitting, to ensure that results are interpreted with caution. By understanding both the pros and cons of backtesting, traders can make informed decisions about their strategies and set realistic expectations for their performance in live markets.

Example of Backtesting Multiple Strategies

These statistical tools should have you pretty well set up to at least compare and contrast various strategies and you should at least know whether the strategy passes the test of time. Always remember to test market turmoil or crashes in the past. See Listings 4-6 and 4-7.

Listing 4-6. Example of a Backtesting Run

```go
package main

import (
    "fmt"
)
func main() {

    // create all indicator data from price action data
    // this is done loading a CSV file with Open High Low Close
    // two variable length moving averages are set as arguments
    indicatorData, err := buildIndicators(5, 9)
    if err != nil {
        fmt.Println("Error fetching data:", err)
        return
    }

    // below two strategies are run sequentially
    EmaStrategy := &MovingAverageCrossoverStrategy{}
    EmaStrategy.SetShortLookback(5)
    EmaStrategy.SetLongLookback(9)
    GCStrategy := &GoldenCrossMaStrategy{}
    GCStrategy.SetShortLookback(50)
    GCStrategy.SetShortLookback(200)

    // Assuming returns is a slice of float64 representing the
        strategy's returns
    var profits []float64
    // Assuming returns is a slice of float64 representing the
        strategy's trades
    var trades []Trade
    // Fill the returns slice with your strategy's returns
    profits, trades = Backtest(EmaStrategy, indicatorData)
```

```go
// output statistics to STDOUT
err = generate_report("Ema100Strategy", profits)
if err != nil {
    panic (err)
}

// storing all executed trades into a CSV file
// this is particularly useful when comparing against a chart
filename := "ema_trades.csv"
err = saveTradesToCSV(trades, filename)
if err != nil {
    fmt.Println("Error saving trades to CSV:", err)
} else {
    fmt.Printf("Trades saved to %s\n", filename)
}

// Assuming returns is a slice of float64 representing the
    strategy's returns
var gc_profits []float64
// Fill the returns slice with your strategy's returns
profits = BacktestGoldenCross(GCStrategy, indicatorData)

// output statistics to STDOUT
err = generate_report("GoldenCross", gc_profits)
if err != nil {
    panic(err)
}

// storing all executed trades into a CSV file
// this is particularly useful when comparing against a chart
filename = "golden_cross_trades.csv"
err = saveTradesToCSV(trades, filename)
if err != nil {
    fmt.Println("Error saving trades to CSV:", err)
} else {
    fmt.Printf("Trades saved to %s\n", filename)
}
```

```
    // export forensic analysis
    filename = "indicators.csv"
    err = saveIndicatorsToCsv(indicatorData, filename)
    if err != nil {
        fmt.Println("Error saving indicators to CSV:", err)
    } else {
        fmt.Println("Indicators saved to %s", filename)
    }

}
```

Listing 4-7. The Output of Running the Code from Listing 4-6

```
$ ./runStrategy
Strategy:  Ema100
PnL: 14419.56
Sharpe Ratio: 1.29
MAR Ratio: 0.00
Trades saved to ema_trades.csv
Strategy:  GoldenCross
PnL: 0.00
Sharpe Ratio: 0.00
MAR Ratio: 0.00
Trades saved to golden_cross_trades.csv
```

A Taste Before Serving the Meal

Real-time trading simulation, often referred to as paper trading or virtual trading, is a crucial component in the development and implementation of an automated trading strategy. By simulating trades using real-time market data, and without risking actual capital, traders can gain invaluable insights into the performance of their strategy under current market conditions. This section explores the importance of real-time trading simulation in building confidence, and managing risk. This can mean that traders can sleep comfortably at night, knowing that their automated trading system is well-equipped to navigate the unpredictable world of financial markets.

Ensuring System Stability

The stability of an automated trading system is of paramount importance, particularly when it comes to executing trades without constant supervision. Real-time trading simulation allows traders to stress-test their systems under actual market conditions, identifying any potential technical issues or bottlenecks that could compromise the performance. By addressing these issues in a simulated environment, traders can ensure that their system remains stable and reliable when it comes time to deploy it in live trading.

Hidden Difficulties

After a particular strategy or a number of strategies go through the grueling test phase and subsequent improvement cycle(s), there might still be unexpected behaviors that are difficult to see. This is the primary reason that it is important to re-run backtesting over the time period that real-time testing was performed. There are numerous reasons for this, but the two mains are slippage and forward look bias.

Slippage can be caused by numerous factors, but it often refers to the difference between the price at the point of order and the price at the time of its fill. More often than not, a trader or investor will see an initial loss. Slippage is hard to quantify and model; it is therefore an important aspect of testing to continuously go back and monitor the difference between backtesting and real-time testing in order to quantify or set expectations.

If a strategy performs similarly in backtesting and remains fairly consistent in real-time trading, the testing framework and the strategy may be sound. If, however, backtesting and real-time testing consistently seem to perform differently where backtesting trades are being profitable and real-time trades are not, it is time to revisit the strategy and make sure no *forward look bias* is introduced.

Forensic Analysis

When strategies work over numerous indicators and concurrent calculations, it may be difficult to track simply looking at trades and charts.

You might need to consider running the calculations under a more granular timeframe in order to be able to catch the nature of slippage or forward look bias. Having a charting tool with real-time data may offer insight as to where the issue is hiding.

Note that a trader may be lucky and find that the slippage ends up helping a trader. You should not count on this, however, as the markets have a tendency to go the other way.

Table 4-1 shows a snippet of the CSV file called ema_trades.csv. In this case, hourly data is used as an interval. Note that the time recorded goes down to second granularity. In this case, only the trade execution times are recorded. As most exchanges offer the order details report, it is important to track down the exact time of the fill (note a trade may be partially filled over multiple fills that sum up to the order amount). The finer the granularity in time, the easier it is to track slippage and other unexpected results.

Table 4-1. *List of Trades Executed by the Backtests from Listing 4-6*

Datetime	Indicator	Price	Quantity	Position Length
2023-03-01T18:45:00Z	buy	1653.17	1	0
2023-03-02T01:00:00Z	sell	1647.36	1	26
2023-03-02T03:00:00Z	buy	1656.39	1	0
2023-03-02T10:15:00Z	sell	1654.07	1	30
2023-03-03T05:30:00Z	buy	1648.72	1	0
2023-03-03T10:15:00Z	sell	1600.66	1	20

Table 4-2 shows a snippet of the CSV file containing all indicators. The importance here is that a trader might need a continuous timeseries with all of the indicators present alongside each other to actively track progress the real-time charts mentioned earlier.

Table 4-2. *A Snippet of the Timeseries Data Containing Indicators*

Datetime	Price	Rsi	Sma5	Sma50	Sma200
2023-03-03T11:45:00Z	1565.51	23	1563.81	1628.63	1642.72
2023-03-03T12:00:00Z	1562.76	22.3	1565.64	1627.38	1642.5
2023-03-03T12:15:00Z	1568.09	26.94	1566.34	1626.2	1642.29
2023-03-03T12:30:00Z	1567.01	26.6	1565.72	1624.96	1642.07
2023-03-03T12:45:00Z	1566.25	26.34	1565.92	1623.73	1641.83
2023-03-03T13:00:00Z	1567.2	27.28	1566.26	1622.54	1641.58

Potential Pitfalls

Real-time trading simulation is an indispensable tool for ensuring the success of an automated trading strategy. By building confidence, identifying potential issues, managing risk, and ensuring system stability, real-time trading simulation provides traders with the peace of mind they need to sleep comfortably at night.

The importance of a fine-tuned, real-time trading simulation cannot be overstated. It serves as a critical step in validating your strategy and ensuring that you are well-prepared to navigate the complex and ever-changing landscape of financial markets with confidence and ease.

As ever, having a wonderfully positive PnL experience in paper trading means almost zero in the trading world. See Listing 4-8.

Listing 4-8. Real-Time or Paper Trading Test Sample Code

```
func StartBot(ctx context.Context, symbol string, interval string,
rsiBuyThreshold float64, rsiSellThreshold float64, fastPeriod int,
slowPeriod int, capital float64) {

    client := getClient()

    select {
    case <-ctx.Done():
        fmt.Println("has just been canceled")
    default:
        time.Sleep(100 * time.Millisecond)
        runStrategy(client, symbol, interval, capital)
    }

}

func runStrategy(client *binance.Client, symbol string, interval string,
capital float64) bool {
    // Fetch klines data for the specified symbol and interval
    klines, err := client.NewKlinesService().Symbol(symbol).
    Interval(interval).Do(context.Background())
    if err != nil {
        log.Fatal(err)
    }
```

```go
// Extract the closing prices from the klines data
var closingPrices []float64
for _, kline := range klines {
    closePrice, _ := strconv.ParseFloat(kline.Close, 64)
    closingPrices = append(closingPrices, closePrice)
}

// create all indicator data from price action data
indicatorData, err := buildIndicators(5, 9, closingPrices)
if err != nil {
    fmt.Println("Error fetching data:", err)
    return
}

positionOpen := false
entryPrice := 0.0
counter := 0
profit := 0.0

if !positionOpen && strategy.ShouldEnterMarket(indicatorData) {

    _, err := checkFunds(client, capital)
    if err {
        return true
    }
    // booking an order commenting out while tesing!
    //buy(symbol, capital, client)
    positionOpen = true
    fmt.Println("Entry price: ", price)
} else if positionOpen && strategy.ShouldExitMarket(indicatorData) {

    // selling position
    positionOpen = false
    // commenting out while testing!
    //sell(symbol, capital, client)
    fmt.Println("Exit price: ", price)

}
```

```go
        return false
}

func buy(symbol string, capital float64, client *binance.Client) {
    // Place a market buy order for the specified symbol and capital
    log.Printf("Buying %s with %f USDT\n", symbol, capital)
    if debug {

    } else {
        order, err := client.NewCreateOrderService().Symbol(symbol).
        Side(binance.SideTypeBuy).Type(binance.OrderTypeMarket).
        QuoteOrderQty(strconv.FormatFloat(capital, 'f', 2, 64)).Do(context.
        Background())
        if err != nil {
            log.Fatal(err)
        }
        log.Printf("Market buy order %s executed at price %s\n", order.
        OrderID, order.Price)
    }
    inPosition = true

}

func checkFunds(client *binance.Client, capital float64) (error, bool) {
    // Check if there are available funds to buy
    balance, err := client.NewGetAccountService().Do(context.Background())
    if err != nil {
        log.Fatal(err)
    }

    var availableBalance float64
    for _, b := range balance.Balances {
        if b.Asset == "USDT" {
            availableBalance, _ = strconv.ParseFloat(b.Free, 64)
            break
        }
    }
```

```go
        log.Printf("Current balance (%f) to buy with capital %f",
        availableBalance, capital)

        if availableBalance < capital {
            log.Printf("Not enough available balance (%f) to buy with capital
            %f", availableBalance, capital)
            return nil, true
        }
        return err, false
    }

func sell(symbol string, capital float64, client *binance.Client) {
    // Place a market sell order for the specified symbol and quantity
    log.Printf("Selling %s with %f USDT\n", symbol, capital)
    if debug {

    } else {
        order, err := client.NewCreateOrderService().Symbol(symbol).
        Side(binance.SideTypeSell).Type(binance.OrderTypeMarket).
        QuoteOrderQty(strconv.FormatFloat(capital, 'f', 2, 64)).Do(context.
        Background())
        if err != nil {
            log.Fatal(err)
        }

        log.Printf("Market sell order %s executed at price %s\n", order.
        OrderID, order.Price)
    }

    inPosition = false

}
```

Dinner Is Served

First things first—did the best performing strategy out of all the ones that were backtested and forward tested beat the market?

This seems to be one of the most important questions on traders' minds when it comes to trading. The reason is, if your money (trading in and out of the markets and leveraging the best-performing strategy at hand) is not beating a trade on the S&P500, it is a failure.

Depending on the financial instrument you are trading, that benchmark can be S&P500, the ten-year treasury, or BTCUSD. This requires a little bit of thinking in making sure you are comparing apples to apples.

Also worthy of note—if you're trading high frequency (say, anything under four-minute intervals), you could be subjected to the phenomenon of "up days" and "down days." For instance, the Federal Reserve Bank's FOMC meetings can move markets drastically depending on the forward guidance given by the chairman. You need to make sure a long enough set of historical data is used at all times and ensure such market movements do not overly bias the analysis one way or another.

Skin in the Game

When it comes to trading, the grizzled vets have many unwritten rules. They are not scientific law, but money and human emotions make humans act in a weird way. When they say, "put some skin in the game", it applies in many ways, but truth be told, there is a difference between monopoly money and real money.

You might tend to find that a strategy that has worked almost perfectly in backtesting, that went through the process to refine and finetune, and that finally proves its worth in real-time testing, still fails to work in real trades with money.

As no amount of testing will ever make you feel the pain of missing a trade, or worse yet, missing an exit, it is recommended that you put on a small amount of money (an amount that is painful enough when it is gone) into the hands of the algorithm for a while.

Fear vs. Greed

For some traders, PnL is not everything. Sure, winning is an important aspect of trading. But health is probably more meaningful to most. For some traders, their quality of life can degrade considerably when real money is being put to risk.

It is therefore not uncommon to find successful traders that opt for consistency rather than maximum returns. Since markets never go up in a straight line nor go down in a straight line, coupled with the fact everything is cyclical, there is a good chance that favorable conditions will be back at some point. Having a highly consistent and profitable strategy is also a very good approach.

Which Products to Trade

There are numerous ways in which trades can be expressed. For instance, let's say you decides to trade cryptocurrencies. There are thousands that exist in the market. It will also likely be the case where the particular strategy developed will work on most. How can you decide what coin to choose?

Just as you quantify and test your trading strategy, you need to do the same for the assets themselves. Take, for instance, the traditional finance assets. A risk curve can be drawn based on risk versus returns (see Figure 4-11). The further out on the risk curve, the higher return probabilities, but also the higher probability to be wiped out.

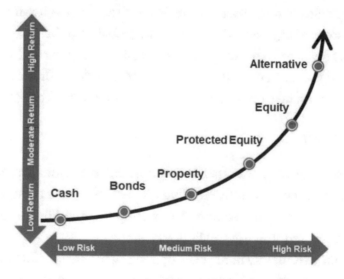

Figure 4-11. *Risk curve on traditional finance instruments*

The same curve can be constructed for cryptocurrencies; see Figure 4-12.

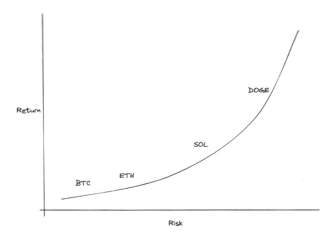

Figure 4-12. *Crypto-assets risk curve example*

It is therefore possible to adapt your strategy and build in implicit risk by choosing the coins out in the further part of the curve and maximize returns. If you can withstand the gut checks.

Aside from the coins to trade based on the level of risks, derivative markets are also available for some of the coins. Derivatives are probably for better suited for more advanced traders. However, trade futures markets can take on long and short positions to maximize winnings in both up and down turns of the cycles with added leverage. In options markets, you can take on bigger risks and take on leverage only risking a premium.

Machine Learning

As mentioned earlier, the sheer number of assets in the world today makes it difficult or costly to cover all assets concurrently. Trading a select few instruments is tiring enough, as you have seen in the previous sections. Attempting to extend the practice beyond the select few instruments requires automation with smarts.

This chapter has delt mainly in the view of making life easier and better for those who love to code (in GoLang preferably). The "smarts" is where it normally takes some fuzzy logic and experience around the markets. That said, the world has seen massive progress with machine learning. It is safe to say that it has become a thing in the world of trading. While varied results and comments are coming from those who love to code in the financial industry, it is prevalent and growing. It is safe to assume there are probably billions invested today to bring ML algorithms to the trading world and teach it as much information as possible. If hardware resources allow, just imagine having three million Warren Buffets working for you 24 hours, 7 days a week.

Although this chapter does not include the knowledge and experience from any members of Berkshire Hathaway, let's see what can be observed in the world where machine learning meets GoLang. A brief search on the frameworks yields results that are not very promising. A very large community seems to exist around most of the well-known Python frameworks. For GoLang, however, the top search results from Google do not demonstrate the fact that there is a vibrant community behind them.

Further digging seems to point toward the direction of Python for any machine learning frameworks. Machine learning algorithms do not gain much in terms of faster compilation or gains of performance on CPU. As 99.9 percent of the runtime is spent on GPUs, most ML developers do not mind doing their work in Python, it seems. In short, the GoLang communities for ML frameworks remain very small and are not maintained often.

Running a quick search on Google or YouTube will return a plethora of links and videos, with trading PnL that will get you dreaming of Lambo's. Before putting real money at work, think about placing the million-dollar strategies in the framework you've learned in this chapter. With creative use of ChatGPT, you should be able to test the strategies easily. There must be a good reason that the ML superpowers have not yet turned into mega-hedge funds.

It might be a matter of time however...

Dessert!

The Exponential Age Is Here

Raoul Pal, the CEO from Real Vision and a staunch advocate of digital currencies, rightly highlights the *exponential age*. In essence, it refers to a period of immense technological evolution that we're currently living in, where innovation isn't linear but exponential, leading to rapid changes in various sectors, particularly in finance and technology.

Cryptocurrencies are evolving, and they no longer simply store value. They are programmable platforms that allow developers to build decentralized applications (dApps) on top of their networks.

As per Metcalfe's Law, the value of a network is proportional to the square of the number of connected users of the system. Cryptocurrencies have recently seen significant adoption, not just among individual users, but also among institutional investors and businesses. This widespread adoption is a testament to their potential and is likely to drive their growth in the coming years.

Cryptocurrencies are becoming an integral part of the global financial system, a trend often referred to as *financialization*. They are enabling new financial structures and systems that are more accessible, transparent, and efficient. Just like how the Eurodollar system reshaped global finance in the last century, these cryptos, and the larger blockchain technology, have the potential to redefine finance in this century.

Trading leveraging successful processes and strategies will be profitable if done properly. The true benefit of the application of these practices on the crypto-verse is the fact that the ecosystem is growing exponentially. Trading algorithmically in a growing ecosystem should by definition be a great opportunity. As with all financial systems, they are not without their risks and challenges, which need to be thoroughly understood and navigated. We can only hope the ecosystem grows into a regulated and safe environment for all.

The Proverbial "Cherry on Top"

In terms of GoLang, no more spaces and tabs. Enough said? It is nice to be reacquainted with curly brackets! Other than the aesthetics of the code, it is nice to have a compiler and fewer runtime errors that take hours to debug. But above all, it is fast. Mind blowing compared to Python.

Truth be told, the community is smaller than Python and there remains a few problems in the quality of libraries. Especially for those financially oriented, Python, Java, or C++ is still the weapon of choice it seems. Possibly stemming from the fact that the other languages are still dominant in the trading field, documentation is sparse and features are missing from key exchanges.

That said, being fast in compilation and execution really is a killer combination. Simply put, a lot more can be done than before. As time-to-market is potentially the most critical aspect in developing strategies, this fast tracking of the processes will at some point yield dollars in return. While rushing through the steps is not the best practice when it comes to building trading strategies, it certainly helps turn epiphanies into working models without losing context.

The real and only difficulty today in building strategies using Go, perhaps the only missing feature as compared with Python, is the ability to build interactive charts on the go like Python does using Jupyter notebooks and the various charting libraries. Go plugins certainly exist to leverage Jupyter functionalities, but the charting tools are unfortunately not available.

Do note that there are some easy-to-use tools with plugins for GoLang to run on a Jupyter notebook. Figure 4-13 shows one example, called gophernotes.

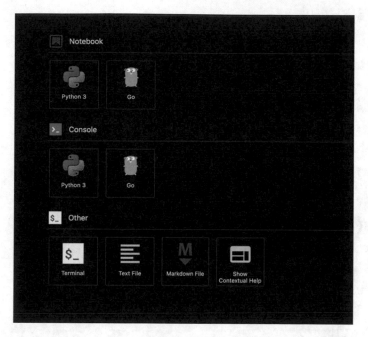

Figure 4-13. *Installing the kernel as described at https://github.com/ gopherdata/gophernotes*

Listing 4-9 shows the sample charting code and Figure 4-14 shows a resultant chart.

Listing 4-9. Sample Charting Code

```go
package main

import (
    "encoding/csv"
    "image/color"
    "io"
    "log"
    "os"
    "strconv"
    "time"
```

```go
    "gonum.org/v1/plot"
    "gonum.org/v1/plot/plotter"
    "gonum.org/v1/plot/vg"
)

type OHLC struct {
    Time    time.Time
    Open    float64
    High    float64
    Low     float64
    Close   float64
}

func readData(filename string) ([]OHLC, error) {
    file, err := os.Open(filename)
    if err != nil {
            return nil, err
    }
    defer file.Close()

    reader := csv.NewReader(file)
    // assuming first row is header
    reader.Read()

    data := []OHLC{}
    for {
            row, err := reader.Read()
            if err == io.EOF {
                    break
            }
            if err != nil {
                    return nil, err
            }

            t, _ := time.Parse("2006-01-02 15:04:05", row[1])
            o, _ := strconv.ParseFloat(row[3], 64)
            h, _ := strconv.ParseFloat(row[4], 64)
```

```go
        l, _ := strconv.ParseFloat(row[5], 64)
        c, _ := strconv.ParseFloat(row[6], 64)

        data = append(data, OHLC{t, o, h, l, c})
    }

    // only the latest 100 data points
    return data[len(data)-100:], nil
}

func plotData(data []OHLC) {
    p := plot.New()

    p.Title.Text = "ETHUSD Hourly OHLC"
    p.X.Label.Text = "Index"
    p.Y.Label.Text = "Price"

    // Define the points for each line
    openPoints := make(plotter.XYs, len(data))
    highPoints := make(plotter.XYs, len(data))
    lowPoints := make(plotter.XYs, len(data))
    closePoints := make(plotter.XYs, len(data))

    for i := range data {
        openPoints[i].X = float64(i)
        openPoints[i].Y = data[i].Open
        highPoints[i].X = float64(i)
        highPoints[i].Y = data[i].High
        lowPoints[i].X = float64(i)
        lowPoints[i].Y = data[i].Low
        closePoints[i].X = float64(i)
        closePoints[i].Y = data[i].Close
    }

    // Add the lines to the plot
    lines := []struct {
        xy      plotter.XYs
        name    string
        color color.Color
```

```go
    }{
            {openPoints, "Open", color.RGBA{R: 0, G: 0, B: 255, A: 255}},
            // blue
            {highPoints, "High", color.RGBA{R: 0, G: 255, B: 0, A: 255}},
            // green
            {lowPoints, "Low", color.RGBA{R: 255, G: 0, B: 0, A: 255}},
            // red
            {closePoints, "Close", color.RGBA{R: 255, G: 165, B: 0,
            A: 255}}, // orange
    }

    for _, line := range lines {
            l, err := plotter.NewLine(line.xy)
            if err != nil {
                    log.Fatal(err)
            }
            l.LineStyle.Width = vg.Points(1)
            l.LineStyle.Color = line.color
            p.Add(l)
            p.Legend.Add(line.name, l)
    }

    if err := p.Save(10*vg.Inch, 4*vg.Inch, "ohlc.png"); err != nil {
            log.Fatal(err)
    }

    displayPlot(p)
}

func main() {
    data, err := readData("/tmp/ETHUSD_hourlies.csv")
    if err != nil {
            log.Fatal(err)
    }
    plotData(data)
}

main()
```

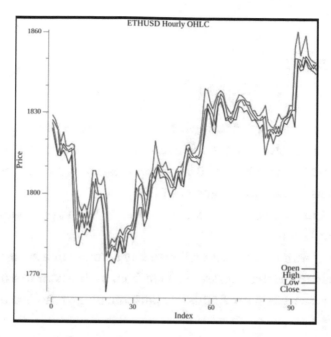

Figure 4-14. *Easily chart using plotutil*

Realistically, the only complaint would be the lack of a large community contributing tools and millions of charting examples. In the world of finance, it is probably safe to say some form of model or strategy you want to employ has already been implemented. If somebody has already paved the way, it is often a big shortcut and there are literally thousands of hours' worth of explanations on YouTube and other media platforms.

This should not scare anybody, however. The missing libraries can probably be overcome by writing libraries to run against APIs (thank you ChatGPT), or perhaps completely transcribe them if they are easy enough. It might very well be a matter of time before the world gives GoLang its due attention and provides for a healthy community of contributors.

If I may, I would like to finish with a simple little note—the language is simply a pleasure to work with.

Appendix

Finance Jargon

Glossary

Amortization: The process of spreading the cost of an intangible asset over its useful life.

Ask: The price at which a seller is willing to sell an asset or a security.

Asset allocation: The strategy of dividing an investment portfolio among different asset classes, such as stocks, bonds, and cash.

Bear market: A market condition characterized by falling prices and pessimism among investors and traders.

Bid: The price at which a buyer is willing to buy an asset or a security.

Bonds: Debt securities that represent a loan from an investor to a borrower, such as a government or a corporation. Bonds pay periodic interest and return the principal amount at maturity.

Breakout: A trading strategy that involves buying or selling an asset or a security when its price moves beyond a certain level of resistance or support, indicating a change in trend or momentum.

Broker: An intermediary who facilitates the buying and selling of assets or securities between buyers and sellers, usually for a commission or a fee.

Bull market: A market condition characterized by rising prices and optimism among investors and traders.

Capital expenditure: Money spent by a business to acquire or improve long-term assets, such as equipment or buildings.

Compound interest: Interest that is calculated on both the initial principal and the accumulated interest of a loan or investment.

Correction: A temporary decline in the price or value of an asset or a security after a period of rise or overvaluation.

Credit default swap: A financial contract that transfers the risk of default from a debt issuer to another party, who agrees to pay the debt in case of default in exchange for a periodic fee.

Day trading: The practice of buying and selling assets or securities the same trading day, closing all positions before the market closes.

Dividend: A portion of a company's profits that is distributed to its shareholders.

Earnings per share: A measure of a company's profitability, calculated by dividing its net income by the number of outstanding shares.

FICO score: A numerical rating of a person's creditworthiness, based on their credit history and current financial situation. FICO scores range from 300 to 850, with higher scores indicating lower risk.

Fill: The execution of an order by a broker or an exchange.

Fundamental analysis: The study of the intrinsic value and performance of assets or securities, based on various factors such as financial statements, earnings, dividends, economic conditions, industry trends, and so on.

Gross domestic product: The total value of all goods and services produced within a country in a given period of time.

Hedge fund: A type of investment fund that uses sophisticated strategies and techniques to generate high returns, often with high risk and low transparency.

Inflation: A general increase in the prices of goods and services over time, resulting in a decrease in the purchasing power of money.

Junk bond: A bond that has a low credit rating and a high risk of default, but also offers a high yield to attract investors.

Key performance indicator: A measurable value that shows how effectively a company or an individual is achieving its goals or objectives.

Leverage: The use of borrowed money to increase the potential return of an investment or a business operation.

Limit order: An order to buy or sell an asset or a security at a specified price or better.

Liquidity: The ease with which an asset or a security can be bought or sold without affecting its price significantly, depending on the availability of buyers and sellers in the market.

Long position: The state of owning or buying an asset or a security, expecting its price to rise in the future.

Margin: The amount of money that a trader or an investor must deposit with a broker or an exchange to open or maintain a leveraged position.

Market capitalization: The total value of all shares of a company or an index, calculated by multiplying the share price by the number of shares outstanding.

Market order: An order to buy or sell an asset or a security at the best available price in the market at the time of execution.

Net present value: The difference between the present value of an investment's cash inflows and outflows, used to evaluate its profitability and feasibility.

Opportunity cost: The value of the next best alternative that is forgone as a result of making a decision.

Portfolio: A collection of investments held by an individual or an organization.

Quantitative easing: A monetary policy tool that involves the central bank buying large amounts of government bonds or other securities to increase the money supply and lower interest rates.

Rally: A sustained increase in the price or value of an asset or a security after a period of decline or consolidation.

Resistance: A price level at which an asset or a security faces difficulty in rising above due to selling pressure.

Return on equity: A measure of a company's profitability, calculated by dividing its net income by its shareholders' equity.

Scalping: A trading strategy that involves taking small profits from frequent trades over a short period of time, exploiting minor price movements and high leverage.

Securities and Exchange Commission: The U.S. federal agency that regulates the securities markets and protects investors from fraud and abuse.

Short selling: The practice of selling an asset or a security that a trader does not own, hoping to buy it back later at a lower price and profit from the price difference.

Slippage: The difference between the expected price of an order and the actual price at which it is executed, which can be caused by market volatility, low liquidity, or delays in execution.

Spread: The difference between the bid and ask prices of an asset or a security, which reflects the liquidity and competitiveness of the market.

Stop order: An order to buy or sell an asset or a security when its price reaches a certain level, which can be used to protect profits or limit losses.

Support: A price level at which an asset or a security faces difficulty in falling below due to buying pressure.

Swing trading: The practice of buying and selling assets or securities over a period of several days or weeks, taking advantage of short-term price fluctuations.

Technical analysis: The study of past price movements and patterns to predict future price movements and trends of assets or securities, using various tools and indicators such as charts, moving averages, trend lines, and so on.

Time value of money: The concept that money available today is worth more than the same amount in the future, due to its potential earning capacity.

Trend: The general direction of the price movement of an asset or a security over time, which can be upward (bullish), downward (bearish), or sideways (range-bound).

Underwriting: The process of evaluating the risk and profitability of a loan, insurance policy, or security issue, and setting its terms and conditions accordingly.

Volatility: The degree of variation in the price or value of an asset or a market over time, often measured by standard deviation or beta.

One-liner

Trading one-liners are witty or humorous remarks related to trading or the markets. They can be used to lighten the mood, poke fun at oneself or others, or make a point. Here are some examples of trading one-liners:

- The market is a device for transferring money from the impatient to the patient. —Warren Buffett

- I'm not a great investor. I'm just good at not losing money. —George Soros

- The four most dangerous words in investing are "this time it's different." —Sir John Templeton

- How do you make a small fortune in the stock market? Start with a large one. —Anonymous

- Buy low, sell high. Easier said than done. —Anonymous

- The trend is your friend until the end when it bends. —Ed Seykota

- In trading, the impossible happens about twice a year. —Henri M Simoes

- There are two types of traders: those who admit they don't know what they're doing and those who lie about it. —Anonymous

- The only thing standing between you and your goal is the bullshit story you keep telling yourself as to why you can't achieve it. —Jordan Belfort

- The stock market is a device for transferring money from the ignorant to the informed. —Andre Kostolany

Extra Indicators of Interest

Tom Demark's Indicators

Many successful and famous global investors speak of Tom Demark's work, and the use of his indicators. When they speak, we listen. See Figure 4-15.

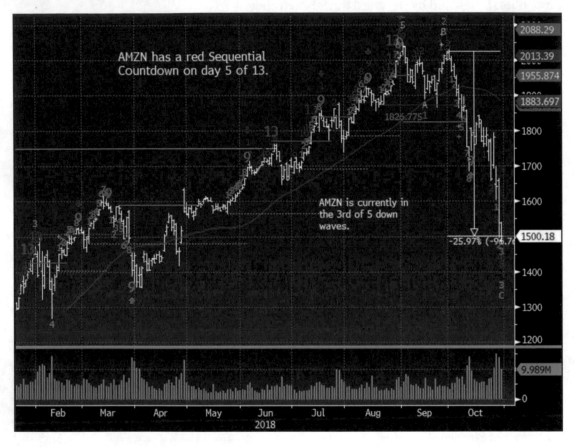

Figure 4-15. *Demark's sequential countdown*

Some call it "a hack for everything." A study in trend fatigue. A lot of famous fund managers have used this indicator in conjunction with daily and weekly timeframes.

Extra Statistics

Several statistical evaluation metrics are commonly used to assess the effectiveness of these strategies. The following are not used in this chapter, but remain relevant and of interest to many leading economists around the world:

- **Sortino ratio**: Similar to the Sharpe ratio, the Sortino ratio also measures risk-adjusted performance. However, it only considers downside risk by using the downside deviation instead of the standard deviation. This ratio is particularly useful for investors who are more concerned about downside risk.

  Sortino Ratio = (Portfolio Return - Risk-free Rate) / Downside Deviation

- **Information ratio**: The Information ratio measures the risk-adjusted performance of an active investment strategy relative to a benchmark. It is calculated as the excess return of the portfolio over the benchmark return, divided by the tracking error (the standard deviation of the excess returns). A higher Information ratio indicates better risk-adjusted performance compared to the benchmark.

  Information Ratio = (Portfolio Excess Return) / Tracking Error

- **Treynor ratio**: Developed by Jack L. Treynor, the Treynor ratio measures the risk-adjusted performance of a portfolio using beta as a risk measure. Beta represents the sensitivity of the portfolio's returns to market movements. The Treynor ratio is calculated as the excess return of the portfolio (portfolio return minus risk-free rate) divided by its beta. A higher Treynor ratio indicates better risk-adjusted performance.

  Treynor Ratio = (Portfolio Return - Risk-free Rate) / Portfolio Beta

- **Maximum drawdown**: Maximum drawdown is a measure of risk that represents the largest peak-to-trough decline in the value of a portfolio over a specified period. It helps investors understand the worst-case loss they could have experienced if they had invested in a particular strategy. Lower maximum drawdowns are generally preferred, as they indicate lower risk.

  Maximum Drawdown = (Peak Portfolio Value - Trough Portfolio Value) / Peak Portfolio Value

Side Notes on Geth

GoLang, also known as Go, is particularly well-suited for blockchain projects due to its performance characteristics and ease of use. One of the main reasons for its popularity in the blockchain space is that a significant portion of Ethereum, the world's second-largest cryptocurrency by market capitalization, is written in GoLang. This section explores the connection between Ethereum and GoLang and discusses why this makes Go a cool choice for blockchain projects.

Ethereum's GoLang Implementation: Geth

Ethereum, a decentralized platform that runs smart contracts, has multiple implementations in different programming languages. One of the most popular and widely-used implementations is Geth, which is written in GoLang. Geth, short for Go Ethereum, is the official command-line interface for running an Ethereum node and interacting with the Ethereum blockchain.

By choosing GoLang for Geth, the Ethereum development team leveraged the language's efficiency, speed, and simplicity to create a robust and high-performance implementation of the Ethereum protocol. As a result, GoLang has become an essential part of the Ethereum ecosystem, with many developers using the language to build decentralized applications (dApps), smart contracts, and other blockchain-related projects on the Ethereum platform.

GoLang's Advantages for Blockchain Development

The success of Geth and its impact on the Ethereum ecosystem have helped to establish GoLang as a popular choice for blockchain development. Some of the key advantages of GoLang for blockchain projects include:

- **Performance**: GoLang is designed for high performance and efficient resource usage, making it ideal for handling the computational and network demands of blockchain projects.

- **Concurrency**: GoLang's built-in support for concurrency and parallelism enables developers to easily manage multiple tasks simultaneously, which is particularly important for blockchain applications that need to process a high volume of transactions or perform complex calculations.

- **Simplicity and maintainability**: GoLang's clean syntax and strong typing make it easier to write, read, and maintain code, which is crucial for the long-term success of blockchain projects that require regular updates and enhancements.

- **Growing ecosystem**: Thanks to its popularity in the Ethereum community, GoLang has a growing ecosystem of libraries, tools, and resources specifically tailored for blockchain development.

The widespread use of GoLang in Ethereum, particularly in the Geth implementation, has helped to establish the language as a cool choice for blockchain projects. Its performance, concurrency support, simplicity, and maintainability make it an ideal choice for developers working on decentralized applications, smart contracts, and other blockchain-related projects. As we embark on creating a GoLang-based trading tool for cryptocurrency markets, the connection between GoLang and Ethereum's success serves as a testament to the language's potential in the world of blockchain development.

References

1. Peccatiello, A. (2021). "The Macro Compass: A Framework for Global Macro Investing." The Macro Compass. Retrieved from `https://themacrocompass.substack.com/p/the-macro-compass-a-framework-for`

2. Weinstein, S. (1988). *Stan Weinstein's Secrets for Profiting in Bull and Bear Markets.* New York: McGraw-Hill.

3. Ammous, S. (2018). *The Bitcoin Standard: The Decentralized Alternative to Central Banking.* Hoboken, NJ: John Wiley & Sons.

4. Ferguson, N. (2008). *The Ascent of Money: A Financial History of the World.* New York: Penguin Press.

5. Murphy, J. J. (1999). *Technical Analysis of the Financial Markets: A Comprehensive Guide to Trading Methods and Applications.* New York: New York Institute of Finance.

6. Strauss, W., & Howe, N. (1997). *The Fourth Turning: What the Cycles of History Tell Us About America's Next Rendezvous with Destiny*. Crown.

7. DeMARK Analytics. (n.d.). *Sequential*. Retrieved May 10, 2023, from `https://demark.com/sequential-indicator/`

8. Pal, R. (Host). (2022-2023). The exponential age [Video series]. Real Vision. `https://realvision.com/shows/the-exponential-age`

9. Real Vision. (2022-2023). Daily briefing [Video series]. `https://realvision.com/shows/daily-briefing`

10. Real Vision. (2022-2023). Daily briefing [Video series]. `https://realvision.com/shows/daily-briefing`

11. Ethereum Foundation. (n.d.). Go-ethereum. Retrieved May 10, 2023, from `https://geth.ethereum.org/`

## CHAPTER 5

Writing a Kubernetes Operator to Run EVM-Compatible Blockchains

Simplicity is the ultimate sophistication.

—Leonardo da Vinci

With the rising popularity of blockchain technology, there is an increasing need for efficient ways to deploy and manage blockchain networks.

N. Modrzyk, *Go Crazy*, https://doi.org/10.1007/978-1-4842-9666-0_5

Kubernetes is a popular container-orchestration platform that enables efficient deployment and management of containerized applications.

This chapter explains to build a Kubernetes operator to run EVM-compatible blockchain networks.

If you are reading this book, I doubt there is a need to explain what the word *blockchain* means, but you might wonder what an *EVM-compatible* blockchain is.

To make it simple, it is a blockchain that can execute smart contracts and decentralized applications written in the same programming language as the Ethereum blockchain (Solidity). These blockchains expose the same set of `json-rpc` APIs as Ethereum does (see `https://ethereum.org/en/developers/docs/apis/json-rpc/`) and therefore it is possible to interact with EVM-compatible blockchains in the same way you interact with Ethereum.

Some examples of EVM-compatible blockchains include Binance Smart Chain, Polygon, Avalanche, and Celo.

Given that these blockchains applications present commonalities, it's relevant to have a strategy to configure and operate them in a generic way. This is where Kubernetes operators come into play!

You've probably heard of Kubernetes before, but maybe you haven't used it. Or maybe you're using it already, but have never had the opportunity to extend it and customize it for specific needs. This is exactly what you'll learn how to do in this chapter.

Let's get started.

Setting Up Kubernetes on Your Machine

For a long time, I did not know how or where to start with Kubernetes.

I constantly heard about it and honestly believed it was a fantastic tool, but I could not find the right way to start with it. Every blog post I read mentioned nodes, pods, stateful sets, services, ingresses, and config maps, but I did not get the big picture.

Surprisingly, the thing that finally removed my psychological barrier was watching "Kubernetes: The Documentary" (you can find it on YouTube). The next thing I knew, I had installed Minikube and Lens on my machine.

Let's install the necessary components to start building with Kubernetes:

- Docker (`www.docker.com`) to build images.

- Access to an image registry such as `https://hub.docker.com` to deploy the built images. You can create an account for free.

- Minikube (`https://minikube.sigs.k8s.io/docs/start/`) allows you to run Kubernetes on your local machine.

- Kubectl (`https://kubernetes.io/docs/tasks/tools/`) is a command-line tool that interacts with a Kubernetes cluster (or Minikube in this case).

As usual, be sure to install the relevant versions for your operating system. The instructions in this chapter are executed from a MacBook with an Apple ARM chip.

Additionally, a few other tools can greatly improve your day-to-day experience with Kubernetes, and I highly recommend you install them:

- Lens (`https://k8slens.dev`) is the "Kubernetes IDE." It is probably the best tool you can install, especially if you start with Kubernetes.

- Kubectx and Kubens (`https://github.com/ahmetb/kubectx`) allow to switch between clusters and between namespaces, respectively.

- The `https://github.com/ahmetb/kubectl-aliases` site contains a collection of shell aliases to make it easier to send `kubectl` commands (for example, you can type `kpf` instead of `kubectl port-forward`).

First verify that the components were correctly installed. Make sure that Docker is running, then start Minikube by typing `minikube start` in your terminal.

You should see something like Figure 5-1.

```
❯ minikube start
😄  minikube v1.25.2 on Darwin 13.3.1 (arm64)
✨  Using the docker driver based on existing profile
👍  Starting control plane node minikube in cluster minikube
🚜  Pulling base image ...
🔄  Restarting existing docker container for "minikube" ...
🐳  Preparing Kubernetes v1.23.3 on Docker 20.10.12 ...
    ▪ kubelet.housekeeping-interval=5m
🔎  Verifying Kubernetes components...
    ▪ Using image gcr.io/k8s-minikube/storage-provisioner:v5
🌟  Enabled addons: storage-provisioner, default-storageclass
🏄  Done! kubectl is now configured to use "minikube" cluster and "default" namespace by default
```

Figure 5-1. *Minikube has started*

Now open the Lens IDE.

From there, you should be able to connect to your Minikube local cluster and browse the different tabs. Most of them will be empty at this stage (see Figure 5-2).

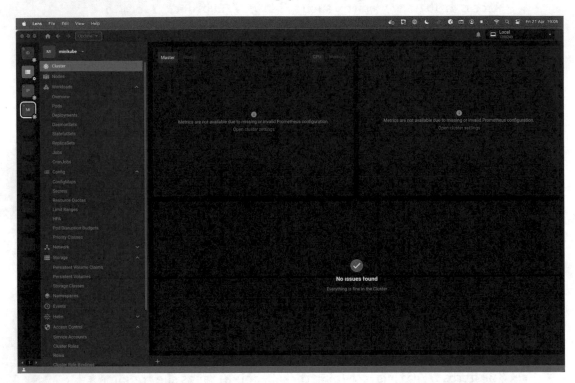

Figure 5-2.   *Lens, the Kubernetes IDE*

Resources Overview

From a certain perspective, Kubernetes can be viewed as an API that lets you manipulate a collection of resources. These resources are grouped into logical categories:

- **Nodes**: These are the machines on which the applications run.

- **Workloads**: At the foundational level, applications are running as containers in so-called *pods,* which are the smallest operational unit of a Kubernetes cluster. Those pods execute workloads and their lifecycle is usually controlled by higher-level resources such as *deployments*, *daemonSets*, *StatefulSets* and the like.

- **Config**: *ConfigMaps* (think of them as a way to provide configurations to your apps) and *Secrets* (think, credentials), as well as *HPAs* (to automate scaling up and down of pods) and *Pod Disruption Budgets* (to better control application upgrades) are the resources you will find in this category.

- **Network**: This category include resources that control how applications are reached out, either from within the cluster (*services*) or from outside the cluster (*ingresses*).

- **Storage**: This category provides resources that abstract and decouple the applications running in pods from the storage requirements they may have, whether they use the disk storage of the nodes they are scheduled to or network storage. *Storage classes, persistent volumes,* and *persistent volume claims* offer ways to configure these aspects.

- **Namespaces**: These are a way to group Kubernetes resources under logical entities.

- **Events**: Give access to the cluster internal events.

- **Access controls**: A group of resources that define and manage user permissions and authentication mechanisms.

- **Custom resource definitions**: Provide a mechanism to extend Kubernetes functionality; this is the category of resources that you will leverage to create the blockchain operator.

Kubernetes is a complex ecosystem, and it is impossible to fully explore all these resources and their possible combinations within the confines of a single chapter. However, in the process of building the operator, you will manipulate many of the important resources. Special attention is given to *StatefulSets* and *Custom Resources Definitions* (or CRDs for short).

A graphical depiction of these concepts is shown in Figure 5-3.

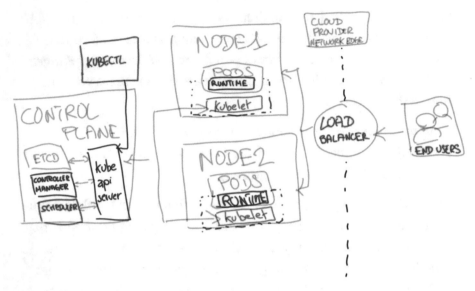

Figure 5-3. *Overview of a Kubernetes deployment*

Let's Run a Pod

In this section, you learn how to deploy a simple application in your local cluster to get your hands dirty and start manipulating native resources, kubectl, and Docker images.

Copy/paste the code in Listing 5-1 into a file and save it as nginx-pod.yaml.

Listing 5-1. A Simple nginx Pod Definition

```
apiVersion: v1
kind: Pod
metadata:
  name: nginx-pod
  labels:
    app: nginx
spec:
  containers:
    - name: nginx-container
      image: nginx
      ports:
        - containerPort: 80
```

In this YAML definition, two fields are slightly more meaningful that the others:

- The kind field indicates the specific Kubernetes resource you want to provision. Here, it is a simple Pod.

- The image field within spec.containers informs Kubernetes that you want to run the nginx image located at https://hub.docker. com/_/nginx.

The following code uses kubectl to create the pod in the local Minikube cluster:

```
kubectl apply -f nginx-pod.yaml
```

Look at the result in Lens, which is shown in Figure 5-4.

Figure 5-4. *Nginx pod running in the cluster*

Congratulations! You created your first Kubernetes native resource running in Minikube.

Demystifying Kubernetes Operators

This chapter uses a framework called Operator-SDK (https://sdk.operatorframework.io/) to build the blockchain operator.

When you use a framework, several aspects are abstracted and simplified, as illustrated in Figure 5-5.

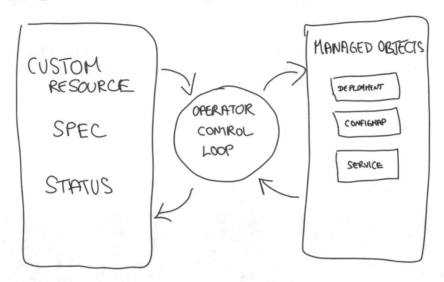

Figure 5-5. *What are Kubernetes operators?*

This provides some benefits. However, as is often the case when using a framework, it is not necessarily obvious what the basic blocks are that *actually* constitute the real thing behind the framework, namely the Kubernetes operator.

This section breaks things down so you can see the basic blocks. That way, when you're using the facilities of Operator-SDK, you understand what you are doing.

At a foundational level, an operator has two parts:

- A Custom Resource Definition (CRD)

- A controller

Custom Resource Definition

To understand this part, you'll start from what you did previously.

When you submitted `nginx-pod.yaml` to `kubectl`, you actually submitted a payload that conforms to the Kubernetes Pod specification, a portion of which is represented in Listing 5-2.

Listing 5-2. The Pod Spec (Excerpt)

```
f:spec:
    f:containers:
        f:args: {}
        f:image: {}
        f:imagePullPolicy: {}
        f:name: {}
        f:ports:
            .: {}
            k:{"containerPort":8443,"protocol":"TCP"}:
                .: {}
            f:containerPort: {}
            f:name: {}
            f:protocol: {}
```

Basically, to make sense to Kubernetes, the nginx-pod.yaml payload *had to* conform to that Pod specification. For instance, under spec.containers, you would not have been allowed to add an arbitrarily new field nor omit a mandatory field (such as Name).

In other words, there are a set of fields, optional or mandatory, that compose the Pod specification and its nested structures. A user must submit a payload that conforms to that specification for the target resource to be created.

Now, as much as Kubernetes knows how to deal with kind:Pod or kind:Deployment, it knows nothing about kind:Blockchain, unless you tell it.

It happens that the way to tell it is to submit a CRD resource to the cluster. That is, a resource of kind CustomResourceDefinition with a spec field that's a *schema* that defines the fields that compose the target resource (Blockchain) that the controller should manage.

For instance, if you want the blockchain resources to contain fields like image, replicas, or p2pPort, you first have to submit a CustomResourceDefinition resource to the cluster, which defines those fields as part of the schema of a blockchain kind.

After that, Kubernetes will understand what a blockchain kind is and will accept payloads that conform to the blockchain spec.

Controller

The ability to submit a blockchain resource payload to the cluster is the essential first part of making an operator. But that's not very helpful until Kubernetes knows *what to do* with it. That's why you have controllers.

A *controller* is essentially a program running within a pod that listens to events broadcasted by Kubernetes within the cluster and takes the necessary actions.

The events include the creation, update, or deletion of resources. The resulting actions include creating native resources (like deployment, service, or configmap) to reflect the state described by the resource definition. For that, the controller will use the Kubernetes API, which can be programmed using the Go SDK.

The process of reflecting in the cluster the state described in the specification is called the *reconciliation loop*. Technically, a controller's `Reconcile` function is continuously called and it is the controller 's job to bring the current state to the desired state described in the resource definition.

If the current state does not match the desired state, the controller takes the necessary actions. For instance, if the desired state is to have three pod replicas and only two are running, the controller will ask Kubernetes to create another pod.

Bootstrapping the Project with Operator-SDK

Go to `https://sdk.operatorframework.io/build/` and follow the instructions to install Operator-SDK.

Next, create a directory called `blockchain-operator` in your preferred location and initialize the project with:

```
operator-sdk init --domain gocrazy.com --repo github.com/gocrazy/
blockchain-operator --plugins=go/v5-alpha
```

`--domain` is used as the prefix of the API group your custom resources will be created in and `--repo` is necessary since scaffolded files require a valid module path. `--plugins=go/v5-alpha` is required only if your local environment is Apple Silicon.

The directory structure shown in Figure 5-6 will be generated.

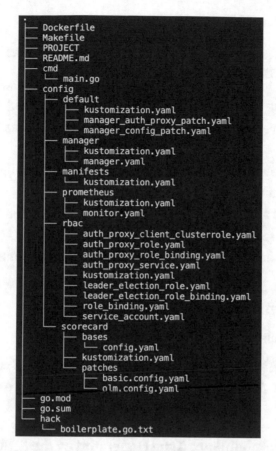

```
├── Dockerfile
├── Makefile
├── PROJECT
├── README.md
├── cmd
│   └── main.go
├── config
│   ├── default
│   │   ├── kustomization.yaml
│   │   ├── manager_auth_proxy_patch.yaml
│   │   └── manager_config_patch.yaml
│   ├── manager
│   │   ├── kustomization.yaml
│   │   └── manager.yaml
│   ├── manifests
│   │   └── kustomization.yaml
│   ├── prometheus
│   │   ├── kustomization.yaml
│   │   └── monitor.yaml
│   ├── rbac
│   │   ├── auth_proxy_client_clusterrole.yaml
│   │   ├── auth_proxy_role.yaml
│   │   ├── auth_proxy_role_binding.yaml
│   │   ├── auth_proxy_service.yaml
│   │   ├── kustomization.yaml
│   │   ├── leader_election_role.yaml
│   │   ├── leader_election_role_binding.yaml
│   │   ├── role_binding.yaml
│   │   └── service_account.yaml
│   └── scorecard
│       ├── bases
│       │   └── config.yaml
│       ├── kustomization.yaml
│       └── patches
│           ├── basic.config.yaml
│           └── olm.config.yaml
├── go.mod
├── go.sum
├── hack
│   └── boilerplate.go.txt
```

Figure 5-6. *Directory structure generated by Operator-SDK*

At this point, you only have generic boilerplate code, which consists essentially of a manager (defined in cmd/main.go), config YAML files, and the project's utilities (makefile, dockerfile, go.mod).

I suggest you take a quick look at the cmd/main.go file to see how the manager is created. Again, there is nothing specific to your needs in this main.go file at this stage. This is just a matter of getting familiar with the code.

Creating an API

Now is the time to start defining the new kind of resources you want to manage with your operator: the Blockchain kind.

The following command is exactly about this:

```
operator-sdk create api --group learn --version v1alpha1 --kind Blockchain
--resource --controller
```

This command instructs Operator-SDK to create resource and controller boilerplate files for a new custom resource of kind Blockchain under the learn group of the gocrazy.com domain.

This will generate api/ and internal/ folders, as well as config files specifically for the Blockchain custom resource under config/.

The command will also update the cmd/main.go file to register the controller for the Blockchain custom resource.

At this stage, you need to focus on two files in order to implement the logic of the controller:

- api/v1alpha1/blockchain_types.go

- internal/controller/blockchain_controller.go

The first file is used to implement the spec of the Blockchain custom resource. This is where you define the fields and types that compose a resource of kind Blockchain, as shown in Listing 5-3.

Listing 5-3. The BlockchainSpec Type Generated by the SDK Operator

```
// BlockchainSpec defines the desired state of Blockchain
type BlockchainSpec struct {
  // INSERT ADDITIONAL SPEC FIELDS - desired state of cluster
  // Important: Run "make" to regenerate code after modifying this file

  // Foo is an example field of Blockchain. Edit blockchain_types.go to
    remove/update
  Foo string 'json:"foo,omitempty"'
}
```

The second file is where you implement the controller's *reconciliation* logic mentioned earlier. This implementation will take place in the Reconcile function, as shown in Listing 5-4.

Listing 5-4. Blockchain Controller's Reconciliation Function

```
func (r *BlockchainReconciler) Reconcile(ctx context.Context, req ctrl.
Request) (ctrl.Result, error) {
    _ = log.FromContext(ctx)

    // TODO(user): your logic here

    return ctrl.Result{}, nil
}
```

Generating the Manifests

From the boilerplate code stored in api/v1alpha1/blockchain_types.go, Operator-SDK can already generate a CustomResourceDefinition with a schema following the fields of the BlockchainSpec struct.

You do this by running make manifests, which will generate a CustomResourceDefinition called learn.gocrazy.com_blockchains.yaml for the Blockchain kind. The manifest will be generated in config/crd/bases.

Whenever you modify blockchain_types.go, you need to also run make manifests to regenerate the CRD for the Blockchain custom resource.

Take a look at the generated file and notice how the properties of the BlockchainSpec struct are described under openAPIV3Schema.properties.spec.

learn.gocrazy.com_blockchains.yaml is the definition that will instruct Kubernetes about your custom Blockchain kind.

Configuring the Makefile

The development workflow involves running these make commands:

- make manifests will regenerate the files under config/.

- make generate will regenerate the api/v1alpha1/zz_generated.
  deepcopy.go file.

- make docker-build will build the Docker image for your controller
  based on the Dockerfile provided at the root of the project.

- `make docker-push` will push the image to a registry of your choice (you see how to set this up soon).

- `make install` will install your CRD into the cluster, along with the required RBAC resources.

- Finally, `make deploy` will deploy your updated controller to the cluster.

There are also commands to tear down the resources, like `uninstall` and `undeploy`.

Each command can be run independently. However, during development, it is very likely that you will need to run most of them in sequence.

Personally, I find it convenient to add a new command called `update` to the makefile, which will execute the other commands in the desired order.

If you agree, just add a new `update` entry within the `undeploy` entry (see Listing 5-5).

Listing 5-5. Using Update to Run Commands

```
.PHONY: update
update: manifests generate docker-build docker-push install deploy
  kubectl rollout restart deployment blockchain-operator-controller-manager -n
blockchain-operator-system
```

You will notice that I also added a `kubectl rollout restart` command to restart the controller every time a new image is pushed to Docker Hub.

The reason for this is because, out of simplicity, it's easier to tag the controller image with `latest` instead of updating the `VERSION` field in the makefile each time you build a new image. As a result, the controller will not automatically restart (which is necessary for you to see the changes).

Finally, you need to tell Operator-SDK where to push the controller-built image. You need to update the `IMG` field in the makefile by referencing your Docker Hub account:

```
IMG ?= <dockerhub-account>/blockchain-operator:latest
```

It's time to give the workflow a try. Run `make update` once. If everything was set up correctly, you should be able to see the result in Lens, as depicted in Figures 5-7 and 5-8.

Figure 5-7. *The Blockchain CRD is installed*

Figure 5-8. *The Blockchain controller is running under the blockchain-operator-system namespace*

Implementing the Operator Reconciliation Logic

Your local environment is now set up, so you can focus on implementing the logic of your controller. In the coming sections, most of the changes will be implemented in the following:

- `blockchain_types.go`: Where you will iteratively define the spec of the Blockchain custom resource.

- `blockchain_controller.go`: Where you will implement the reconciliation logic.

Let's take a look at the target state you need to reconcile. To guide you in the implementation of the reconciliation logic, refer to Listing 5-6 for a StatefulSet definition.

Listing 5-6. The StatefulSet State that the Blockchain Operator Will Reconcile

```yaml
apiVersion: apps/v1
kind: StatefulSet
metadata:
  name: ethereum-goerli
  namespace: ethereum
  labels:
    app: ethereum-goerli
spec:
  serviceName: ethereum-goerli
  replicas: 1
  selector:
    matchLabels:
      app: ethereum-goerli
  template:
    metadata:
      labels:
        app: ethereum-goerli
    spec:
      containers:
        - name: client
          command: ['geth']
          args:
            - '--goerli'
            - '--syncmode=light'
            - '--datadir=data'
            - '--cache=128'
          image: ethereum/client-go:stable
          imagePullPolicy: Always
          resources:
            limits:
```

```
            cpu: "500m"
            memory: 1Gi
          requests:
            cpu: "500m"
            memory: 1Gi
        ports:
          - containerPort: 30303
            name: p2p
            protocol: TCP
          - containerPort: 8545
            name: rpc
            protocol: TCP
        volumeMounts:
          - name: data
            mountPath: /data
  volumeClaimTemplates:
    - metadata:
        name: data
      spec:
        accessModes: [ "ReadWriteOnce" ]
        storageClassName: standard
        resources:
          requests:
            storage: 1Gi
```

Let's break things down:

```
kind: StatefulSet
```

The target resource will be of kind StatefulSet (https://kubernetes.io/docs/
concepts/workloads/controllers/statefulset/).

Using a StatefulSet native resource is relevant in this case, because blockchain
nodes usually need storage as they sync blocks from their peer-to-peer network.
Persisting the data across the client application restarts is therefore important.

StatefulSets are like deployments, but with one key difference. They are associated with a storage resource. However, when deleting a pod replica managed by the StatefulSet, the associated storage resource is not automatically deleted (it needs to be deleted manually if required).

Another difference is that the pod names use an index that is bound to the number of replicas so that the names are deterministic.

The next section in the listing is:

```
metadata:
  name: ethereum-goerli
  namespace: ethereum
  labels:
    app: ethereum-goerli
```

As the name suggests, the code intends to run the Ethereum Goerli testnet. Furthermore, the resource will be scheduled to run in a dedicated namespace (called ethereum).

The next section specifies how many replicas you want to create. This is a piece of information that you expose in the Blockchain spec.

```
replicas: 1
```

Then, the selector field lets you define some key-value labels that can be used by other resources to select the group of pods that will be managed by your StatefulSet.

```
  selector:
    matchLabels:
      app: ethereum-goerli
```

For instance, you can use them to expose the ethereum-goerli pods over the network via a service.

The following section specifies the command, args, and image fields that tell Kubernetes which software application and version you want to run and how you want to start the container.

```
command: ['geth']
args:
  - '--goerli'
  - '--syncmode=light'
  - '--cache=128'
image: ethereum/client-go:stable
```

The `resources` section defines how much CPU and memory should be allocated to the designated container. You expose this detail in your CRD.

```
resources:
  limits:
    cpu: "500m"
    memory: 1Gi
  requests:
    cpu: "500m"
    memory: 1Gi
```

The following section, `ports`, specifies which ports should be exposed by the container running in the pod. You can also make it possible to configure this detail in the Blockchain CRD.

```
ports:
  - containerPort: 30303
    name: p2p
    protocol: TCP
  - containerPort: 8545
    name: rpc
    protocol: TCP
```

Then, the `volumeMounts` field allows you to specify one or more volumes to be mounted into the container running in the pod.

```
volumeMounts:
  - name: data
    mountPath: /data
```

Finally, the volume in question is created by the `volumClaimTemplates` definition:

```
volumeClaimTemplates:
  - metadata:
      name: data
    spec:
      accessModes: [ "ReadWriteOnce" ]
      storageClassName: standard
      resources:
        requests:
          storage: 1Gi
```

To understand this last part, you can think of it in these terms: Upon creation, the `StatefulSet` will submit a claim for storage to Kubernetes using a specific `storageClassName`. This claim will be satisfied once Kubernetes creates a persistent volume.

This example references the `standard` storage class, which is preinstalled when you install Minikube. This class uses a default directory on your machine to persist the data written by the container. This allows you to run your blockchain client on your local machine and mimic what would happen in a real Kubernetes cluster (see Figure 5-9).

Figure 5-9. *The standard storage class available by default in Minikube*

Now update your `BlockchainSpec` struct and capture some of the details that your controller will use. Get rid of the boilerplate code and make it look like Listing 5-7.

Listing 5-7. Defining the API of the Blockchain Custom Resource

```
// BlockchainSpec defines the desired state of Blockchain
type BlockchainSpec struct {

    // Number of pod replicas to run
    Replicas *int32 'json:"replicas,omitempty"'
```

```
// url to the Docker image of the client blockchain to run
Image string 'json:"image,omitempty"'

// arguments that will be passed to the client container
ClientArgs []string 'json:"client-args,omitempty"'

// entry point for the main blockchain client container
Command []string 'json:"command,omitempty"'
}
```

Notes from the code follow:

- The Replicas field is an int32 pointer. As you will see, this the type expected by the StatefulSetSpec, as defined in the v1 package of the Kubernetes Go SDK.

- The image field is a string that points to the actual Docker image that the main container in your StatefulSet will run.

- ClientArgs is a list of strings that you will pass as arguments to the main container.

- command is a list of strings to pass as the entry point command to the main container.

Now to confirm that you are able to read the values from a custom Blockchain resource submitted to Kubernetes, update the BlockchainReconciler::Reconcile function to simply read those values.

Just remove the boilerplate code generated by Operator-SDK and update the function, as shown in Listing 5-8.

Listing 5-8. Logging the Values to Make Sure Things Work

```
// Reconcile is part of the main kubernetes reconciliation loop
which aims to
// move the current state of the cluster closer to the desired state.
func (r *BlockchainReconciler) Reconcile(ctx context.Context, req ctrl.
Request) (ctrl.Result, error) {

    log.SetPrefix("BlockchainReconciler")
    blockchain := &learnv1alpha1.Blockchain{}
```

```go
err := r.Get(ctx, req.NamespacedName, blockchain)

if err != nil {
        return reconcile.Result{}, err
}

log.Println("namespace", blockchain.Namespace, blockchain.
GetNamespace(), req.NamespacedName)
log.Println("name", blockchain.Name)
log.Println("replicas", *blockchain.Spec.Replicas)
log.Println("image", blockchain.Spec.Image)

for _, value := range blockchain.Spec.Command {
        log.Printf("command %s\n", value)
}

for _, value := range blockchain.Spec.ClientArgs {
        log.Printf("ClientArgs %s\n", value)
}

return reconcile.Result{}, nil
}
```

The updated code reads as follows:

- First, you populate a blockchain variable by fetching values using the BlockchainReconciler Get function.

- Once the code holds a blockchain instance, it prints the values of the different fields.

- If the field is of primitive type (like the image field, which is of type string), the code simply prints its value from Blockchain.spec.

- If the field is of composite type (like ClientArgs), then it iterates over the slice and prints each element in it using the range keyword.

Okay, so you have updated the BlockchainSpec struct and the controller reconciliation logic. It is time to run make update to regenerate the manifests and controller image, deploy a new CRD for your custom resource, and restart the controller.

Wait until the controller manager has restarted and is ready (in Lens) and then test the flow by submitting a sample `Blockchain` custom resource to the cluster.

Under `config/samples/`, you should have a `learn_v1alpha1_blockchain.yaml` sample file generated by Operator-SDK. Make it look like Listing 5-9.

Listing 5-9. A Sample Blockchain Custom Resource to Test the Flow

```
apiVersion: learn.gocrazy.com/v1alpha1
kind: Blockchain
metadata:
  labels:
    app.kubernetes.io/name: blockchain
    app.kubernetes.io/instance: blockchain-sample
    app.kubernetes.io/part-of: blockchain-operator
    app.kubernetes.io/managed-by: kustomize
    app.kubernetes.io/created-by: blockchain-operator
  name: blockchain-sample
  namespace: ethereum
spec:
  replicas: 1
  image: ethereum/client-go:stable
  command: ['geth']
  client-args:
    - '--goerli'
    - '--syncmode=light'
    - '--cache=128'
    - '--datadir=data'
```

As you can see in the definition, this `blockchain-sample` resource should be created under the ethereum namespace.

You don't have this namespace yet in your Minikube cluster. You can create it from the command line using `kubectl`, as follows:

```
kubectl create namespace ethereum
```

The remaining part of the sample test resource provides the relevant details for the number of replicas, the image to run, the command to invoke, and the arguments to be passed to the Geth process (see Figure 5-10).

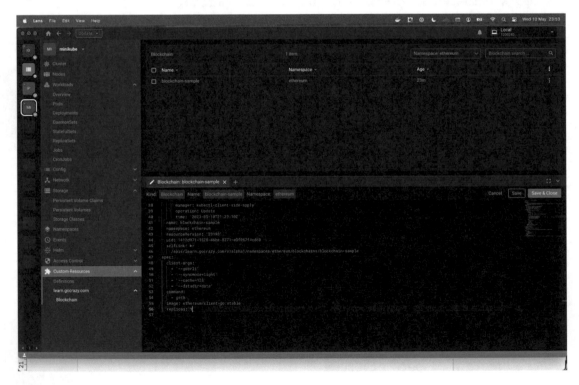

Figure 5-10. *The resources will be deployed under the ethereum namespace*

Now you can create the `blockchain-sample` resource in the cluster by invoking `kubectl` from the command line:

```
kubectl apply -f config/samples/learn_v1alpha1_blockchain.yaml
```

Doing this will store the custom resource in the Minikube cluster, as shown in Figure 5-11.

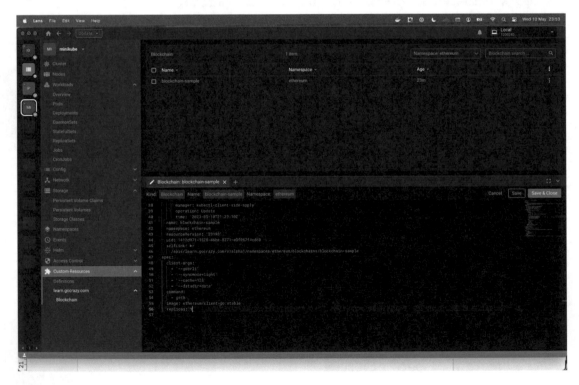

Figure 5-11. *A blockchain-sample custom resource deployed to Minikube*

From there, navigate to the Pods tab and check the log of the manager container for the `blockchain-operator-controller-manager` pod.

You should see log output like the one shown in Figure 5-10.

The controller has effectively been notified of the existence of the `blockchain-sample` custom resource and can fetch all the relevant details about it. That basically means the points are connected and that the flow is working properly.

This is good news, because you no longer have to worry about it. Rather, you can focus on iteratively improving the blockchain resource spec and reconciliation logic (see Figure 5-12).

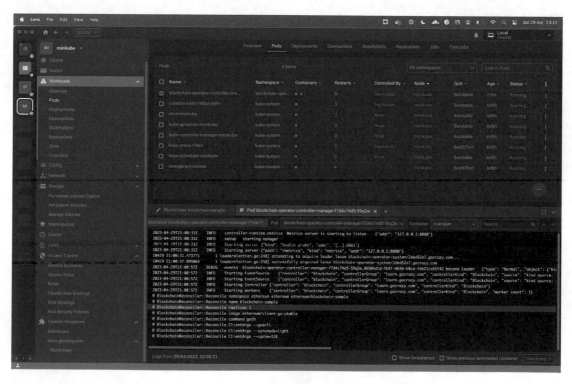

Figure 5-12. *blockchain-sample custom resource details*

Using the Kubernetes Go SDK

In this section, you are going to use the Kubernetes API to manage the native resource that your operator needs to reconcile, that is the `StatefulSet`.

To reach that goal, the first thing you need to ensure is that your blockchain controller has the right to manage (that is, create/read/update/delete) StatefulSet resources.

Using Operator-SDK, you grant these permissions by adding +kubebuilder annotations to the code.

Update the annotations that precede the BlockchainReconciler main Reconcile function so that they look like the ones in Listing 5-10.

Listing 5-10. The kubebuilder Annotations that Manage RBAC

```
//+kubebuilder:rbac:groups=learn.gocrazy.com,resources=blockchains,verbs=
get;list;watch;create;update;patch;delete
//+kubebuilder:rbac:groups=learn.gocrazy.com,resources=blockchains/
status,verbs=get;update;patch
//+kubebuilder:rbac:groups=learn.gocrazy.com,resources=blockchains/
finalizers,verbs=update
//+kubebuilder:rbac:groups=apps,resources=statefulsets,verbs=get;list;
watch;create;update;patch;delete
```

Note that the last annotation grants the controller the rights to manage statefulsets resources.

To learn more about RBAC and annotations, refer to https://kubebyexample. com/learning-paths/operator-framework/operator-sdk-go/rbac-operator-authorization.

Now you can implement the reconciliation logic to handle StatefulSet. You need to update the Reconcile function, as shown in Listing 5-11.

Listing 5-11. Updating the BlockchainReconciler Main Function

```
// Check if the statefulset already exists, if not create a new one
    foundSts := &appsv1.StatefulSet{}
    err = r.Get(context.TODO(), types.NamespacedName{Name: blockchain.Name,
    Namespace: blockchain.Namespace}, foundSts)
    if err != nil && errors.IsNotFound(err) {
        // Create a new StatefulSet
        sts := r.ReconcileStatefulSet(blockchain)
```

```
        err = r.Client.Create(context.TODO(), sts)
        if err != nil {
                log.Println("Failed to create new StatefulSet", err,
                "Namespace", sts.Namespace, "Name", sts.Name)
                return reconcile.Result{}, err
        }
        // StatefulSet created successfully - return and requeue
        return reconcile.Result{Requeue: true}, nil
 } else if err != nil {
        log.Println("Failed to get StatefulSet", err)
        return reconcile.Result{}, err
 }
```

Note the following about this code:

1. First, it checks if a StatefulSet with the same name in the target namespace already exists.

2. If not, it creates one.

3. If Statefulset already exists, the code will update it, as you will see soon.

The ReconcileStatefulSet function is not implemented yet. Listing 5-12 adds it.

Listing 5-12. The ReconcileStatefulSet Function

```
func (r *BlockchainReconciler) ReconcileStatefulSet(b *learnv1alpha1.
Blockchain) *appsv1.StatefulSet {
    log.Println("Creating a new StatefulSet")

    // Make sure to run at least 1 replicas
    if b.Spec.Replicas == nil {
            b.Spec.Replicas = pointer.Int32(1)
    }

    // provisioning a PVC to store this statefulset's data
    pvc := v1.PersistentVolumeClaim{
            ObjectMeta: metav1.ObjectMeta{
                    Name: "data",
            },
```

```go
        Spec: v1.PersistentVolumeClaimSpec{
                AccessModes:        []v1.PersistentVolumeAccessMode{v1.
                ReadWriteOnce},
                StorageClassName: pointer.String("standard"),
                Resources: v1.ResourceRequirements{
                    Requests: v1.ResourceList{
                        v1.ResourceStorage: apiResource.MustParse(fmt.
                        Sprintf("%dGi", 1)),
                    },
                },
            },
        },
    }

    // Specifying resources for the main container
    reqs := &v1.ResourceRequirements{
        Limits: v1.ResourceList{
            "cpu":    apiResource.MustParse("500m"),
            "memory": apiResource.MustParse("1Gi"),
        },
        Requests: v1.ResourceList{
            "cpu":    apiResource.MustParse("500m"),
            "memory": apiResource.MustParse("1Gi"),
        },
    }

    sts := &appsv1.StatefulSet{
        ObjectMeta: metav1.ObjectMeta{
            Name:      b.Name,
            Namespace: b.Namespace,
        },
        Spec: appsv1.StatefulSetSpec{
            Replicas: b.Spec.Replicas,
            Selector: &metav1.LabelSelector{
                MatchLabels: b.ObjectMeta.Labels,
            },
```

```go
        Template: corev1.PodTemplateSpec{
            ObjectMeta: metav1.ObjectMeta{
                Labels: b.ObjectMeta.Labels,
            },
            Spec: corev1.PodSpec{
                Containers: []corev1.Container{{
                    Image:           b.Spec.Image,
                    ImagePullPolicy: "Always",
                    Name:            "app",
                    Command:         b.Spec.Command,
                    Args:            b.Spec.ClientArgs,
                    Ports: []corev1.ContainerPort{{
                        ContainerPort: 30303,
                        Name:          "p2p",
                        Protocol:      "TCP",
                    }, {
                        ContainerPort: 8545,
                        Name:          "api",
                        Protocol:      "TCP",
                    }},
                    Resources: *reqs,
                    VolumeMounts: []corev1.VolumeMount{{
                        Name:      "data",
                        MountPath: "/data",
                    }},
                }},
            },
        },
        VolumeClaimTemplates: []v1.PersistentVolumeClaim{
            pvc,
        },
    },
}
```

```
    // Set Learn instance as the owner and controller
    controllerutil.SetControllerReference(b, sts, r.Scheme)
    return sts
}
```

Don't forget to update the `import` statements in the `blockchain_controller.go` file. Make sure the following dependencies are included (see Listing 5-13).

Listing 5-13. Importing the Required Dependency from the Kubernetes Go SDK

```
import (
    "context"
    "fmt"
    appsv1 "k8s.io/api/apps/v1"
    corev1 "k8s.io/api/core/v1"
    v1 "k8s.io/api/core/v1"
    "k8s.io/apimachinery/pkg/api/errors"
    apiResource "k8s.io/apimachinery/pkg/api/resource"
    metav1 "k8s.io/apimachinery/pkg/apis/meta/v1"
    "k8s.io/apimachinery/pkg/types"
    "k8s.io/utils/pointer"
    "log"
    "sigs.k8s.io/controller-runtime/pkg/controller/controllerutil"
    "sigs.k8s.io/controller-runtime/pkg/reconcile"

    learnv1alpha1 "github.com/gocrazy/blockchain-operator/api/v1alpha1"
    "k8s.io/apimachinery/pkg/runtime"
    ctrl "sigs.k8s.io/controller-runtime"
    "sigs.k8s.io/controller-runtime/pkg/client"
)
```

There is quite a lot of code in the `ReconcileStatefulSet` function.

By creating the `StatefulSet,` this function implements a good part of the operator logic. Here are the important pieces of this function:

1. First, you need to make sure that the `StatefulSet` will create at least one pod (one replica) by affecting `b.Spec.Replicas = pointer.Int32(1)` in case the `Replicas` field is not provided when the user submitted the custom resource.

2. Second, you create a `PersistentVolumeClaim` object using the *standard* storage class with the name `data` and 1 Gi of initial storage request.

3. Then, you create a `ResourceRequirements` object, where you request 500 millicores of CPU and 1 Gi of memory to be allocated to the main container running the client blockchain.

    Note that these values are actually too low to properly run a blockchain client and they are used only for the sake of illustration.

    Be sure to consider the resource requirements for the blockchain software that you intend to run (see `https://geth.ethereum.org/docs/getting-started/hardware-requirements` for instance).

    Also keep in mind that, even if Minikube is for local development purposes, it can be started with specific resource allocation by using the `--memory` and `--cpus` flags.

4. Next, create the `StatefulSet` using the `appsv1.StatefulSet` API from the Kubernetes Go SDK.

    Provide the `StatefulSet` name and namespace in the blockchain custom resource. You set the number of pod replicas and apply the custom resource labels.

    Then, using `Template.Spec`, you add one container by specifying the image, commands, and args defined in the custom resource. The `Ports` and `Resources` for now have been hard-coded as part of the function. You'll update these parts very soon.

    You then configure the storage by referencing the `PersistentVolumeClaim` you created earlier and making sure the blockchain main container is allowed to read and write to that storage by mounting it to the `/data` path.

5. Finally, use the `controllerutil.SetControllerReference` function to indicate that the `StatefulSet` resource is in fact managed by a higher-level resource, which is your Blockchain custom resource. This has the direct consequence that whenever the parent custom resource is deleted, the child `StatefulSet` resource will also be automatically deleted.

Time for a test!

Run `make update` to generate and install every asset, build and deploy the new controller, and restart the controller manager.

Then create the custom resource in Minikube using `kubectl apply -f config/samples/learn_v1alpha1_blockchain.yaml`.

You can observe the changes in action by interacting with Lens.

Navigate to the Pods tab and note that the `blockchain-sample-0` pod is running. Check the logs for the app container and ta-da! The Ethereum `Goerli` testnet is running in your Minikube local cluster (see Figure 5-13).

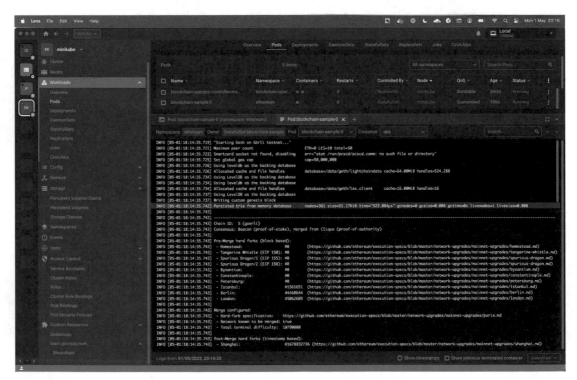

Figure 5-13. *Ethereum Goerli running in Minikube*

You can also execute a shell on the pod and run a few commands. Note that the Geth files are found in the data directory that is mounted to your container.

If you execute the du -h /data command at regular intervals, you should see that the disk usage under /data/geth/lightchaindata keeps increasing as new blocks are produced and stored (see Figure 5-14).

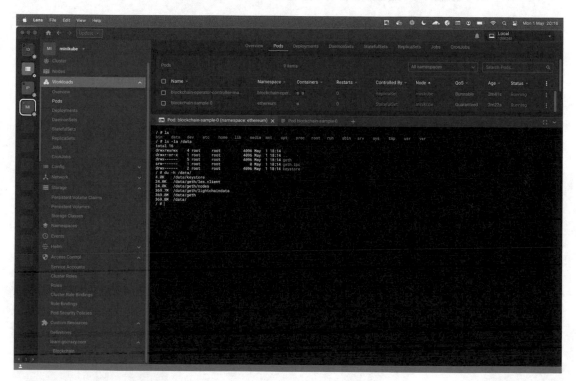

Figure 5-14. *Opening a shell on the "app" container*

Finally, browse to the Persistent Volume Claim and Persistent Volume tabs and observe the child resources have been created there (see Figures 5-15 and 5-16).

Figure 5-15. *Persistent Volume Claim child resource*

Figure 5-16. *Persistent Volume child resource*

Interacting with the JSON-RPC API

As stated at the beginning of this chapter, the goal is to run EVM-compatible blockchains.

In that regard, those blockchains should adhere to the Ethereum JSON-RPC API https://geth.ethereum.org/docs/interacting-with-geth/rpc such that it should be possible to call the RPC methods and process the API results in the same fashion regardless of the actual concrete blockchain client managed by the operator.

You can do a simple test by calling the eth_blockNumber rpc method. This is a simple method that does not require parameters and returns the block number at the tip of the chain.

In order to do this, you need to start your Geth client with a few more arguments. Update the sample resource located at config/samples/learn_v1alpha1_blockchain.yaml and add the new client arguments. For clarity, I reproduced the full spec in Listing 5-14.

Listing 5-14. Enabling the HTTP Server on the Blockchain Resource

```
spec:
  replicas: 1
  image: ethereum/client-go:stable
  command: ['geth']
  client-args:
    - '--goerli'
    - '--syncmode=light'
    - '--cache=128'
    - '--datadir=data'
    - '--http'
    - '--http.api=eth,net,web3'
    - '--log.debug=true'
```

Adding these configs will enable the HTTP server for the eth, net, and web3 namespaces of the Geth json-rpc API. The API will be available on the default port, 8545.

Now, since your operator controller does not support updates yet (you will add this feature in the coming sections), you need to restart from a clean slate, before submitting your changes.

Go ahead and delete the blockchain-sample custom resource using Lens. This should automatically remove the child resources: the statefulset, the replicaset, and the pod. However, the persistent volume claim resource won't be deleted automatically. You need to delete it manually.

Next, apply the custom resource again using the following:

```
kubectl apply -f config/samples/learn_v1alpha1_blockchain.yaml
```

Using Port-Forward

The blockchain-sample-0 pod should be back in action. To reach out to its json-rpc API, you can use a convenient Kubernetes feature known as port-forwarding (see https://kubernetes.io/docs/tasks/access-application-cluster/port-forward-access-application-cluster/).

As mentioned earlier, the client API is available on port 8545. You will map the local 8545 port to the same port on the pod by opening another terminal:

```
kubectl port-forward blockchain-sample-0 8545:8545
```

From now on, you should be able to reach the json-rpc API by sending curl requests to http://localhost:8545. You can try it using the snippet in Listing 5-15.

Listing 5-15. Testing the Blockchain with a Sample eth_blockNumber Request

```
curl http://localhost:8545/ \
  -X POST \
  -H "Content-Type: application/json" \
  --data '{"method":"eth_blockNumber","params":[],"id":1,"jsonrpc":"2.0"}'
```

You should get a response similar to this one (the value will be different of course):

```
{"jsonrpc":"2.0","id":1,"result":"0x73dcd0"}
```

I encourage you to explore the `json-rpc` API. You will take another look at it when implementing health checks for your blockchain pods in the coming sections.

For now, let's go back to the controller and tidy up the loose ends.

Parameterizing Resources and Ports

In the previous sections, you hard-coded a couple of settings for `StatefulSet` in the `ReconcileStatefulSet` function—namely the resources requirements and the container ports.

You now learn how to expose those details via the Blockchain CRD.

You'll see how to update the `BlockchainSpec` struct and add new fields to accommodate the changes. After the `Command` field, make sure to add the new fields in Listing 5-16.

Listing 5-16. Improving the BlockchainSpec

```
// number of cpus to allocate to the main blockchain container
Cpu string 'json:"cpu,omitempty"'

// memory to allocate to the main blockchain container
Memory string 'json:"memory,omitempty"'

// container port for the json-rpc api
ApiPort int32 'json:"api-port,omitempty"'
```

Now you need to update the `ReconcileStatefulSet` function and make the necessary changes to account for the newly added fields.

After the `pvc` definition, add the logic to set default values for the CPU and memory (see Listing 5-17).

Listing 5-17. Reconciling CPU and Memory

```
// Specifying default resources for the main container
if b.Spec.Cpu == "" {
  b.Spec.Cpu = "500m"
}

if b.Spec.Memory == "" {
  b.Spec.Cpu = "1Gi"
}
```

As you know, in Golang non-initialized primitive type variables are assigned a default value (empty string for string types, 0 for numeric types, so forth), so you need to check on the default value and reassign the concrete value passed via the custom resource.

You can use these new fields when creating the v1.ResourceRequirements object (see Listing 5-18).

Listing 5-18. Specifying Resources

```
reqs := &v1.ResourceRequirements{
  Limits: v1.ResourceList{
    "cpu":    apiResource.MustParse(b.Spec.Cpu),
    "memory": apiResource.MustParse(b.Spec.Memory),
  },
  Requests: v1.ResourceList{
    "cpu":    apiResource.MustParse(b.Spec.Cpu),
    "memory": apiResource.MustParse(b.Spec.Memory),
  },
}
```

Similarly, you need to add logic to handle a default value for the API port (see Listing 5-19).

Listing 5-19. Reconciling the API Port

```
if b.Spec.ApiPort == 0 {
  b.Spec.ApiPort = 8545
}
```

That should be it. Run make update again to deploy the updated CRD and the controller.

Next, navigate to the Pods tab in Lens, click the blockchain-sample-0 pod, and then click the pencil icon in the window. It that opens and shows the pod specification. Visually confirm that the correct config is applied to that pod (see Figure 5-17).

```yaml
containers:
  - name: app
    image: ethereum/client-go:stable
    command:
      - geth
    args:
      - '--goerli'
      - '--syncmode=light'
      - '--cache=128'
      - '--datadir=data'
      - '--http'
      - '--http.api=eth,net,web3'
      - '--log.debug=true'
    ports:
      - name: p2p
        containerPort: 30303
        protocol: TCP
      - name: api
        containerPort: 8545
        protocol: TCP
    resources:
      limits:
        cpu: 600m
        memory: 500Mi
      requests:
        cpu: 600m
        memory: 500Mi
```

Figure 5-17. *Container settings correctly configured*

Implementing the Update Logic

How does it feel?

Not too bad, right? You have an operator that can abstract a lot of the complexity of setting up and configuring a `statefulset` and its associated storage. As well, you have a workflow that makes it very easy to update your Blockchain API and test your changes quickly in Minikube.

However, the implementation is lacking the ability to update the derived resources whenever the custom resource changes.

Now you'll add this feature to your controller logic.

In the Reconcile function of the `blockchain_controller.go` file, after this code block:

```
...
} else if err != nil {
    log.Println("Failed to get StatefulSet", err)
      return reconcile.Result{}, err
}
```

Add the code lines in Listing 5-20.

Listing 5-20. Reconciling Subparts of the StatefulSet

```
// sts already exists. Updating to reflect the Blockchain spec
// Ensure the number of replicas matches the spec
r.reconcileReplicas(blockchain, foundSts)
// Ensure the container image size is the same as the spec
r.reconcileImage(blockchain, foundSts)
// Ensure the container ClientArgs are the same as the spec. The order does
not matter
r.reconcileArgs(blockchain, foundSts)
// Ensure the container command is the same as the spec. The order
does matter
r.reconcileCommand(blockchain, foundSts)
// Ensure the container resources are the same as the spec.
r.reconcileResources(blockchain, foundSts)
// Ensure the container ports are the same as the spec.
// r.reconcileContainerPorts(blockchain, foundSts)

return ctrl.Result{}, nil
```

As you see, for each property you expose via the Blockchain CRD, you want to have a dedicated reconcile function that receives a pointer to the `learnv1alpha1.Blockchain` struct and to the existing `StatefulSet`.

Listing 5-21 shows the implementation of the `reconcileReplicas` function.

Listing 5-21. Reconciling the Replicas Field

```
func (r *BlockchainReconciler) reconcileReplicas(blockchain *learnv1alpha1.
Blockchain, sts *appsv1.StatefulSet) (ctrl.Result, error) {
  specReplicas := *blockchain.Spec.Replicas
  stsReplicas := *sts.Spec.Replicas

  if stsReplicas != specReplicas {
    sts.Spec.Replicas = &specReplicas
    err := r.Client.Update(context.TODO(), sts)
    if err != nil {
      log.Println("Failed to update StatefulSet Replicas", err,
      "Namespace", sts.Namespace, "Name", sts.Name)
      return reconcile.Result{}, err
    }
    log.Println("Spec updated", "Replicas", *sts.Spec.Replicas)
  }

  // Spec unchanged or updated - return and requeue
  return reconcile.Result{Requeue: true}, nil
}
```

The logic is straightforward:

1. The code reads the `replicas` value from the deployed custom resource.

2. The code reads the `replicas` value from the existing `StatefulSet`.

3. If the two values are different, the code updates the replicas value for the `StatefulSet`.

4. Then, the code sends a message to the Kubernetes API server via the `BlockchainReconciler` and requests to update the `StatefulSet`. In turn, this will result in an increase or a decrease of the number of pods and persistent volume claims running in the `ethereum` namespace.

At a macro level, the logic will be the same for each reconcile* function. That's about reading the relevant value from the deployed custom resources and reading the corresponding value from the running statefulset, then comparing those two values. If there is a mismatch, the code requests an update to StatefulSet.

Go ahead and implement the reconcileImage function (see Listing 5-22).

Listing 5-22. Reconciling the Image Field

```
func (r *BlockchainReconciler) reconcileImage(blockchain *learnv1alpha1.
Blockchain, sts *appsv1.StatefulSet) (ctrl.Result, error) {
    specImage := blockchain.Spec.Image
    stsImage := sts.Spec.Template.Spec.Containers[0].Image
    if stsImage != specImage {
        sts.Spec.Template.Spec.Containers[0].Image = specImage
        err := r.Client.Update(context.TODO(), sts)
        if err != nil {
            log.Println("Failed to update StatefulSet Image", err,
            "Namespace", sts.Namespace, "Name", sts.Name)
            return reconcile.Result{}, err
        }
    }
    return reconcile.Result{Requeue: true}, nil
}
```

As you can see, the function follows the same logic as before, but this time you read the Image value set on the first (single) container managed by the StatefulSet.

The next two update functions—reconcileArgs and reconcileCommand—are just slightly more complicated, as the values you need to compare are slices.

To help with the comparison, you'll use a short compareSlices helper function.

This function compares two string slices and reports whether they are equal. You will parameterize this function with a withPreOrdering bool parameter to indicate whether the order of the elements also matters when doing the comparison.

Here it is in Listing 5-23.

Listing 5-23. A compareSlices Helper Function

```go
func compareSlices(s1 []string, s2 []string, withPreOrdering bool) bool {
    if len(s1) != len(s2) {
        return false
    }

    // Sort the slices so that their elements are in the same order
    if withPreOrdering {
        sort.Strings(s1)
        sort.Strings(s2)
    }

    // Compare the elements of the sorted slices
    for i, v := range s1 {
        if v != s2[i] {
            return false
        }
    }
    return true
}
```

1. The function first checks if the lengths of the slices match. If they don't, the slices can't be equal so the code returns false prematurely.

2. The code then sorts the slices only if withPreOrdering is passed as true (the default is false). By doing this, ["a", "b"] and ["b", "a"] are considered equal.

3. Then the code loops over the elements and compares them.

4. The code returns true if it reaches the end of the function (which means all the comparisons succeeded).

Thanks to this helper function, you can now implement reconcileArgs and reconcileCommand easily.

For the former one, you use compareSlices with preOrdering=true because the order of the arguments passed to the client software does not matter and should not cause the pods to restart.

By ordering the elements before comparing them, you ensure that the elements are compared one-to-one (see Listing 5-24).

Listing 5-24. Reconciling the ClientArgs Field

```
func (r *BlockchainReconciler) reconcileArgs(blockchain *learnv1alpha1.
Blockchain, sts *appsv1.StatefulSet) (ctrl.Result, error) {
  specClientArgs := blockchain.Spec.ClientArgs
  stsClientArgs := sts.Spec.Template.Spec.Containers[0].Args
  argsEquals := compareSlices(specClientArgs, stsClientArgs, true)

  if !argsEquals {
    sts.Spec.Template.Spec.Containers[0].Args = specClientArgs
    err := r.Client.Update(context.TODO(), sts)
    if err != nil {
      log.Println("Failed to update StatefulSet ClientArgs", err,
      "Namespace", sts.Namespace, "Name", sts.Name)
      return reconcile.Result{}, err
    }
  }
  return reconcile.Result{Requeue: true}, nil
}
```

Listing 5-25 shows the implementation of the reconcileCommand function.

Listing 5-25. Reconciling the Command Field

```
func (r *BlockchainReconciler) reconcileCommand(blockchain *learnv1alpha1.
Blockchain, sts *appsv1.StatefulSet) (ctrl.Result, error) {
    specCommand := blockchain.Spec.Command
    stsContainerCommand := sts.Spec.Template.Spec.Containers[0].Command
    argsEquals := compareSlices(specCommand, stsContainerCommand, false)
    if !argsEquals {
        sts.Spec.Template.Spec.Containers[0].Command = specCommand
        err := r.Client.Update(context.TODO(), sts)
```

```
        if err != nil {
                log.Println("Failed to update StatefulSet Command", err,
                "Namespace", sts.Namespace, "Name", sts.Name)
                return reconcile.Result{}, err
        }
    }
    return reconcile.Result{Requeue: true}, nil
}
```

Finally, you will implement the reconcileResources function. You will not update Cpu and Memory independently, but rather consider that any mismatch of Cpu or Memory with respect to the custom resource spec should trigger a reconciliation (see Listing 5-26).

Listing 5-26. Reconciling the CPU and Memory Fields

```
func (r *BlockchainReconciler) reconcileResources(blockchain
*learnv1alpha1.Blockchain, sts *appsv1.StatefulSet) (ctrl.Result, error) {

    specCpu := blockchain.Spec.Cpu
    stsContainerResources := sts.Spec.Template.Spec.Containers[0].Resources
    stsResourceRequestCpu := stsContainerResources.Requests.Cpu().String()

    specMemory := blockchain.Spec.Memory
    stsResourceRequestMemory := stsContainerResources.Requests.Memory().
    String()

    if specCpu != stsResourceRequestCpu || specMemory !=
    stsResourceRequestMemory {

        reqs := &v1.ResourceRequirements{
            Limits: v1.ResourceList{
                "cpu":    apiResource.MustParse(specCpu),
                "memory": apiResource.MustParse(specMemory),
            },
            Requests: v1.ResourceList{
                "cpu":    apiResource.MustParse(specCpu),
                "memory": apiResource.MustParse(specMemory),
            },
        }
```

```
      sts.Spec.Template.Spec.Containers[0].Resources = *reqs
      err := r.Client.Update(context.TODO(), sts)
      if err != nil {
            log.Println("Failed to update StatefulSet Resources", err,
            "Namespace", sts.Namespace, "Name", sts.Name)
            return reconcile.Result{}, err
      }
   }
   return reconcile.Result{Requeue: true}, nil
}
```

You only have the `reconcileContainerPorts` function left to implement. I leave this one for you to implement as an exercise! The logic is the same as the other functions. The only detail to consider more carefully is how you select the container port to compare when reading from the `StatefulSet`, since you are exposing two ports (`api` and `p2p`).

Once this is done, go ahead and run `make update` to redeploy the controller.

Then, edit the spec in the `learn_v1alpha1_blockchain.yaml` file, try changing the number of replicas or the Cpu values for instance, and submit the modified sample resource to the cluster via `kubectl`.

You can observe the changes in Lens, as shown in see Figure 5-18.

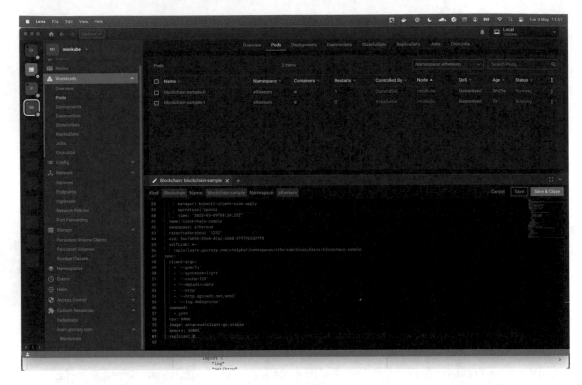

Figure 5-18. *An update to the custom resource triggering the creation of a new replica*

Well done! With the implementation of the update logic, your blockchain operator is becoming more mature.

Of course, there are many things you could do to improve the blockchain spec and the reconciliation logic. I can only encourage you to continue on this path and improve the code you've added to `blockchain_controller.go`.

It's now time to turn your attention to the topic of health checks.

Implementing Health Checks

Container health checks are an essential aspect of managing applications in a Kubernetes cluster.

In a containerized environment, it is important to ensure that the application running inside the container is healthy and functioning as expected.

Health checks are built on top of a Kubernetes mechanism known as *probes*.

There are two types of probes: readiness probes and liveness probes. The former determines whether the container is ready to serve traffic while the latter determines whether the container is still alive and functioning correctly.

Health checks involve periodically probing the container to verify that the application is running as expected.

In practice, this is achieved by running another container (another application) alongside the main container within a single pod and having this second container (also referred to as a "sidecar" container) send requests to the main container and check its responses.

If the responses are satisfying, the sidecar container will return HTTP OK to the readiness probe and the entire pod will be marked healthy.

Any other response code will notify Kubernetes that the pod is not healthy and should not be used to serve traffic.

Note that the sidecar container can reach the main container using the loopback address (localhost) given that both containers are running alongside within the same pod.

(Since the health-check container is an autonomous application, you deploy it independently of the blockchain operator. For that purpose, we create a distinct mini sub-project to develop it.)

Creating a Minimal Go HTTP Server

Go ahead and create a new project named health-checks.

The goal here is to illustrate the practical steps to implement and configure health checks with readiness probes. As such, this project is small. You'll use it in your main blockchain-operator project.

A health check application is essentially a server application that exposes a single endpoint, performs the required checks, and returns an HTTP status code.

The program prompts ChatGPT to generate minimal Go HTTP server code to start. Here is the prompt:

Can you generate a template code for a minimal go http server listening on port 8080. The server implements a single API endpoint called "readiness".

Listing 5-27 shows the code that ChatGPT generated.

Listing 5-27. A Minimal HTTP Server Generated by AI

```go
package main

import (
    "log"
    "net/http"
)

func readinessHandler(w http.ResponseWriter, r *http.Request) {
    w.WriteHeader(http.StatusOK)
    w.Write([]byte("OK"))
}

func main() {
    http.HandleFunc("/readiness", readinessHandler)

    log.Println("Starting server on :8080...")
    if err := http.ListenAndServe(":8080", nil); err != nil {
        log.Fatal(err)
    }
}
```

This is all you need to start. Save this snippet of code in a `main.go` file. You will also add a minimal `Dockerfile` to build the `health-check` image (see Listing 5-28).

Listing 5-28. The Dockerfile that Builds the Health-Check Image

```dockerfile
# Use an official Go 1.19 module image as a parent image
FROM golang:1.19 as builder

WORKDIR /workspace

COPY go.mod go.mod
COPY go.sum go.sum

RUN go mod download

COPY main.go main.go

# Build the Go app
# RUN go build -o server .
```

```
RUN CGO_ENABLED=0 GOOS=${TARGETOS:-linux} GOARCH=${TARGETARCH} go build -a -o
server main.go

# Expose port 8080 to the outside world
EXPOSE 8080

# Define environment variables
ENV PORT=8080

# Use distroless as minimal base image to package the manager binary
# Refer to https://github.com/GoogleContainerTools/distroless for
more details
FROM gcr.io/distroless/static:nonroot
WORKDIR /
COPY --from=builder /workspace/server .
USER 65532:65532

# Run the Go app when the container starts
CMD ["/server"]
```

Like you did for the blockchain operator, you will need access to a Docker registry to publish and serve the health-check Docker image.

Be sure to create a registry for the health-check application and name it blockchain-health-checks.

For future reference, use the following commands to build and publish the health-check Docker image to your registry:

- docker build -t <dockerhub-account>/blockchain-health-checks:latest

- docker push <dockerhub-account>/blockchain-health-checks:latest

Or create a makefile and save those commands in it for convenience.

Performing a net_peerCount Health Check

As mentioned earlier, you are not going to develop a complex application in this last section. All you need to understand is the principle of having a health-check sidecar container to respond to Kubernetes readiness probes to only allow the traffic to be routed toward healthy pods among a group of pod replicas.

Given this consideration, the `health-checks` application will only perform a single check—whether or not the blockchain node running as the main container in the pod has enough peers.

This is in fact a relevant check for a blockchain node, since without a decent number of peers, the node cannot receive new blocks fast enough from the peer-to-peer network. As a direct consequence, the node would lag behind the other nodes that compose the decentralized network. It would serve out-of-sync or inconsistent data.

You certainly don't want that, so add a peer count check to your application and return HTTP OK only if the number of peers is above a defined number; otherwise, have it return HTTP 503 (`service unavailable`)

To request the number of peers connected to a node, you can send a `net_peerCount` HTTP request to the node. This is a `json-rpc` API that should be available on most EVM-compatible networks. In order to send `json-rpc` requests to the node, you can use the convenient `github.com/ethereum/go-ethereum/ethclient` library.

Again, use ChatGPT to generate the appropriate code:

Here is the prompt:

```
can you generate some code using "github.com/ethereum/go-ethereum/
ethclient" that sends a 'net_peerCount' request to a node reachable at
http://localhost:8545 and assess whether the number of peers returned is
above a defined threshold ?
```

Listing 5-29 shows what you get.

Listing 5-29. HTTP Request and Comparison with the AI-Generated Result

```
package main

import (
    "context"
    "fmt"
    "log"
```

```go
    "math/big"

    "github.com/ethereum/go-ethereum/ethclient"
)

func main() {
    // Connect to the Ethereum node
    client, err := ethclient.Dial("http://localhost:8545")
    if err != nil {
        log.Fatal(err)
    }

    // Send the net_peerCount request
    peerCount, err := client.NetPeerCount(context.Background())
    if err != nil {
        log.Fatal(err)
    }

    // Define the threshold for minimum number of peers
    minPeers := big.NewInt(10)

    // Compare the peer count with the minimum threshold
    if peerCount.Cmp(minPeers) > 0 {
        fmt.Printf("Number of peers (%d) is above the threshold (%d)\n",
            peerCount, minPeers)
    } else {
        fmt.Printf("Number of peers (%d) is below the threshold (%d)\n",
            peerCount, minPeers)
    }
}
```

This is a pretty good starting point for the purposes here. Just one thing is incorrect and does not compile. That is peerCount.Cmp(minPeers), because peerCount is a uint64 and does not have a Cmp method.

You will now incorporate this code as part of the existing readinessHandler function and make a few modifications.

Listing 5-30 shows the updated code of the readinessHandler function.

Listing 5-30. Updating the readinessHandler Function

```
func readinessHandler(w http.ResponseWriter, r *http.Request) {
    client, err := ethclient.Dial("http://localhost:8545")
    if err != nil {
        http.Error(w, fmt.Sprint("Failed to connect to localhost: %v",
        err), http.StatusServiceUnavailable)
        return
    }

    // first query the latest block
    peerCount, err := client.PeerCount(context.Background())
    if err != nil {
        http.Error(w, fmt.Sprint("Failed to read peer count: %v", err),
        http.StatusServiceUnavailable)
        return
    }

    // Define the threshold for minimum number of peers
    var minPeers uint64 = 10

    // Compare the peer count with the minimum threshold
    if peerCount < minPeers {
        http.Error(w, fmt.Sprint("Number of peers is too low: %d",
        peerCount), http.StatusServiceUnavailable)
        return
    }

    w.WriteHeader(http.StatusOK)
    w.Write([]byte("OK"))
}
```

Let's see what is happening here:

1. The code establishes a connection to the node running in the
    main container by connecting to a localhost on port 8545.

2. Then it sends a net_peerCount HTTP request (see https://geth.
    ethereum.org/docs/interacting-with-geth/rpc/ns-net#net-
    peercount) to the node via the client.PeerCount helper function.

3. Finally, it compares the peerCount result against a defined
    threshold and returns an HTTP OK response if it passes the test.

4. In all the other cases, it returns HTTP 503 Service Unavailable.

Also, don't forget to update the import statement and make sure to include github.
com/ethereum/go-ethereum/ethclient, as shown in Listing 5-31.

Listing 5-31. Updating the import Statement

```
import (
    "context"
    "fmt"
    "log"
    "net/http"
    "github.com/ethereum/go-ethereum/ethclient"
)
```

And that's it. You are done with the health-checks application.
As an exercise, I suggest the following improvements:

1. The minPeers threshold variable is hard-coded in the
    readinessHandler function. Update the function to read the
    value from an environment variable so that it can be passed from
    outside the container.

2. Implement additional checks and make sure all the checks
    pass before returning HTTP OK. For instance, EVM-compatible
    blockchains expose the https://ethereum.org/en/developers/
    docs/apis/json-rpc/#eth_syncing json-rpc method, which can
    be used to determine if the chain is synced or is lagging behind
    the other peers of the network.

Make sure to build the image and host it in a public Docker registry.
You will now use it to configure a readiness probe in the Blockchain operator.

Configuring the Readiness Probe

Back to the blockchain-operator project.

In the ReconcileStatefulSet function, under the App container, you need to configure a second container to run the health-checks image in the same pod as the blockchain app (see Listing 5-32).

Listing 5-32. Adding the health-checks Sidecar Container to the StatefulSet

```
{
Image:                "<your-dockerhub-account>/blockchain-health-
checks:latest",
ImagePullPolicy: "Always",
Name:                "health-checks",
Ports: []corev1.ContainerPort{{
    ContainerPort: 8080,
    Name:            "readiness",
    Protocol:        "TCP",
}},
ReadinessProbe: &v1.Probe{
    ProbeHandler: v1.ProbeHandler{
    HTTPGet: &v1.HTTPGetAction{
        Path: "/readiness",
        Port: intstr.IntOrString{
                    IntVal: 8080,
            },
        },
    },
        PeriodSeconds:      5,
        SuccessThreshold: 3,
        FailureThreshold: 3,
        },
    }
```

Note that this code uses the ReadinessProbe field of the new container to configure a readiness probe that will be executed every five seconds.

The overall flow is as follows:

1. Every five seconds, Kubernetes will send a HTTP GET request to the health-checks container on the /readiness endpoint.

2. In turn, the server application running in that container will intercept the request and execute the readinessHandler function.

3. As part of the logic defined in the readinessHandler function, the server will send the net_peerCount json-rpc Post request to http://localhost:8545, where the HTTP server of your blockchain container app is running.

4. Upon receiving the response from the blockchain node:

    If the number of peers connected to the blockchain client is above the threshold, the health-checks app will return HTTP OK to Kubernetes.

    Otherwise, the health-checks app will return HTTP 503 to Kubernetes.

    • If the readiness probe receives an HTTP 503 status code three times in a row, the entire pod is marked as unhealthy and as a consequence Kubernetes won't send any traffic to it.

    • However, if the readiness probe receives an HTTP OK status code three times in a row, the entire pod is marked as healthy again and Kubernetes will start sending traffic to it.

Give the workflow a try. Run make update again and check the state in Lens. Here is what you can observe:

1. At first, a newly created pod will be marked as unhealthy. This is because it takes a little time for the HTTP server to start up within the Geth client. It also takes a little time for the node to connect to the peer-to-peer network and pass the threshold (see Figure 5-19).

2. After a few seconds, Geth is bootstrapped and the readiness probe will start to receive success notifications. Eventually, the two containers in the pod turn green and the entire pod is marked as healthy (see Figure 5-20).

Figure 5-19. *A readiness probe failing at startup*

Figure 5-20. *All containers are healthy and the pod can handle traffic*

On that point, this chapter concludes. There are plenty of features you could incorporate into your operator to make it more powerful. I suggest a few here:

1. Leverage service-, endpoint-, and ingress-native resources as part of the operator reconciliation logic to expose the pods internally and externally to the cluster.

2. Take advantage of the horizontal pod autoscaler resources to upscale or downscale the number of replicas based on metrics like CPU and memory usage.

3. Expose an API in the Blockchain spec to let the user of your CRD choose which class of storage they want to use.

Kubernetes is a fantastic piece of machinery and I cannot wait to see what you build with it.

Summary

This chapter reviewed and implemented a lot of concepts:

1. It started by reviewing concepts related to a standard Kubernetes deployment.

2. Then it showed you how to deploy standard pods and services on Kubernetes.

3. It moved to implementing a custom operator, interacting with a locally deployed blockchain.

4. It showed you how to fine-tune the operator to properly propagate updates.

5. Finally, the chapter showed you how to implement a custom health check for your operator.

Go Beyond : Connecting to C for a Performance Boost

Once we accept our limits, we go beyond them.

—Albert Einstein

One of the features of Go that hasn't been covered much so far is its out-of-the-box integration with other native languages, like C, or even more native, like metal for GPU programming on macOS-based machines.

© Nicolas Modrzyk 2023

N. Modrzyk, *Go Crazy*, https://doi.org/10.1007/978-1-4842-9666-0_6

This means you'll get a little out of your comfort zone, especially having all those battery-included memory safety nets provided by Go, but you also get to do more, and differently.

As specified in the official documentation, using C is often not the best choice, and maybe having a server running in another language or simply writing a new version of your favorite algorithm is the best route.

But you may be short on time or have a proven library with proper C bindings, yet you want the Go code and its build framework to handle clean interfacing.

So here goes—this chapter covers C, C++, and metal code integration with your Go code, so you can achieve anything from image computations to simple GPU computing.

C is for Change

To improve is to change; to be perfect is to change often.

—Winston Churchill

Cgo is the GoLang core library that enables you to create Go programs calling properly interfaced C code.

To use Cgo, you basically write normal Go code that imports a pseudo-package called C. The Go code can then refer directly to C functions and types such as C.int, variables such as C.stdout, or functions such as C.putchar.

Calling C

This first example prints a statement on the output. It simply calls the C code directly from your main Go function.

You should still be in the GoLang editor, and the C code is inlined in the hello.go file, as shown in Listing 6-1.

Listing 6-1. Calling the Inline C Code

```
package main

//#include<stdio.h>
//void inC() {
//    printf("Once we accept our limits, we go beyond them!\n");
```

```
//}
import "C"

func main() {
    C.inC()
}
```

See how the C code is written in the Go file, each line prepended with //? The C code uses printf from the stdio core C library, so the header to include the C package stdio.h is included at the top of the inline C code.

There is nothing extra to set up and the executed code indeed prints the quote on the standard output.

Note the use of the Go import C, which tells Go which part of the code is coming from C and should be resolved after compiling the inline C code.

Calling C Code Located in a C File

This second example expands on the first one, this time splitting the C code into a separate C file. See Listing 6-2.

Listing 6-2. C Code in a Separate File

```
#include<stdio.h>

void inCFile() {
    printf("Once we accept our limits, we go beyond them!\n");
}
```

The Go code in its own hello.go file and calls the C code from the separate file.

Note that there is no reference to the filename of the C code, as long as the code is in the same folder, and Cgo resolves things automatically, as shown in Listing 6-3.

Listing 6-3. Go Calling C Code in Two Separate Files

```
package main

/*
void inCFile();
*/
```

```
import "C"

func main() {
    C.inCFile()
}
```

Note that the signature of the C function is still included in the Go code. You will see later in the chapter how to have a separate C header file to better the integration.

C Code Calling Go Code

Still building on your impressive progress, you will now get the C code to call the Go code, using Cgo imports in the C file; see Listing 6-4.

Listing 6-4. C Code About to Call Go Code

```
#include<stdio.h>
#include "_cgo_export.h"

void inCFile() {
    printf("Once we accept our limits, we go beyond them!\n");
    callFromC();
}
```

Note how the pre-processing directive _cgo_export.h makes the Go function available to the C code. Then the Go code builds on Listing 6-3, this time adding a function that is exported using the //export annotation on a Go function (see Listing 6-5).

Listing 6-5. Exporting a Go Function for Use from C

```
package main

/*
#include<stdio.h>
void inCFile();
*/
import "C"
import "fmt"
```

```go
func main() {
    fmt.Println("GO: I am about to call C.")
    C.inCFile()
}

//export callFromC
func callFromC() {
    fmt.Println("GO: C is calling me...")
}
```

Executing the code compiled from Listings 6-4 and 6-5 gives you the output of Listing 6-6, where you can see statements coming from the C and Go code.

Listing 6-6. Output of GO Calling C Calling Go

```
GO: I am about to call C.
Once we accept our limits, we go beyond them!
GO: C is calling me...
```

Passing Parameters

You have been coding mostly without parameters so far. Let's see how things work when passing some strings to the C code. Listing 6-7 shows how the C code receives strings via char pointers, char*.

Listing 6-7. Using the Go String and Returning a C String to Go

```c
#include<stdio.h>
#include "_cgo_export.h"

char* inCFile(char *str) {
    char *ret = "C String";
    printf("Received string from Go: %s\n", str);
    return ret;
}
```

You must be extra careful when writing the Go code because C strings take memory, and this memory allocation and deallocation is not handled by the Go garbage collector. You have to free memory allocated to C constructs manually after using it.

Apart from memory management, Listing 6-8 also shows how to:

- Use C.CString to create a C string from a Go string

- Use C.GoString to create a Go string from a C string

Listing 6-8. Passing Strings from Go to C to Go

```
package main

/*
#include<stdio.h>
#include <stdlib.h>
char* inCFile(char *str);
*/
import "C"
import (
    "fmt"
    "unsafe"
)

func main() {
    cstr := C.CString("Go string!")
    defer C.free(unsafe.Pointer(cstr))

    cString := C.inCFile(cstr)
    gostr := C.GoString(cString)
    fmt.Println("Received string from C: " + gostr)
}
```

Compiling and executing this new code gives the output in Listing 6-9.

Listing 6-9. Output of the Strings Passing Program

```
Received string from Go: Go string!
Received string from C: C String
```

Make sure you see and understand that the defer call frees the memory allocated for the C string, using a pointer reference.

Using a Header File

In this next example, Greet, you use a header file for the C file and reference that from both the Go and C code.

You will also get the return value of the greeting, generated in the C code, via a memory pointer, not directly by its value.

Listing 6-10 shows the contents of hello.h file and Listing 6-11 shows the C file.

Listing 6-10. Greet Header, hello.h

```
int greet(const char *name, char *out);
```

Listing 6-11. Greet C Code, hello.c

```
#include "hello.h"
#include <stdio.h>

int greet(const char *name, char *out) {
    return sprintf(out, "%s", name);
}
```

The C code itself is quite succinct; you use sprintf to format a string, and the output of the formatting is a char* pointer. The returned value of the C code is the size of the string located at the char pointer location.

Listing 6-12 shows the Go code, where C.malloc prepares a pointer to a string (a char*), and C.GoBytes retrieves the string from the pointer and the size of the returned value of the C call.

Listing 6-12. Greet's Go Code

```
package main

// #cgo CFLAGS: -Wall
// #include <stdlib.h>
// #include "hello.h"
import "C"
```

```go
import (
    "fmt"
    "unsafe"
)

func main() {
    name := C.CString("Einstein used to say: Once we accept our limits, we
    go beyond them.")
    defer C.free(unsafe.Pointer(name))

    ptr := C.malloc(C.sizeof_char * 1024)
    defer C.free(unsafe.Pointer(ptr))

    size := C.greet(name, (*C.char)(ptr))

    b := C.GoBytes(ptr, size)
    fmt.Println(string(b))
}
```

This is a lot of extra work just for a simple string, but you should now understand how to handle pointers to strings back and forth between C and Go.

Using a C Struct from Go

The following example achieves the same output, except this time you use a C struct to pass the data to the C code.

The C struct will be defined in the header file, as shown in Listing 6-13.

Listing 6-13. Passing Data to C Code via a C Struct

```c
struct Greetings {
    const char *name;
    const char *quote;
};

int greet(struct Greetings *g, char *out);
```

The C code simply prints a string using data from the C struct (see Listing 6-14).

Listing 6-14. C Code Handling a C struct

```
#include "hello.h"
#include <stdio.h>

int greet(struct Greetings *g, char *out) {
    return sprintf(out, "%s used to say: %s", g->name, g->quote);
}
```

The Go code is more involved, but it uses the same pieces you have seen up to now in this chapter:

- CString to create a C string from within Go

- C.free to release memory taken by the C string (no garbage collection here)

- C.malloc to allocate memory for a pointer

The new pieces of Listing 6-15 are as follows:

- C.struct_Greetings is made accessible by Cgo from the C code of Listing 6-13, namely the Greetings struct.

- C.GoBytes creates a C byte array with the C pointer and makes a Go string out of it.

Listing 6-15. Using C structs from Go

```
package main

// #cgo CFLAGS: -g -Wall
// #include <stdlib.h>
// #include "hello.h"
import "C"
import (
    "fmt"
    "unsafe"
)
```

```go
func main() {
    name := C.CString("Einstein")
    defer C.free(unsafe.Pointer(name))

    quote := C.CString("Once we accept our limits, we go beyond them.")
    defer C.free(unsafe.Pointer(quote))

    g := C.struct_Greetings{
        name:  name,
        quote: quote,
    }

    ptr := C.malloc(C.sizeof_char * 1024)
    defer C.free(unsafe.Pointer(ptr))

    size := C.greet(&g, (*C.char)(ptr))

    b := C.GoBytes(ptr, size)
    fmt.Println(string(b))
}
```

Unfortunately, there is no easy way to call and use a Go struct from C. Your best bet is to copy fields back and forth between Go and C.

Note   The Cgo preprocessing seems to get confused when using separate .h and .c files, but putting it all together in one file allows for using the `typedef` struct, instead of struct, which makes for slightly cleaner Go code.

Listing 6-16 shows how to call the C struct from Go.

Listing 6-16. Slightly Simpler with C Code Within Go

```go
package main

// #include <stdio.h>
// #include <stdlib.h>
// #include <string.h>
// typedef struct {
```

```go
//     const char *name;
//     const char *quote;
//} Greetings;
// int greet(Greetings *g, char *out) {
//     return sprintf(out, "%s used to say: %s", g->name, g->quote);
//}
import "C"
import (
    "fmt"
    "unsafe"
)

func main() {
    name := C.CString("Einstein")
    defer C.free(unsafe.Pointer(name))

    quote := C.CString("Once we accept our limits, we go beyond them.")
    defer C.free(unsafe.Pointer(quote))

    g := C.Greetings{
        name:  name,
        quote: quote,
    }

    ptr := C.malloc(C.sizeof_char * 1024)
    defer C.free(unsafe.Pointer(ptr))

    size := C.greet(&g, (*C.char)(ptr))

    b := C.GoBytes(ptr, size)
    fmt.Println(string(b))
}
```

This is not a surprise anymore: in a few pages, you will be dealing with writing code and implementing squares and averages and other statistical functions running on the GPU threads natively.

To prepare for this, you'll have a little adventure computing squares in Go via C. This exercise takes you directly to calling C library functions from Go.

Listing 6-17 shows how you can call `sqrt`, the square root function, from the core C math library.

Listing 6-17. Calling C Library Functions Directly

```
package main

/*
#include <math.h>
*/
import "C"
import "fmt"

func main() {
    number := 32.0
    result := float64(C.sqrt(C.double(number)))
    fmt.Printf("Square root of %.2f = %.2f\n", number, result)
}
// Output:
// Square root of 32.00 = 5.66
```

As observed, there is a need to convert between C and Go types, using `C.double` and `float64`, but the code is quite concise and clear. The output is inline in the comments of the listing, and as you can see, computing the square value of a single float is .. well .. fast.

Using the same C math library, and still in preparation for later GPU code, you'll try now to compute the power of 2 of each element of an array.

Here again you use the `math.h` library, this time from within the C code where the main algorithm will be written this time. Then you'll retrieve the array values in Go.

Each power of 2 is computed in-place, and thus you can simply use the array created in Go (see Listing 6-18).

Listing 6-18. Computing Powers of Two Using the C Math Library on a Go Array

```
package main

/*
#cgo CFLAGS: -g -Wall
#include <stdlib.h>
#include <math.h>
```

```
void square_array(double* arr, int length) {
    for (int i = 0; i < length; i++) {
        arr[i] = pow(arr[i], 2);
    }
}
*/

import "C"
import (
    "fmt"
    "unsafe"
)

func squareArray(arr []float64) {
    length := len(arr)
    cArr := (*C.double)(unsafe.Pointer(&arr[0]))
    C.square_array(cArr, C.int(length))
}

func main() {
    array := []float64{2.0, 3.0, 4.0, 5.0}
    squareArray(array)
    fmt.Printf("squared array:%v", array)
}
```

You can also enjoy a bit of speed Look how fast the C code can handle a 1M items array, using the updated main function from Listing 6-19.

Listing 6-19. 1M Lines of Powers

```
func main() {
    const size = 1000000
    array := make([]float64, size)
    for i := 0; i < size; i++ {
        array[i] = float64(i)
    }

    squareArray(array)
    fmt.Printf("Last item of squared array:%f", array[size-1])
}
```

That new listing generates a random array of 1M value and then prints out the last value on the output to give you an idea of the speed. Here again, the last statement prints out almost before compilation has begun.

But enough of C exercises, let's move on to something more exciting—applying image transformation using a library coded in C.

Matisse, ImageMagick, and Sepia

Building on this first batch of small examples, let's put it all together and call a known library with C bindings, in order to do some image processing with ImageMagick.

One sunny moment, moving inexorably toward sepia.

—Jonathan Galassi

ImageMagick is known for its CLI implementation directly in a shell, or sometimes via Php. It's no surprise that the Php code also calls the C-based binding.

The example code will turn a picture from color to sepia using those same ImageMagick C bindings.

While the code itself is quite straight forward, the setup is a bit more involved.

ImageMagick on OSX

Let's go over the OSX version first, and then you will see the similarities and differences when running the same code on Linux and Raspberry Pi. See Listing 6-20.

Listing 6-20. Go Code to Use ImageMagick on OSX

```
package main

/*
#cgo CFLAGS: -g -Wall -I/opt/homebrew/include/ImageMagick-7
#cgo LDFLAGS: -L/opt/homebrew/lib -lMagickWand-7.Q16HDRI
-lMagickCore-7.Q16HDRI
#include <MagickCore/magick-baseconfig.h>
#include <MagickWand/MagickWand.h>

void convertToSepia(const char* inputFile, const char* outputFile, const
double ratio);

*/
import "C"

func main() {
    inputFile := C.CString("../gopher3.jpeg")
    outputFile := C.CString("../gopher3-sepia.jpeg")
    ratio := C.double(0.98)

    C.convertToSepia(inputFile, outputFile, ratio)
}
```

You can see that:

- You use `C.CString` and `C.double` again to pass parameters to the C code. (I left out `C.free` … but make sure to put them back in place where needed for those strings.).

- The `convertToSepia` function is declared in the Go code and will be implemented in the C code.

- ImageMagick library headers for OSX are:

  - `MagickCore/magick-baseconfig.h`

  - `MagickWand/MagickWand.h`

- You silently used them before, now you actively require them

  - Settings for CFlags: This is where you find the header files for the library. This is depending on the package installer used to install ImageMagick, here Homebrew on OSX.

    - Set an extra `-I` for each library header location

  - Settings for LDFlags determine where to find the library when creating the binary image.

    - Set `-L` to specify a library path

    - Set `-l` to specify library names

  - Finally, the extra library headers to include ImageMagick in the Go file:

    - `#include <MagickCore/magick-baseconfig.h>`

    - `#include <MagickWand/MagickWand.h>`

On to the C code now, which is pure ImageMagick code.

The C code in Listing 6-21 is mostly platform independent, so you can write very similar code for Linux and later on for the Raspberry Pi

Listing 6-21. ImageMagick Code (Not OSX Specific)

```
#include <MagickWand/MagickWand.h>

void convertToSepia(const char* inputFile, const char* outputFile, const
double ratio) {
    MagickWandGenesis();

    MagickWand *wand = NewMagickWand();
    MagickReadImage(wand, inputFile);

    int sepia = 65536 * ratio;
    MagickSepiaToneImage(wand, sepia);

    MagickWriteImage(wand, outputFile);

    wand = DestroyMagickWand(wand);
    MagickWandTerminus();
}
```

Sequentially, the code:

- Initializes the ImageMagick library.

- Reads the input file.

- Sets the Sepia tone. The magic value 65536 is the base for the image, and then you multiply this by a value between 0 and 2, where values for sepia, it's mostly between 0.8 and 1.2.

- Writes the result to the output file.

- Cleans up.

The installation steps for OSX are briefly shown in Listing 6-22.

Listing 6-22. Install ImageMagick C library on OSX Using Homebrew

```
#!/bin/bash
brew install imagemagick
```

With a sepia ration setting of 0.86, you would get something like the output of Figure 6-1—quite deep rendering.

Figure 6-1. *Matisse in sepia*

ImageMagick on Linux

Unfortunately, the packaging for ImageMagick, and any C library, is platform dependent. So, the headers and flags for Linux are different, as shown in Listing 6-23.

Listing 6-23. Headers to Use ImageMagick on Linux

```
//on linux arm ubuntu
#cgo CFLAGS: -g -Wall -I/usr/include/ImageMagick-6 -I/usr/include/aarch64-
linux-gnu/ImageMagick-6
#cgo LDFLAGS: -lMagickWand-6.Q16
#include <magick/magick-baseconfig.h>
#include <wand/MagickWand.h>
```

ImageMagick on Raspberry Pi

Again, those headers change when running on Raspberry Pi, as shown in Listing 6-24.

Listing 6-24. Headers and Flags for Raspberry Pi

```
//on raspberry pi
#cgo CFLAGS: -g -Wall -I/usr/include/ImageMagick-6 -I/usr/include/arm-
linux-gnueabihf/ImageMagick-6
#cgo LDFLAGS: -lMagickWand-6.Q16
#include <magick/magick-baseconfig.h>
#include <wand/MagickWand.h>

void convertToSepia(const char* inputFile, const char* outputFile, const
double ratio);
```

That being said, the code runs fast on each platform and Matisse can be turned to sepia on each of the different OSes.

GPU Coding on OSX

Right in the middle of this big Go/C battle, you are going to get even more involved by doing some processing on the GPU.

Unfortunately, this part will only focus on GPU coding using the metal API provided by Apple on its M1/M2 based Mac, not particularly because there is a lack of bindings for other platform, like CUDA, but because this one-off library makes it easy to achieve it, and to illustrate the perfect point that using more processing efficient hardware should not be that hard after all.

- The blog post presenting the library is here: `https://adrianhesketh.com/2022/03/31/use-m1-gpu-with-go/`

- The companion project hosted on GitHub is here: `https://github.com/a-h/gpu`

The M1 based basic MacBook air has 32 GPU cores, and the code presented earlier makes it easy to use all those cores for custom computations.

The first example is taken directly from the examples, both the previous library one and the metal library one: adding two arrays together within GPU code.

Basics: Adding Values from Two Arrays

The code for the GPU kernels looks almost like C code, with one more added library—
the metal_stdlib, which is the GPU library from Apple.

The design of the GPU library is such that each input and output has been turned
into a long 1D matrix, and the computation inside the kernel code is done on that
1D matrix.

So, proper indexes to locate a specific element from the input (so originally, whether
1D, 2D, or 3D) are computed via a custom made idx function that is included each time
in the GPU kernel code.

Obviously, the process function is the most interesting part of Listing 6-25.

Listing 6-25. Metal Code for Adding Two Matrixes

```
#include <metal_stdlib>
using namespace metal;

typedef struct Params {
  int w_in, h_in, d_in;
  int w_out, h_out, d_out;
} Params;

int idx(int x, int y, int z, int w, int h, int d) {
  int i = z * w * h;
  i += y * w;
  i += x;
  return i;
}

kernel void process(device const Params* p,
    device const float* input,
    device float* output,
    uint3 gridSize[[threads_per_grid]],
    uint3 gid[[thread_position_in_grid]]) {

  // Only process once per row of data.
  if(gid.x != 0) {
    return;
  }
```

```
    // Since we know we're in the first column...
    // we can process the whole row.
    int input_index = idx(0, gid.y, gid.z,p->w_in, p->h_in, p->d_in);

    float a = input[input_index];
    float b = input[input_index+1];

    int output_index = idx(0, gid.y, gid.z, p->w_out, p->h_out, p->d_out);

    output[output_index] = a + b;
}
```

This first metal example is taken almost directly from the GPU library examples: https://github.com/a-h/gpu/blob/main/examples/add/add.metal
The Go code itself has some specificities:

- It uses go:embed to import an external file as a string

- The GPU code is compiled directly from the Go code, via gpu.Compile

- The code then creates an input and an output of custom sizes and types via gpu.NewMatrix

- The code is run on the GPU when calling gpu.NewMatrix

Listing 6-26 shows the contents of the Go part calling the metal code.

Listing 6-26. Go Code Calling the Metal Kernel Code

```
package main

import (
    _ "embed"
    "fmt"
    "github.com/a-h/gpu"
)

//go:embed add.metal
var source string
```

```
func main() {
    // Compilation has to be done once.
    gpu.Compile(source)

    count := 100000000
    input := gpu.NewMatrix[float32](2, count, 1)

    z := input.D - 1
    for y := 0; y < input.H; y++ {
       for x := 0; x < input.W; x++ {
          input.Set(x, y, z, float32(y))
       }
    }
    output := gpu.NewMatrix[float32](1, input.H, 1)

    // Run code on GPU, includes copying the matrix to the GPU.
    gpu.Run(input, output)

    fmt.Printf("Output: %d\n", int(output.Get(0, input.H-1, 0)))
}
// Output: 200000000
```

Running this code, you can confirm and see the GPU activity generated by opening the GPU view in the Activity Monitor of OSX, and typing Command+4 or using Window ➤ GPU History (see Figure 6-2).

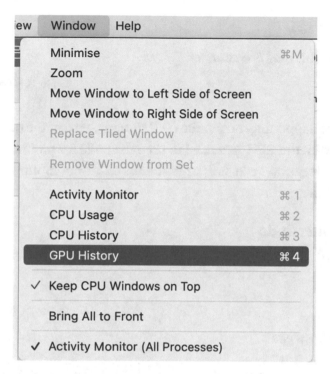

Figure 6-2. *GPU Activity from the Activity Monitor Menu*

You can see the GPU threads in action in real time when running the Go code (see Figure 6-3).

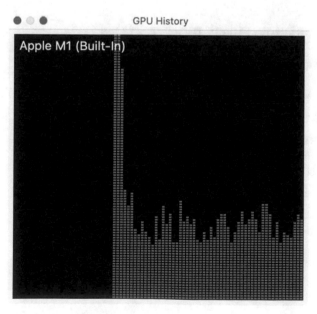

Figure 6-3. *GPU use*

Back to the Plot

Character is plot, plot is character.

—By F. Scott Fitzgerald

To visualize what is happening, not on the GPU directly, but on the output of the computed values with the GPU, you need to prep the code for plotting data.

You will use plotter and add helper functions to format inputs (and outputs), as shown in Listing 6-27.

Listing 6-27. Plotter Code

```
package metal

import (
    "fmt"
    "github.com/a-h/gpu"
    "gonum.org/v1/plot"
    "gonum.org/v1/plot/plotter"
    "gonum.org/v1/plot/vg"
    "image/color"
)

func PlotMe(title string, input plotter.XYs) {

    p := plot.New()

    p.Title.Text = title
    p.X.Label.Text = "i"
    p.Y.Label.Text = "value"

    l, _ := plotter.NewLine(input)
    l.LineStyle.Width = vg.Points(1)
    l.LineStyle.Color = color.RGBA{R: 255, A: 255}
    p.Add(l)

    p.Save(16*vg.Inch, 4*vg.Inch, fmt.Sprintf("%s.png", title))
}
```

```go
func FloatsToXY(input []float32) plotter.XYs {
    pts := make(plotter.XYs, len(input))
    for i := range pts {
        pts[i].Y = float64(input[i])
        pts[i].X = float64(float32(i))
    }
    return pts
}

func MatrixToXY(input *gpu.Matrix[float32]) plotter.XYs {
    pts := make(plotter.XYs, input.H)
    for i := range pts {
        pts[i].Y = float64(input.Get(i, 0, 0))
        pts[i].X = float64(float32(i))
    }
    return pts
}
```

This is mostly direct from plotter, converting a gpu.Matrix or an array of floats to what the plotter library expects.

Building on Chapter 4, you'll now implement loading and processing some hourly data of ETDUSD quotes, open and close.

You load data from a CSV file. You could of course use a specific Go library, but let's do this directly using core Go code this time, as shown in Listing 6-28.

Listing 6-28. Loading ETHUSD Data from CSV File

```go
package metal

import (
    "encoding/csv"
    "os"
    "strconv"
)

func GetOpensCloses(filename string) ([]float32, []float32) {
    file, _ := os.Open(filename)
    defer file.Close()
```

```go
    reader := csv.NewReader(file)
    data, _ := reader.ReadAll()

    var openPrice []float32
    var closePrice []float32

    for i, row := range data {
        if i == 0 {
            continue
        }

        o, _ := strconv.ParseFloat(row[3], 32)
        openPrice = append(openPrice, float32(o))

        c, _ := strconv.ParseFloat(row[6], 32)
        closePrice = append(closePrice, float32(c))
    }
    return openPrice, closePrice
}
```

Bridging Listings 6-27 and 6-28, you can now write a simple Go script that uses those two helper functions and generates a graph from open quotes. See Listing 6-29.

Listing 6-29. Loading and Plotting ETHUSD Hourly Open Quotes

```go
package main

import (
    _ "embed"
    "github.com/hellonico/libgpu/pkg/metal"
)

func main() {

    opens, _ := metal.GetOpensCloses("sample-data/ETHUSD_hourlies.p.csv")

    metal.PlotMe("simple opens", metal.FloatsToXY(opens))

}
```

This time the output is slightly more visual, and you can see the quotes graph in the simple opens.png file in Figure 6-4.

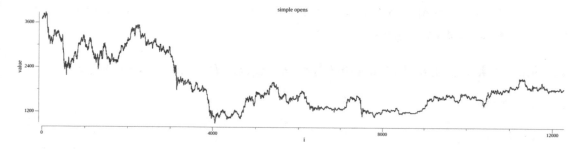

Figure 6-4. *Simple plot for open quotes*

But let's go back for more and start processing data on the GPU and use the helper functions to plot the diverse outputs.

Generic GPU Processing Go Code

The few coming examples are all based on an almost identical Go template:

- Load data from the CSV file

- Format it as an input matrix for GPU processing

- Do the processing

- Plot the output

Only the GPU/metal code will really change, so the Go code is included only once in the book and not repeated after.

This Go code iteration is indeed quite generic and builds on the first GPU example that you had for adding values. It does the following:

- Embeds the metal code as a string using the nicely named embed.

- Compiles the embedded metal code for the GPU kernel via gpu. Compile.

- Loads data from the sample CSV code to the input matrix.

- Prepares the output matrix.

- Runs the metal code.

- Displays the output in a chart.

297

The full code is shown in Listing 6-30, but make sure you adapt it, depending on the metal code you are working on.

Listing 6-30. Go Code to Call GPU Processing and Plot the Output Matrix

```go
package main

import (
    _ "embed"
    "fmt"
    "github.com/a-h/gpu"
    "github.com/hellonico/libgpu/pkg/metal"
)

//go:embed normalize.metal
var source string

func main() {

    gpu.Compile(source)

    opens, _ := metal.GetOpensCloses("sample-data/ETHUSD_hourlies.p.csv")

    input := gpu.NewMatrix[float32](1, len(opens), 1)
    output := gpu.NewMatrix[float32](1, len(opens), 1)

    for x := 0; x < input.H; x++ {
        input.Set(x, 0, 0, opens[x])
    }

    gpu.Run(input, output)

    for y := 0; y < output.H; y++ {
        fmt.Printf("Normalize: %v\n", output.Get(y, 0, 0))
    }

    fmt.Printf("Normalized for %d values\n", len(opens))

metal.PlotMe("Normalized", metal.MatrixToXY(output))

}
```

Opens ETHUSD Hourlies Quotes: Moving Average

The next metal code computes the moving average for your dataset. The code was also generated by ChatGPT using this prompt:

Using metal, generate the moving average of a 1x10 matrix.

As usual, you can then adapt the code proposed to your needs:

- The moving average window size is passed as a parameter in the second column (I assume no input data in that second column)

- You update the value of the window size accordingly

You would thus have code similar to Listing 6-31.

Listing 6-31. Plain Moving Average Metal Code

```
kernel void process(device const Params* p,
                    device const float* input,
                    device float* output,
                    uint3 gridSize[[threads_per_grid]],
                    uint3 gid[[thread_position_in_grid]]) {
    // Only process once per row of data.
    if(gid.x != 0) {
        return;
    }

    // Size of the moving average window
    const uint windowSize = input[0,1];

    for (uint i = windowSize; i <= p->h_in; i++) {
        float sum = 0.0;

        for (uint j = i - windowSize; j < i; j++) {
            sum += input[j];
        }

        output[i] = sum / windowSize;
    }
}
```

Note that the metal code:

- Assumes you know where the relevant input is (first column).

- Does a simple loop over all the input values and recomputes the loop each time.

Plotting the generating output from the code gives you two days, as shown in Figure 6-5.

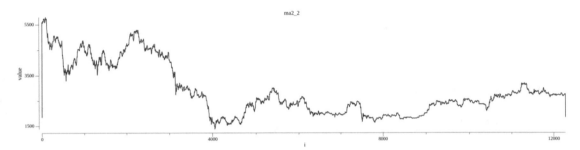

FIgure 6-5. *Two days moving average*

And for 100 days moving average, you get the image in Figure 6-6.

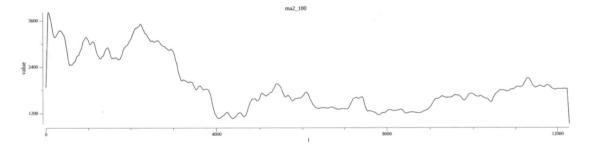

Figure 6-6. *100 days moving average*

You can see a smoother line graph in Figure 6-6, as it should be on the 100 days moving average graph.

Slightly Better Moving Average on the GPU

The metal code was quite fast, but it doesn't maximize the usage of the GPU by using proper GPU threads.

It uses a sequential C loop to compute each of the output values, while they could be computed in parallel by different GPU threads.

Let's take another approach and specify which index of the output matrix you are working on in the kernel code, and then limiting the moving average computation loop, thus allowing more threads to run in parallel (see Listing 6-32).

Listing 6-32. Maximizing GPU Thread Use

```
kernel void process(device const Params* p,
                    device const float* input,
                    device float* output,
                    uint3 gridSize[[threads_per_grid]],
                    uint3 gid[[thread_position_in_grid]]) {

    int input_index = idx(gid.x, gid.y, 0,p->w_in, p->h_in, p->d_in);

    // Size of the moving average window
    const float windowSize = input[0,1];

    float sum = 0.0;
    for (int i = -windowSize / 2; i <= windowSize / 2; ++i) {
        int index = idx(gid.x, gid.y+i, 0,p->w_in, p->h_in, p->d_in);
        if (index >= 0 && index < p->h_in) {
            sum += input[index];
        }
    }

    output[input_index] = sum / windowSize;

}
```

The custom plotting code turns the output into a visual plot. Figure 6-7 shows the Moving Average for a ten-day window size.

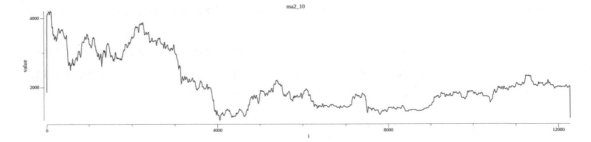

Figure 6-7. *Faster ten days moving average*

Sweet and fast.

Normalized Set

This exercise adds an extra level of difficulty. Say you want to compute the normalized set, from the input, so that all values of the input set are between 0 and 1. As you may know, to achieve this, you need to first compute the sum of squares.

Obviously, you could recompute that sum every single time, given how fast the GPUs are, but let's try to be subtle and create a cache value of the sum of squares (and also the normalization factor and the variance.)

You need to synchronize that value among the GPU threads while still keeping your parallel processing ability. Listing 6-33 shows how it is done.

Listing 6-33. Normalized Set with Cache and Synchronization Between Threads

```
kernel void process(device const Params* p,
    device const float* input,
    device float* output,
    uint3 gridSize[[threads_per_grid]],
    uint3 gid[[thread_position_in_grid]]) {

    int input_index =
        idx(gid.x, gid.y, gid.z,p->w_in, p->h_in, p->d_in);

    int output_index =
        idx(0, gid.y, 0,p->w_out, p->h_out, p->d_out);

    // Compute the sum of squares if it hasn't been cached yet
    if (input_index == 0) {
```

```
    float sumOfSquares = 0.0;
    float mean = 0.0;
    float variance = 0.0;

    for (uint i = 0; i < 100; i++) {
        float value = input[i];
        sumOfSquares += value * value;
        mean += value;
    }
    // mean average
    mean /= p->h_in;

    // The normalized standard deviation
    // (or Coefficient of Variance)
    // is just the standard deviation divided by the mean.
    variance /= p->h_in;

    // Compute the normalization factor
    float normalizationFactor = sqrt(sumOfSquares);

    // variance
    float variance = normalizationFactor / sumOfSquares;

    output[idx(0,1,0,p->w_in, p->h_in, p->d_in)] =
    normalizationFactor / sumOfSquares;
}

// Synchronize to ensure sumOfSquares
// is available to all threads
threadgroup_barrier(mem_flags::mem_threadgroup);

// Read the cached sum of squares value
float normalizationFactor =
    input[idx(0,1,0,p->w_in, p->h_in, p->d_in)];

// Compute the normalized value and
// store it in the output array
output[input_index] = input[input_index] / normalizationFactor;

}
```

In Listing 6-33, you can see how:

- The sum of squares, the normalization factor, and variance are computed only once (and stored using a spare cell of the output matrix).

- `threadgroup_barrier`(`mem_flags::mem_threadgroup`) forces the computation to wait for the cache to be ready.

- The rest of the computation can be as fast as possible using multiple threads thereafter.

The resulting set from the Go code can be turned into a graph again, and Figure 6-8 shows the values of the normalized set.

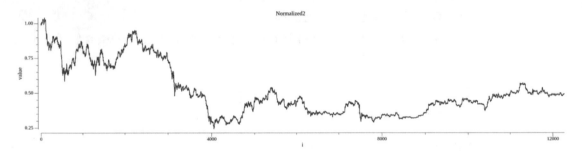

Figure 6-8. *Normalized set using caching and parallel threads*

Pearson Coefficient Moving Factor

The last example mostly comes from ChatGPT tweaks. I wanted to see how good the AI answer would be to compute a moving Pearson correlation coefficient.

The Pearson coefficient identifies if two sets have some kind of correlation, with values between -1 and 1 where:

- -1 means the sets are probably negatively connected. (If one set moves one way then the other set moves the other direction.)

- 0 means no connection between the two sets (totally independent).

- 1 means the sets moves in the same direction and are positively correlated.

The Person coefficient moving factor is one value, but the moving factor version computes the Pearson coefficient at any point in time of the input set.

The AI came pretty close. After a few fixes, you get the code from Listing 6-34.

Listing 6-34. Pearson Correlation Coefficient Using GPUs

```
kernel void process(device const Params* p,
                    device const float* input,
                    device float* output,
                    uint3 gridSize[[threads_per_grid]],
                    uint3 gid[[thread_position_in_grid]]) {

    constexpr uint windowSize = 120;   // Size of the window

    int input_index = idx(gid.x, gid.y, gid.z,p->w_in, p->h_in, p->d_in);

    const uint rows = p->h_in;

    // Number of rows in the output matrix
    const uint outputRows = rows - windowSize + 1;

    uint colIndex = gid.x;

    for (uint rowIndex = 0; rowIndex < outputRows; rowIndex++) {
        float sumX = 0.0;
        float sumY = 0.0;
        float sumXY = 0.0;
        float sumX2 = 0.0;
        float sumY2 = 0.0;

        // Compute the starting index of the window
        uint windowStart = rowIndex;

        // Compute the ending index of the window
        uint windowEnd = rowIndex + windowSize - 1;

        // Compute the sums within the window
        for (uint i = windowStart; i <= windowEnd; i++) {
            float x = input[i * columns + colIndex];
            float y = input[i * columns + (colIndex + 1)];

            sumX += x;
            sumY += y;
```

```
        sumXY += x * y;
        sumX2 += x * x;
        sumY2 += y * y;
    }

    // Compute the Pearson correlation coefficient
    float numerator = (windowSize * sumXY) - (sumX * sumY);
    float denominator = sqrt((windowSize * sumX2 - sumX * sumX) *
    (windowSize * sumY2 - sumY * sumY));

    float correlation = numerator / denominator;

    // Store the correlation in the output matrix
    output[rowIndex * columns + colIndex] = correlation;
    }

}
```

Without going into too many details, you can see that the code is using a flat sequential loop, so an exercise for you would be to write metal code (or prompt ChatGPT) to maximize parallelism.

That being said, the values are correctly generated. The values for the moving Pearson coefficient are shown in Figure 6-9.

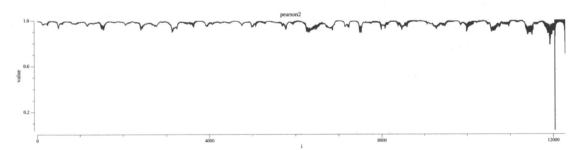

Figure 6-9. *Pearson Correlation Coefficient*

GPU usage goes up a slight bit, as shown in Figure 6-10.

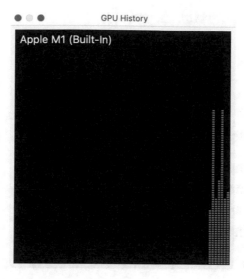

Figure 6-10. *Correlated GPU usage*

As mentioned, it should go much higher if the algorithm is implemented correctly for parallelism.

Sepia Gopher

This last example, which ends your GPU voyage, takes you back to changing color like you did for Matisse and the ImageMagick library.

The metal code is the code from the examples of the GPU library with custom sepia values.

At this stage, you should be very proficient at reading metal code. One small note here is that the kernel only does one pass per four values of the 1D matrix, since the pixel (of four values each) are encoded one after the other, sequentially. See Listing 6-35.

Listing 6-35. Sepia on the GPU

```
kernel void process(device const Params* p,
    device uint8_t* input,
    device uint8_t* output,
    uint3 gridSize[[threads_per_grid]],
```

```
    uint3 gid[[thread_position_in_grid]]) {
  // Only process once per pixel of data (4 uint8_t)
  if(gid.x % 4 != 0) {
    return;
  }

  int input_index = idx(gid.x, gid.y, gid.z, p->w_in, p->h_in, p->d_in);

  uint8_t r = input[input_index+0];
  uint8_t g = input[input_index+1];
  uint8_t b = input[input_index+2];
  uint8_t a = input[input_index+3];

  uint8_t avg = uint8_t((int(r) + int(g) + int(b)) / 3);

  // value for Red
  output[input_index+0] = avg * 0.99;
  // value for Green
  output[input_index+1] = avg * 0.90;
  // value for Blue
  output[input_index+2] = avg * 0.75;
  // value for alpha (seemingly not used here)
  output[input_index+3] = 0;
}
```

And the resulting happy sepia gopher is shown in Figure 6-11.

Figure 6-11. *Sepia gopher here again*

Extreme Calling OpenCV/C++ from Go

A few of my readers know that I am a big OpenCV fan. While it is not recommended to use in mission-critical production code without testing, I am going to sidestep a bit and try to call OpenCV from Go.

What would be the problem, you might ask, since you have just seen how to use ImageMagick? Well, OpenCV is written in C++ and the preprocessing performed by Cgo does not allow calls directly to C++. Hmm.

If the plan doesn't work, change the plan, not the goal.

—Anonymous

A trick that has been documented on StackOverflow:
https://stackoverflow.com/questions/1713214/how-to-use-c-in-go/1721230

As well as on GitHub:

https://github.com/arrieta/golang-cpp-basic-example/

These tricks use a custom library containing a C wrapper around the C++ code, and then call that C wrapper from Go and execute the needed code.

Again, a bit extreme, not really documented, but working crazy well enough that it is worth being presented in this book.

Figure 6-12 shows the folder structure and the files required for this C++ example to work properly.

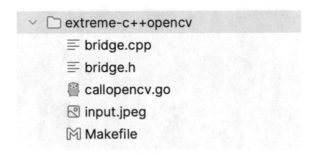

Figure 6-12. *Folder structure for wrapping C++ code*

Here are explanations of each of these files:

- `bridge.cpp`: Contains the C++ code calling the OpenCV C++ code

- `bridge.h`: Contains the C header, with definitions of the functions that will be called from Go to C++

- `callopencv.go`: The usual GoLang file

- `input.jpeg`: The gopher ready to be turned to sepia again

- `Makefile`: The magic glue to compile and link this custom library

Listing 6-36 shows the `bridge.h` file code.

Listing 6-36. The Header File

```
#pragma once
#ifdef __cplusplus
extern "C" {
#endif
```

```c
int callopencv();

#ifdef __cplusplus
}  // extern "C"
#endif
```

Then onto the C++ code that calls the OpenCV functions, as shown in Listing 6-37.

Listing 6-37. Calling Gophers from C++ OpenCV

```cpp
#include <stdio.h>
#include "bridge.h"
#include <opencv2/opencv.hpp>
void convertToSepia(cv::Mat& image) {
    cv::Mat kernel = (cv::Mat_<float>(3, 3) <<
        0.272, 0.534, 0.131,
        0.349, 0.686, 0.168,
        0.393, 0.769, 0.189
    );

    cv::transform(image, image, kernel);
    cv::threshold(image, image, 255, 255, cv::THRESH_TRUNC);
}

int callopencv() {
        // Load the image
        cv::Mat image = cv::imread("input.jpeg");
        if (image.empty()) {
            printf("Failed to load the image.\n");
            return -1;
        }

        // Convert the image to sepia
        convertToSepia(image);

        // Save the sepia image
        cv::imwrite("output.jpg", image);

        return 0;
}
```

The OpenCV code has again been generated by ChatGPT with the following prompt:

```
In opencv C++ code, using opencv operations on mat, show how to load and
turn an image into sepia.
```

Apart from the wrong headers, the generated code of Listing 6-37 contains almost no modifications.

The makefile is the most involved part of this section. It assumes you are using clang++ and that the OpenCV library has been installed using Homebrew (`brew install opencv`). Then the makefile compiles and creates the shared library called `libmyopencv.so`.

Listing 6-38 includes `opencv_highgui`, which is not required for this example, but you may find it useful for other usual OpenCV tasks.

Listing 6-38. Makefile to Compile the Custom Shared Library and Go Code

```
.PHONY: all

all: main

myopencv.so:
    /usr/bin/clang++ -o libmyopencv.so *.cpp  -std=c++20 -O3 -Wall -Wextra
    -fPIC -shared -I/opt/homebrew/include/opencv4 -L/opt/homebrew/lib
    -lopencv_core -lopencv_imgcodecs -lopencv_imgproc -lopencv_highgui

main: myopencv.so
    go build callopencv.go
```

Make (pun intended) sure the path to the `include` and `library` folders are correct. Those shown here are for OSX, so you will need to update those for Linux and others.

Finally, the simple Go code is shown in Listing 6-39.

Listing 6-39. Go Code to Call OpenCV

```
package main

// #cgo LDFLAGS: -L. -lmyopencv
// #include "bridge.h"
import "C"
```

CHAPTER 6   GO BEYOND : CONNECTING TO C FOR A PERFORMANCE BOOST

```
func main() {
    C.callopencv()
}
```

The only new part of the Go code is that it loads the custom library and calls the function defined in the bridge.h header file.

Also note the inclusion of the current folder to locate the library generated by the make call.

Calling make shows the libmyopencv.so library (from the C and C++ code) and the callopencv binary (from the Go code) files that have been generated (see Figure 6-13).

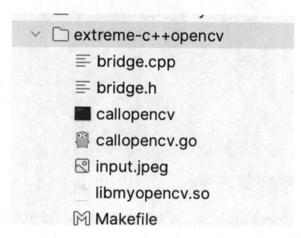

Figure 6-13. *Generated files*

Providing you execute the command from the same folder, you get a newly generated output.jpg file, with a yellowed, but happy, gopher (see Figure 6-14).

Figure 6-14. *Yellow/sepia gopher*

The next step is to tweak the kernel values used for the OpenCV transformation in the `bridge.cpp` file. Then you can turn the gopher blue or red.

The other examples from the `https://github.com/arrieta/golang-cpp-basic-example/` GitHub repository are worth looking at, especially the `goroutines` folder, which uses Go routines to run CPU-heavy tasks and proves that Go handles the load and the scheduling between the tasks very well.

> *The irony is that the actual story starts from the moment we think that everything has ended.*
>
> —Aaliya Mallick

Summary

So, here you are, ending this longer-than-expected chapter. At this point, you should now have complete understanding on how to:

- Write and call C code from Go and vice versa.

- Install and call C-based libraries from Go code and ensure that no memory leaks are unintentionally created.

- Process datasets using metal on Apple GPUs.

- Do some statistical processing on sets using parallel GPUs.

- Do image processing, this time using GPUs.

- Have some new coding ideas by calling C++ from Go and using OpenCV to perform fast image processing.

CHAPTER 7

Alef from Plan 9

Then took the other, as just as fair, And having perhaps the better claim, Because it was grassy and wanted wear; Though as for that the passing there Had worn them really about the same ---

"The Road Not Taken" by Robert Frost

Computer science is a discipline filled with intricate narratives and complexities despite its relatively short history. The evolution of operating systems and programming languages follows a linear trajectory in the textbooks, with disruptive innovations occasionally surfacing along the timeline. Unfortunately, many alternative systems

N. Modrzyk, *Go Crazy*, https://doi.org/10.1007/978-1-4842-9666-0_7

that failed to gain mainstream acceptance are often overlooked and forgotten. Yet, hidden within these off-path branches lie invaluable lessons and insights waiting to be rediscovered.

During my early days as a computer science student in the 1990s, I had the privilege of experiencing firsthand the computer science renaissance. It was a period teeming with innovation, where operating systems, computer architectures, and programming languages bloomed like wildflowers. In this odd chapter, as I reflect upon my fond memories of that era, I find great pleasure in recounting the journey shaped by the offbeat systems of NeXT, Plan 9, and Alef.

The NeXT computer, a technological marvel ahead of its time, played a pivotal role in my exploration of unconventional computing platforms. It was a machine that embodied Steve Jobs' vision, offering advanced features and a powerful development environment. While the world was fixated on mainstream choices, I found solace in the unique capabilities of the NeXT computer. Its sleek design, innovative object-oriented programming model, and unparalleled multimedia capabilities ignited my passion for seeking unconventional paths. While NeXT failed to go mainstream, NeXTSTEP found a home in Mac OSX after Apple acquired NeXT in 1996.

I stumbled upon Plan 9 in a newsletter article that mentioned that Bell Labs had ported Plan 9, an operating system that dared to challenge the established norms of distributed computing. Developed by the brilliant minds at Bell Labs, Plan 9 envisioned a future where seamless communication and collaboration between machines and users would be the norm. Its revolutionary 9P protocol and distributed filesystem model blurred the boundaries between local and remote systems. Plan 9 was designed to be the successor to UNIX, the OS born in Bell Labs in the 1970s. Many of the original developers of UNIX are on the Plan 9 team and saw it as a chance to "fix" UNIX. They took the ideas they had for UNIX to their logical conclusion. As Ken Thompson said jokingly, "I'd remember to spill 'create' correctly this time."

The experience with Plan 9 was nothing short of awe-inspiring, fueling my curiosity and expanding my understanding of distributed systems. At the heart of Plan 9 lay *Alef*, a programming language specifically designed for system programming tasks. Alef drew inspiration from many languages, merging the best features of Pascal, C, and Concurrent Euclid. With its emphasis on concurrent programming and interprocess communication, Alef shattered the conventional notions of sequential execution that had dominated my studies. Its concise syntax and expressive power could tackle complex system-level challenges easily. Through Alef, I delved into the realm of lightweight processes and built distributed applications that harnessed the full potential of Plan 9. Although Alef disappeared after the second edition of Plan 9, its influence lived on Limbo in the Inferno OS and the Go programming language.

As I wrote this unconventional chapter for a book centered on Go, a language with a great Plan 9 and Alef heritage, I went on a nostalgic journey, with memories of the intellectual fervor and the boundless sense of possibility that permeated the computer science landscape of the 1990s. Ideas and concepts from those vibrant days, brimming with a myriad of operating systems, diverse computer architectures, and a cornucopia of programming languages, are now resurfacing as new systems are developed. Though these alternative paths may not have attained widespread acceptance, their impact and the lessons they offer remain undeniably significant and should not be overlooked.

In a world where dominant narratives often overshadow unconventional ideas, it is vital to remember the contributions of the offbeat systems. They remind us that progress is not solely measured by market share or popular opinion, but by the depth of ideas explored and the impact they have on shaping our collective knowledge.

Plan 9 from Bell Labs

UNIX has long reigned as a foundational pillar, shaping the modern computing landscape. The design principles and elegant simplicity of Plan 9 propelled it to great heights, powering many systems across the globe. Yet, within the halls of Bell Labs, a team of visionaries who developed UNIX originally embarked on a bold endeavor to push the boundaries of UNIX. Their creation was none other than Plan 9. Driven by a desire to overcome the limitations of UNIX and explore new frontiers, the team set out to design an operating system that would address the challenges of a distributed and networked world.

At its core, Plan 9 sought to redefine the concept of distributed computing, transcending the traditional boundaries of individual machines. It discarded the notions of a centralized filesystem and embraced a decentralized model, where resources from different systems seamlessly intermingled. The innovative 9P network protocol allowed users and processes to access and manipulate files across networked machines as if they were local, fostering collaboration and communication.

One of the fundamental tenets that set Plan 9 apart was its unified view of resources. In the Plan 9 universe, everything, from devices to files, was represented as a file-like object, opening up a wealth of possibilities for interactivity and abstraction.

The Plan 9 operating system's /net directory treats all network resources as files. This directory serves as a virtual filesystem that encapsulates a wealth of information and functionalities related to networking. By representing network resources as files, Plan 9 simplifies the management and interaction with the network, providing a unified and consistent approach. Within the /net directory, one can discover files representing network interfaces, connections, and services. These files enable users to manipulate network settings, establish connections to remote machines, and perform various network-related tasks using familiar file operations and tools. The file-based representation of network resources in the /net directory exemplifies Plan 9's elegant design philosophy, fostering simplicity and uniformity throughout the operating system (see Figure 7-1).

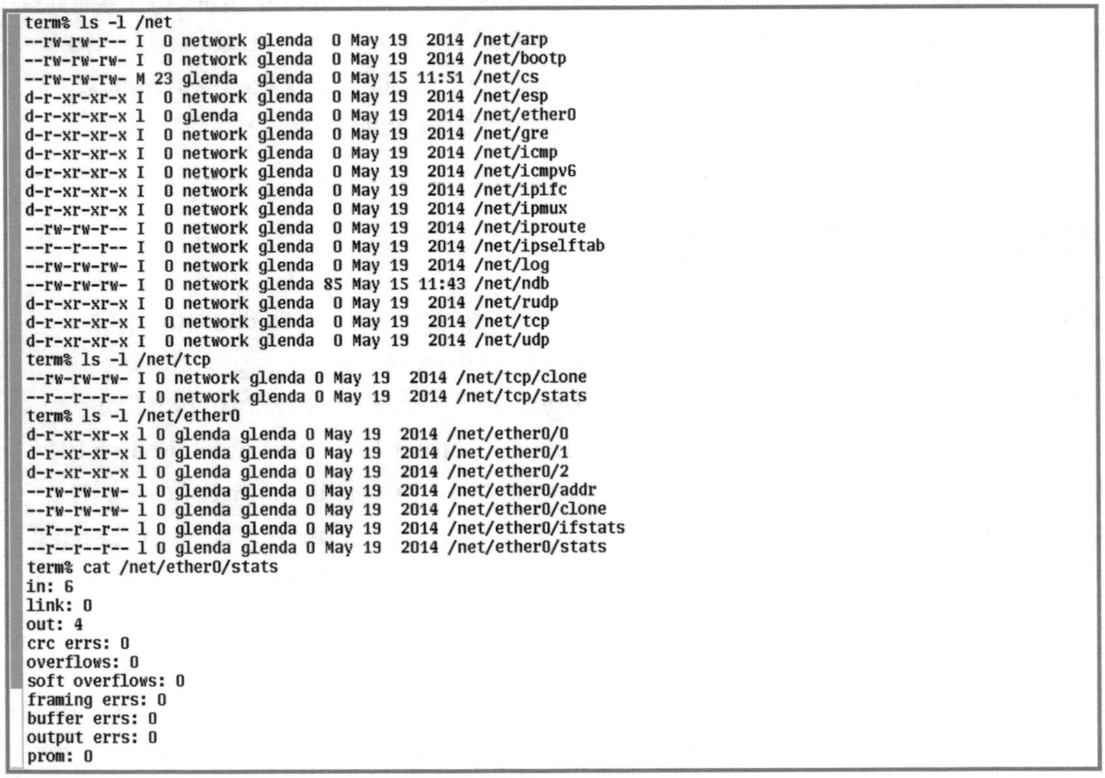

```
term% ls -l /net
--rw-rw-r-- I  0 network glenda  0 May 19  2014 /net/arp
--rw-rw-rw- I  0 network glenda  0 May 19  2014 /net/bootp
--rw-rw-rw- M 23 glenda  glenda  0 May 15 11:51 /net/cs
d-r-xr-xr-x I  0 network glenda  0 May 19  2014 /net/esp
d-r-xr-xr-x 1  0 glenda  glenda  0 May 19  2014 /net/ether0
d-r-xr-xr-x I  0 network glenda  0 May 19  2014 /net/gre
d-r-xr-xr-x I  0 network glenda  0 May 19  2014 /net/icmp
d-r-xr-xr-x I  0 network glenda  0 May 19  2014 /net/icmpv6
d-r-xr-xr-x I  0 network glenda  0 May 19  2014 /net/ipifc
d-r-xr-xr-x I  0 network glenda  0 May 19  2014 /net/ipmux
--rw-rw-r-- I  0 network glenda  0 May 19  2014 /net/iproute
--r--r--r-- I  0 network glenda  0 May 19  2014 /net/ipselftab
--rw-rw-rw- I  0 network glenda  0 May 19  2014 /net/log
--rw-rw-rw- I  0 network glenda 85 May 15 11:43 /net/ndb
d-r-xr-xr-x I  0 network glenda  0 May 19  2014 /net/rudp
d-r-xr-xr-x I  0 network glenda  0 May 19  2014 /net/tcp
d-r-xr-xr-x I  0 network glenda  0 May 19  2014 /net/udp
term% ls -l /net/tcp
--rw-rw-rw- I 0 network glenda 0 May 19  2014 /net/tcp/clone
--r--r--r-- I 0 network glenda 0 May 19  2014 /net/tcp/stats
term% ls -l /net/ether0
d-r-xr-xr-x 1 0 glenda glenda 0 May 19  2014 /net/ether0/0
d-r-xr-xr-x 1 0 glenda glenda 0 May 19  2014 /net/ether0/1
d-r-xr-xr-x 1 0 glenda glenda 0 May 19  2014 /net/ether0/2
--rw-rw-rw- 1 0 glenda glenda 0 May 19  2014 /net/ether0/addr
--rw-rw-rw- 1 0 glenda glenda 0 May 19  2014 /net/ether0/clone
--r--r--r-- 1 0 glenda glenda 0 May 19  2014 /net/ether0/ifstats
--r--r--r-- 1 0 glenda glenda 0 May 19  2014 /net/ether0/stats
term% cat /net/ether0/stats
in: 6
link: 0
out: 4
crc errs: 0
overflows: 0
soft overflows: 0
framing errs: 0
buffer errs: 0
output errs: 0
prom: 0
```

Figure 7-1. *Contents of the /net folder*

Everything is a file in Plan 9. Windows are viewed and interacted with as files in the filesystem. This approach introduces a level of abstraction that allows for unified and consistent handling of graphical user interfaces (GUI) and user interactions. Each window is represented as a file, and operations such as reading, writing, and seeking can be performed on these window files. By treating windows as files, Plan 9 provides a seamless integration of GUI elements into the overall file-based paradigm of the operating system. This design choice simplifies the development of GUI applications and enables efficient communication and sharing of data between different windows and processes. As you can see in Figure 7-2, five windows correspond to five files under /dev/wsys.

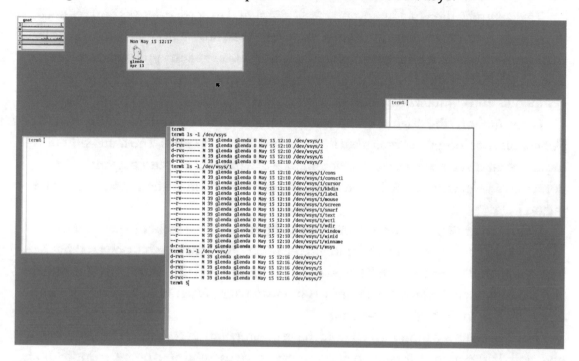

Figure 7-2. *Five windows, five files*

The Network Is the Computer

The development of the Plan 9 operating system began in the late 1980s at Bell Labs, AT&T's research and development arm of AT&T. The same team that created the UNIX operating system initiated the project, including notable individuals like Rob Pike, Dennis Ritchie, and Ken Thompson. "The Network is the Computer" was a popular paradigm in the late 80s, capturing the idea that the true power of computing lay in the collective capabilities of a networked infrastructure. The Internet rapidly expanded during this era, and the vision of interconnected computers held immense promise. The paradigm emphasized the potential of distributed computing, where resources and computing power could be shared seamlessly across a network.

However, as the 90s progressed, a different paradigm gained popularity: centralizing services through web browsers and servers. The rise of the World Wide Web shifted focus from distributed computing to centralized architectures. The browser became the primary interface through which users accessed applications and services hosted on remote servers, similar to the mainframe paradigm that the distributed computation tried to replace.

This centralization had its advantages: it simplified user experiences and reduced the complexity of managing distributed resources. Web browsers and servers provide a convenient and accessible platform for delivering content and applications to users. However, it also resulted in a concentration of power and control within a few dominant companies and centralized platforms.

Consequently, the original vision of distributed computing and the notion that "The Network is the Computer" took a backseat for nearly two decades. The focus shifted toward centralized services and the dominance of a handful of Internet giants. The potential of leveraging the full capabilities of a networked infrastructure seemed to be put on hold.

It was not until the emergence of Web3 and decentralized technologies that the "The Network is the Computer" paradigm regained popularity. Web3, powered by blockchain and other decentralized technologies, rekindled the vision of a distributed and interconnected network. It aimed to empower users, foster trust, and create a more open and equitable digital ecosystem.

Web3 envisions a future where users have greater control over their data, identities, and digital interactions. It seeks to decentralize services, returning power to individual users and enabling more peer-to-peer interactions. With the rise of decentralized applications (dApps) and decentralized protocols, the paradigm of "The Network is the Computer" has resurfaced, fueling innovation and exploring new possibilities in areas such as decentralized finance, digital ownership, and governance.

As you embark on designing a new distributed computing framework with Web3 technologies, it is valuable to revisit the design principles and features of Plan 9. Plan 9 was ahead of its time in many ways, embodying a holistic and elegant approach to distributed systems that still holds relevance today.

One of the most notable aspects of Plan 9 was its "everything is a file" philosophy. This concept treated resources, devices, and even network connections as files within a unified filesystem. By adopting this approach, Plan 9 simplified the interaction with various system components and promoted a consistent and intuitive interface. Bringing this idea to the design of a Web3 distributed computing framework could provide a unified abstraction layer that allows for seamless and uniform interactions with diverse resources and protocols.

Additionally, Plan 9's network transparency and remote file access capabilities are worth considering in the context of Web3. The ability to treat remote resources as if they were local files greatly simplifies distributed computing and fosters collaboration across different nodes and networks. By incorporating similar features into a Web3 framework, you can enable decentralized applications to transparently access and utilize resources across a network, promoting a more inclusive and interoperable ecosystem.

Go, the programming language with lineage traced back to Plan 9 and popularity among Web3 developers, is an ideal platform to welcome back some of the visitors from Plan 9.

The Alef Language

The Alef programming language was created in the late 1980s at Bell Labs, renowned for its groundbreaking contributions to computer industries. Alef was developed as an integral part of the Plan 9 operating system, which aimed to address the challenges posed by distributed systems and parallel computing.

The origins of Alef can be traced back to the collaborative efforts of a talented team of researchers and computer scientists at Bell Labs, primarily Phil Winterbottom with contributions from Rob Pike and others. They sought to design a programming language enabling efficient and scalable concurrent programming in distributed environments. Alef drew inspiration from various programming languages and concurrency models, incorporating ideas from C, Pascal, and concurrent languages like Newsqueak.

While Alef did not achieve widespread adoption, its influence and legacy can be seen in subsequent programming languages. Notably, Alef's design principles and concepts played a significant role in shaping the development of the popular Go programming language. Go adopted Alef's lightweight goroutines and channels, emphasizing concurrent programming as a first-class concept.

Over time, Alef was phased out from later editions of Plan 9 as the operating system integrated distributed primitives and absorbed the concurrent programming features of Alef into its thread library. However, the objective remains to provide readers with a glimpse into the essence of Alef and Plan 9, with the aspiration that their concepts and designs may serve as valuable inspiration for developing novel distributed systems.

> **Note**   This section intends not to provide a complete tutorial on Alef. *Alef Language Reference Manual* by Phil Winterbottom is a great place to dig into the language.

Hello Tuple!

Tuples were a favored data structure in concurrent languages in the 1980s. Using tuples in concurrent programming languages such as Alef stems from their ability to encapsulate multiple values into a single entity, facilitating concise and efficient handling of related data. With their immutability and support for heterogeneity, tuples effectively organize and pass around data within concurrent programs. Instead of the first-class language constructs, there are several projects, as shown in Listing 7-1.

Listing 7-1. Tuples

```
(int, byte*, byte)
func()
{
    return (10, "hello", 'c');
}

void
main()
{
    int a;
    byte* str;
    byte c;
    (a, str, c) = func();
}
```

Channels and Processes

Listing 7-2 shows a simple C program with channels.

Listing 7-2. Channels and Processes

```
#include        <alef.h>

void
receive(chan(byte*) c)
{
    byte *s;
    s = <-c;
    print("%s\n", s);
    terminate(nil);
}

void
main(void)
{
    chan(byte*) c;
    alloc c;
    proc receive(c);
    c <-= "Hello, World!";
    terminate(nil);
}
```

Channels and processes are the cornerstones of Alef, establishing them as first-class constructs within the language. Alef places significant emphasis on concurrent programming, and channels and processes are the key components that enable effective communication and synchronization between concurrent entities.

Channels serve as the primary means of communication and synchronization in Alef. They provide a safe and efficient way for goroutines and processes to exchange data and coordinate their actions. Channels are created using the channel declaration syntax, allowing programmers to define the type of data that can be transmitted. Sending and receiving messages on channels occur through dedicated send-and-receive operations. This design choice ensures explicit synchronization between concurrent entities, promoting orderly communication and preventing race conditions.

The ability to declare and manipulate channels as first-class constructs grants Alef a high degree of flexibility and expressiveness. Channels can be buffered, allowing them to hold a limited number of messages, which introduces a level of decoupling between senders and receivers. Buffered channels enable non-blocking operations when the buffer is not full or empty, facilitating data flow between concurrent components without unnecessary delays.

In Alef, processes are also treated as first-class constructs, elevating their significance in concurrent programming. Processes are separate instances that execute concurrently, and they communicate with each other using channels. This approach enables a higher level of concurrency and encapsulation, as each process maintains its own set of goroutines and executes independently. The isolation of processes enhances reliability, security, and fault tolerance by preventing unintended interference between concurrent entities.

Including processes as first-class constructs enables Alef to handle complex concurrent scenarios more effectively. By organizing concurrent entities into distinct processes, programmers can structure their code in a modular and hierarchical manner, leading to better code organization and maintainability. Spawning and terminating processes provide fine-grained control over concurrent execution, allowing for the dynamic creation and destruction of concurrent units as needed.

Alef's treatment of channels and processes as first-class constructs underpins the language's ability to handle concurrency effectively. Channels facilitate safe communication and synchronization between concurrent components, while processes enable the encapsulation and coordination of concurrent execution. By providing dedicated support for these constructs, Alef empowers programmers to write concurrent programs that are expressive, reliable, and scalable. The integration of channels and processes as first-class entities showcases Alef's commitment to providing a strong foundation for concurrent programming.

Proc and Task

"In Plan 9, fork is not a system call, but a special version of the true system call, rfork (resource fork) which has an argument consisting of a bit vector that defines how the various resources belonging to the parent will be transferred to the child. Rather than having processes and threads as two distinct things in the system, then, Plan 9 provides a general process-creation primitive that permits the creation of processes of all weights."

—Rob Pike

The topic of OS-level threading and goroutines has been a subject of intense discussion within the Go (GoLang) community, focusing on achieving effective parallelism and concurrency. The debate surrounding processes versus threads remains an ongoing issue in contemporary operating systems. In this context, the introduction of user-space cooperative threads and OS-level threads adds complexity to the discussion.

Plan 9 recognized the challenges associated with processes and threads early on. It identified the need for finer control over resources when creating new processes. In most operating systems, the traditional `fork()` system call is a special version of `rfork()` in Plan 9. This distinction allows for more precise management of resources and provides greater flexibility in controlling the behavior of new processes.

By incorporating `rfork()` as a fundamental mechanism, Plan 9 introduced a novel approach to process creation and resource control. This approach became instrumental in addressing the complexities surrounding parallelism and concurrency. Plan 9's innovative design and resource management mechanisms set the stage for exploring and developing efficient and scalable concurrent programming models.

In the Go programming language, goroutines serve as lightweight concurrent units of execution, allowing for highly concurrent and efficient code. Goroutines are not tied to OS-level threads directly but are multiplexed onto a smaller number of threads managed by the Go runtime. This approach mitigates the overhead associated with OS-level threads while still providing concurrency and parallelism in Go programs.

The consideration of process versus thread models, coupled with Plan 9's insights and Go's goroutine model, showcases the ongoing evolution and exploration of parallelism and concurrency in modern operating systems and programming languages. By addressing the complexities early on and providing innovative solutions, Plan 9's influence can be seen in the design of Go, offering developers powerful tools to achieve effective concurrency and parallelism while maintaining fine-grained control over resources (see Figure 7-3).

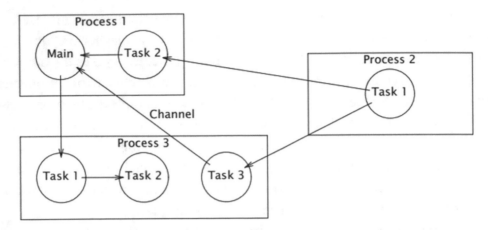

Figure 7-3. *Roots of Go's concurrency model*

As a concurrent programming language, Alef capitalized on the efficient and lightweight process-creation mechanisms by Plan 9. Building on the foundations laid by Plan 9, Alef introduced its own constructs, namely *Proc* and *Task*, to enable concurrent programming. Leveraging Plan 9's innovative resource control and process management capabilities, Alef harnessed the power of lightweight processes to achieve concurrency and parallelism.

With Proc, Alef provided a way to define concurrent processes that could execute independently and concurrently. These processes in Alef exhibited characteristics similar to Plan 9's processes, offering fine-grained control over resources and encapsulating execution units in the language. The Proc construct allowed developers to model concurrent activities and manage them efficiently.

Additionally, Alef introduced the Task construct, inspired by Plan 9's task-oriented approach. With Task, Alef facilitated the creation of concurrent units of execution that could operate in parallel with the main process. Similar to Plan 9's lightweight processes, Task entities in Alef leveraged the efficient process-creation mechanisms, enabling developers to design and coordinate concurrent activities easily, as shown in Listing 7-3.

Listing 7-3. Task Entities in Alef

```
Void
kbdtask(chan(int) kbdc)
{
  int r;
```

```
  for(;;) {
    r = <-kbdc;
    /* process keyboard input */
  }
}

void
mousetask(chan(Mevent) mc)
{
  Mevent m;
  for(;;) {
    m = <-mc;
    /* process mouse input */
  }
}

void
main(void)
{
  chan(int)[100] kbd;
  chan(int) term;
  chan(Mevent) mouse;
  alloc kbd, mouse, term;
  proc kbdproc(kbd, term), mouseproc(mouse, term);
  task kbdtask(kbd), mousetask(mouse);
  <-term; /* main thread blocks here */
  postnote(PNPROC, mousepid, "kill");
  postnote(PNPROC, kbdpid, "kill");
  exits(nil);
}
```

By leveraging Plan 9's efficient and lightweight process-creation capabilities, Alef provided a robust foundation for concurrent programming. The introduction of Proc and Task in Alef allowed developers to harness the power of lightweight processes and achieve concurrency and parallelism in a controlled and efficient manner. Alef's integration of Plan 9's process management mechanisms enhanced its ability to address the challenges of concurrent programming.

Have Fun with Plan 9

Bell Labs initially provided the source code of the first and second editions of Plan 9 to academics under a non-commercial license during the 1990s. However, in subsequent years, Lucent Technologies took the step to release the third and fourth editions of Plan 9 under an open-source license, marking a significant milestone in the operating system's availability. This move allowed a broader community to access and contribute to the development of Plan 9. Since then, the open-source version of Plan 9 has sparked a collective effort within the community to maintain and enhance the operating system. Notably, 9front has emerged as the most active fork of Plan 9, showcasing the ongoing dedication and commitment to advancing the capabilities and evolution of the system.

The source and the ISO images are available from `9p.io` and `9front.org`. Although it is possible to boot the system in modern computers, setting it up and running using virtual environments such as VirtualBox is easier. VirtualBox can be found and download at the following location:

`https://www.virtualbox.org/`

With VirtualBox on your computer, follow these steps to get Plan 9 up and running if you're interested in having a back-to-the-future experience with this future OS from the 90s.

1. Download the Plan 9 ISO. Visit the official Plan 9 website (`https://9p.io/plan9/`) or the Plan 9 from Bell Labs website (`https://9p.io/plan9/download.html`). Download your desired platform's latest stable ISO file (e.g., x86, amd64).

2. Set up a new virtual machine:

   a. Open VirtualBox and click New to create a new virtual machine.

   b. Provide a name for the virtual machine and select the appropriate Type and Version (e.g., Other and Other/Unknown, respectively) (see Figure 7-4).

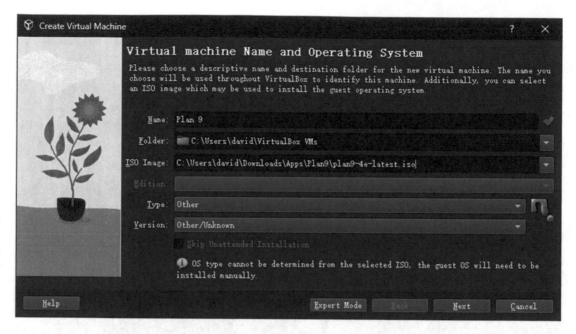

Figure 7-4. *Create the Plan 9 virtual machine*

3. Assign an appropriate amount of memory (RAM) to the virtual machine. Although 32MB is enough, I use 128MB for high resolution (see Figure 7-5).

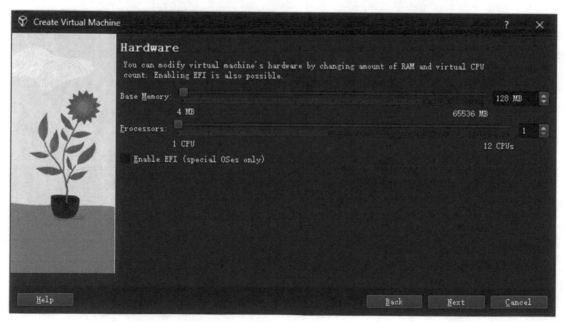

Figure 7-5. *Assign just enough memory*

4. Choose to create a new virtual hard disk and select the
    appropriate disk size and type (see Figure 7-6).

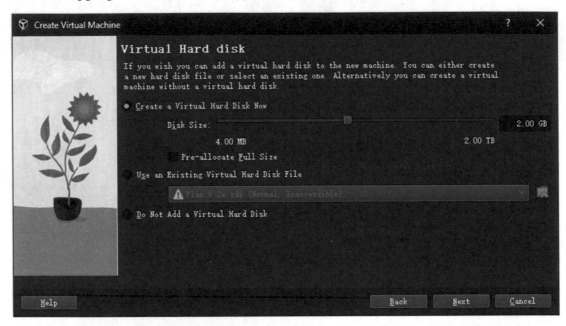

Figure 7-6. *Virtual machine disk size*

5. Click Finish to create the virtual machine (see Figure 7-7).

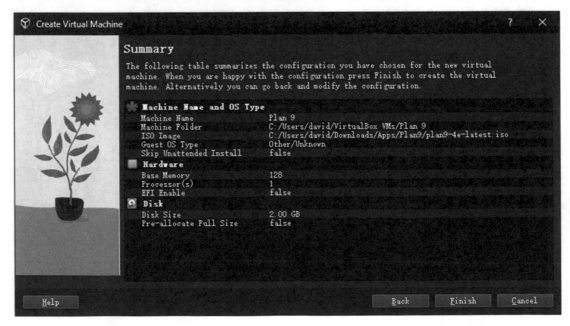

Figure 7-7. *Create the virtual machine*

6. Configure the virtual machine settings:

   a. Select the newly created virtual machine and click Settings
      (see Figure 7-8).

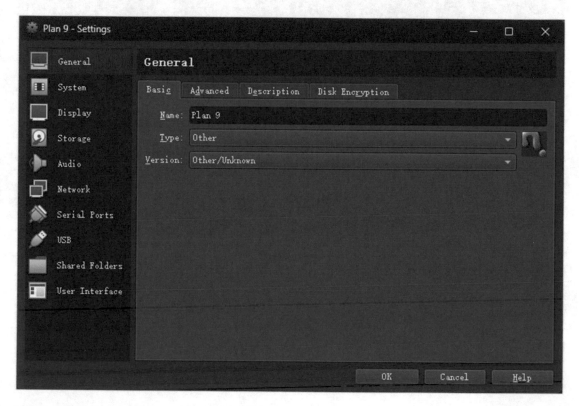

Figure 7-8. *Settings screen of the VM*

b. In the Audio section, select SoundBlaster 16 (see Figure 7-9).

Figure 7-9. *Audio Controller Settings*

c. Click OK to save the settings.

7. Install Plan 9 on the virtual machine:

a. Start the virtual machine by clicking Start. The virtual machine
    will boot from the Plan 9 ISO (see Figure 7-10).

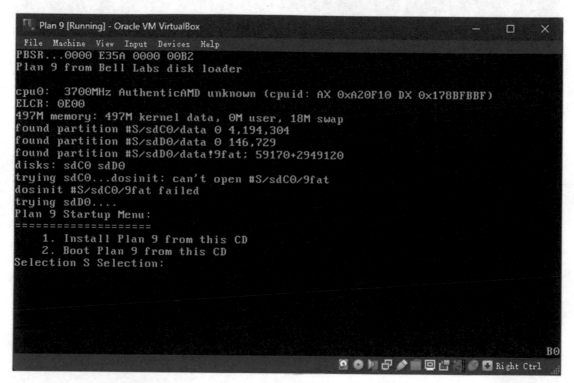

Figure 7-10. *Booting the virtual machine*

b. Select 1 to install Plan 9 to the virtual machine (see Figure 7-11).

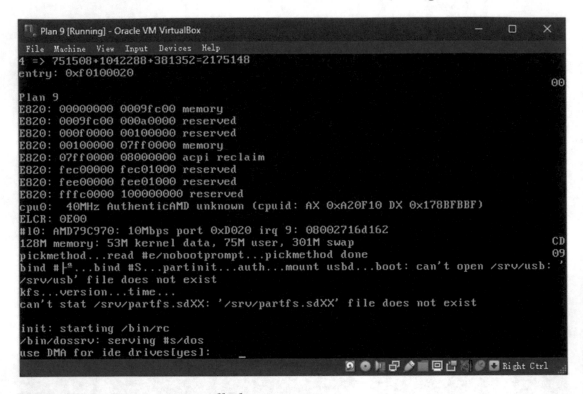

Figure 7-11. *Prepare to install Plan 9*

c. Use the configuration for the drive, mouse, and display (see Figure 7-12).

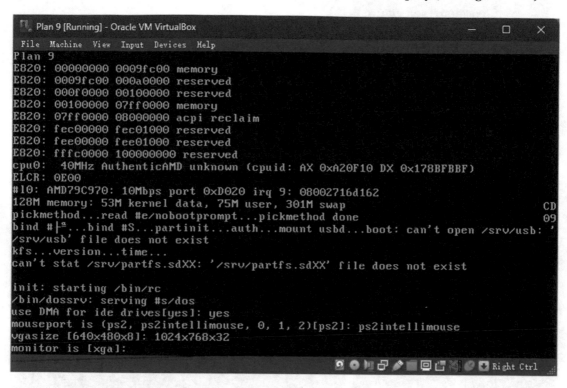

Figure 7-12. *Default configuration for monitor*

8. Boot up the system and begin the installation by configuring the
    filesystem (see Figure 7-13).

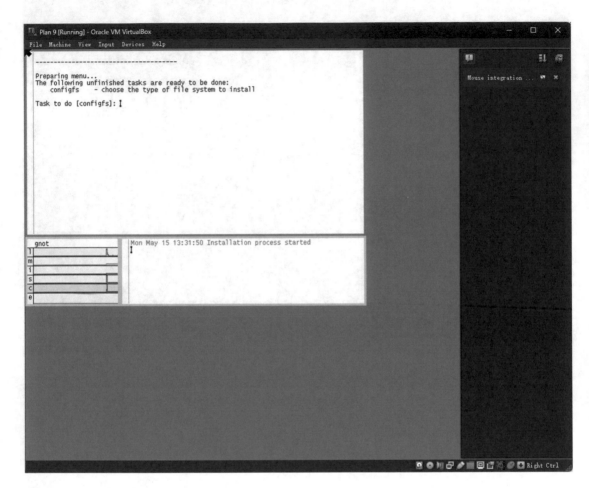

Figure 7-13. *Installing the filesystem*

a. The Fossil filesystem works fine (see Figure 7-14).

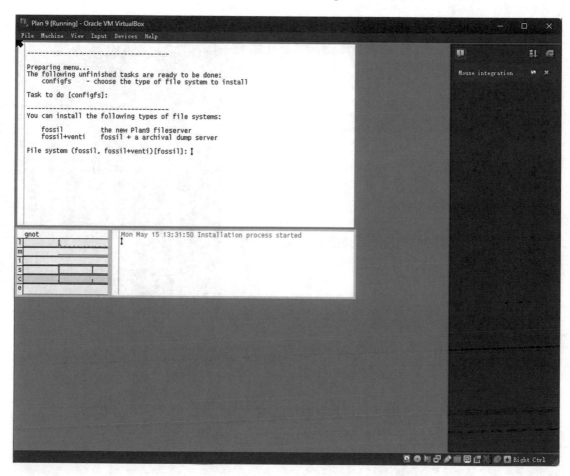

Figure 7-14. *Installing the Fossil filesystem*

9.   Partition the disk. Use sdC0 (see Figure 7-15).

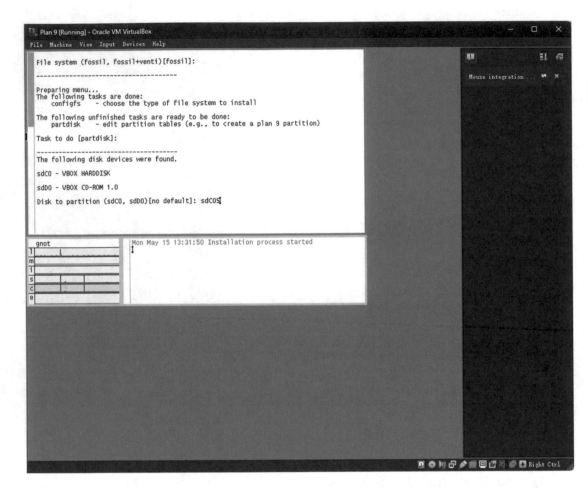

Figure 7-15. *Disk partitioning*

a. Choose Y to install MBR (see Figure 7-16).

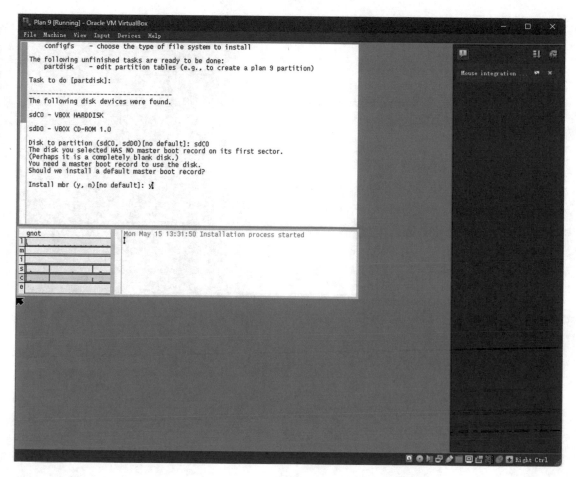

Figure 7-16. *Install the MBR*

b. Choose w and q to use the whole disk (see Figure 7-17).

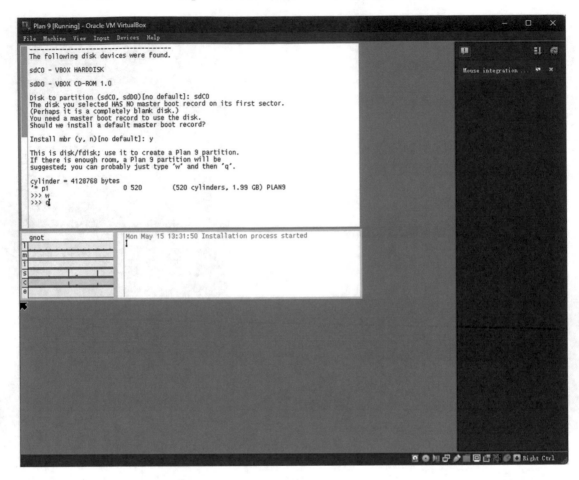

Figure 7-17. *Use the whole disk*

c. Follow all the default with prepdisk (see Figure 7-18).

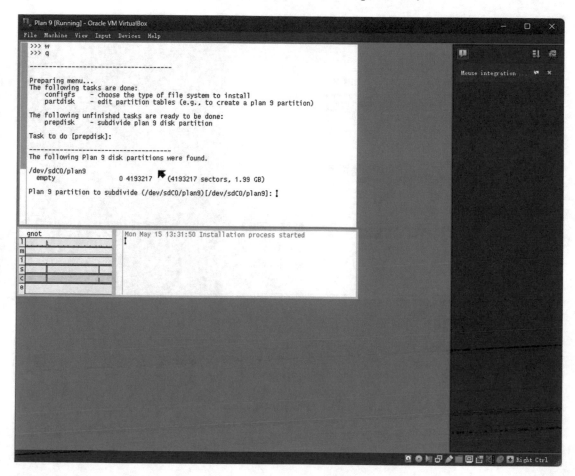

Figure 7-18. *Default for prepdisk*

d. Choose w and q to write the disk partition (see Figure 7-19).

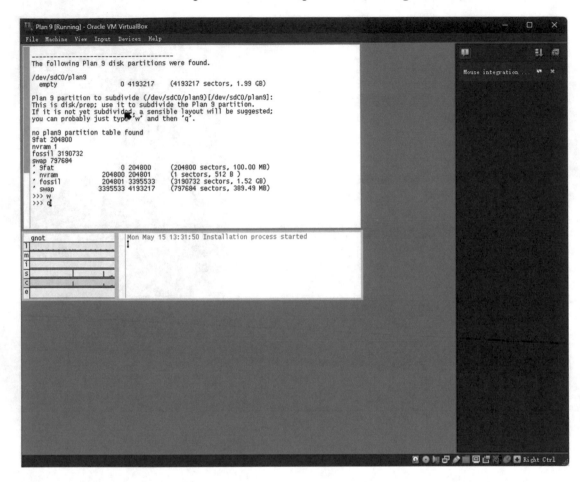

Figure 7-19. *Write the disk partition*

10.   Format the disk (see Figure 7-20).

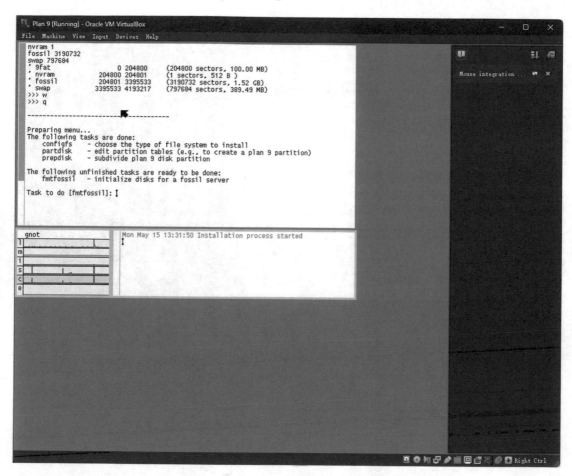

Figure 7-20. *Format the disk*

11.   Mount the filesystem. Use the defaults, as shown in Figure 7-21.

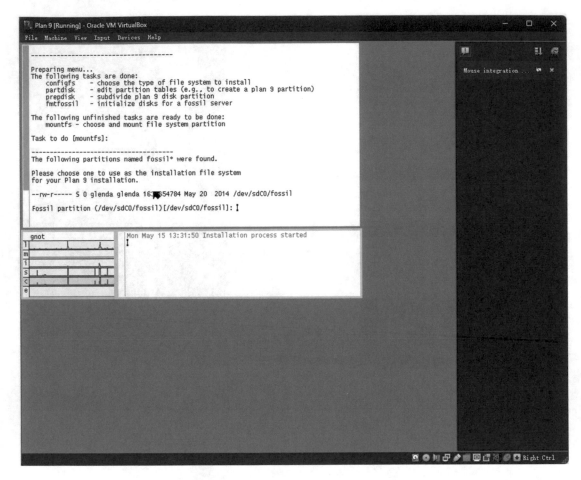

Figure 7-21. *Mounting the filesystem*

12.   Install the distribution from the local media (see Figure 7-22).

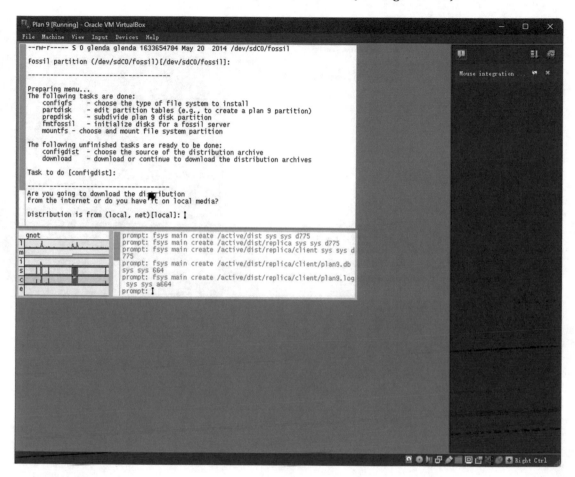

Figure 7-22. *Install from the local distribution*

13.   Mount the local ISO distribution (see Figure 7-23).

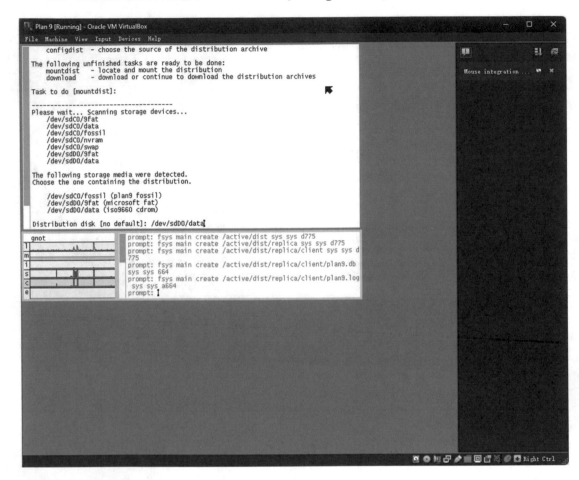

Figure 7-23. *Mount the local ISO*

14.   The root / is the distribution. There is no need to browse (see
       Figure 7-24).

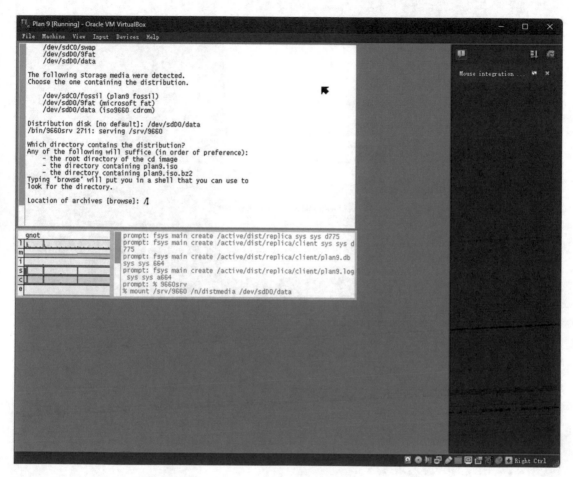

Figure 7-24. *Location of archives at the root FS*

15.   Start copying the OS files with `copydist` (see Figure 7-25).

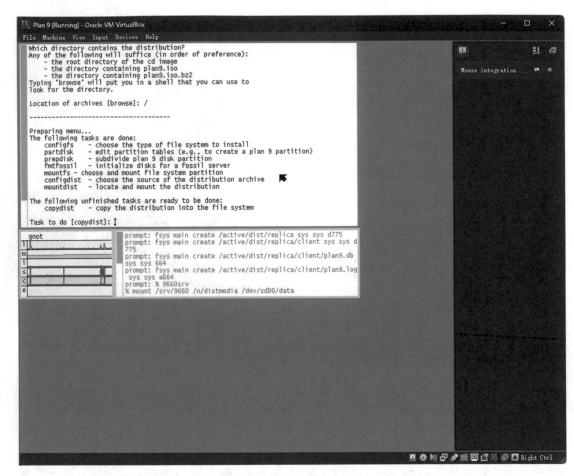

Figure 7-25. *Copying the OS*

16.   Installing the OS. It's going to take a while. Go for a coffee break
        (see Figure 7-26).

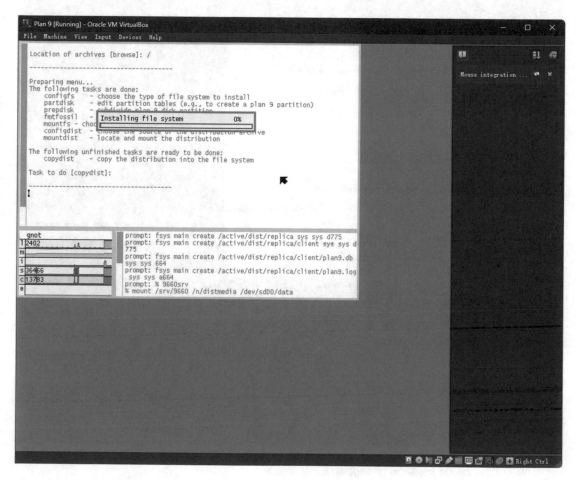

Figure 7-26. *Coffee break*

17. Boot Plan 9 by default (see Figure 7-27).

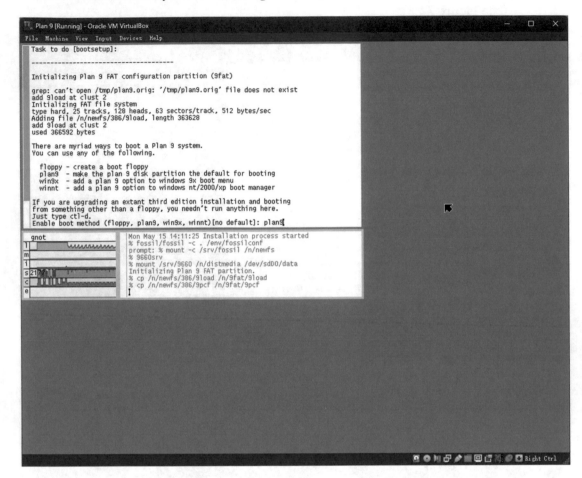

Figure 7-27. *Boot plan 9 by default*

18.   Finish the installation (see Figure 7-28).

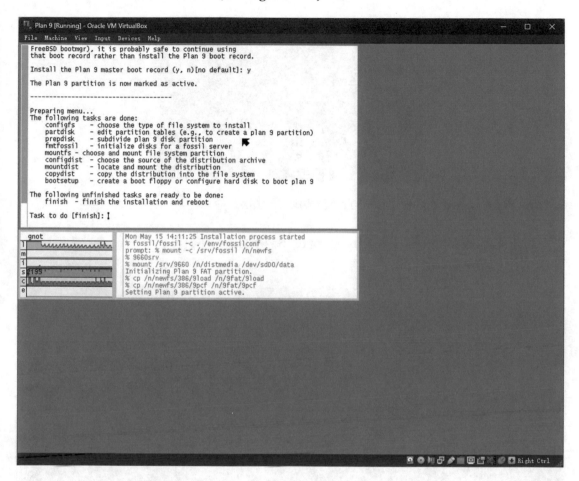

Figure 7-28. *Finish the installation*

19.   Shut down the VM (see Figure 7-29).

Figure 7-29. *Shut down the VM after installation*

20.   Unmount the ISO disk by going to the Storage area (see Figure 7-30).

Figure 7-30. *Unmount the installation disk*

21. Restart the VM.

22. Access Plan 9:

 a. After the virtual machine restarts, boot the local filesystem by pressing Enter, and then use glenda to log in (see Figure 7-31).

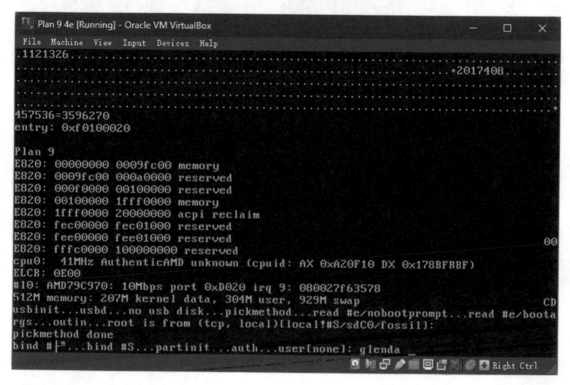

Figure 7-31. *Use glenda to log in to Plan 9*

b. You are welcomed to Plan 9 with the Rio window system. The
    Terminal and the ACME editor are running by default (see
    Figure 7-32).

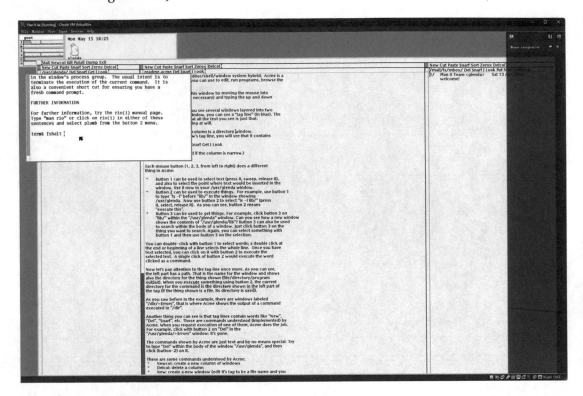

Figure 7-32. *Plan 9 VM is ready!*

23. Shut down the system by typing `fshalt` in the terminal window (see Figure 7-33).

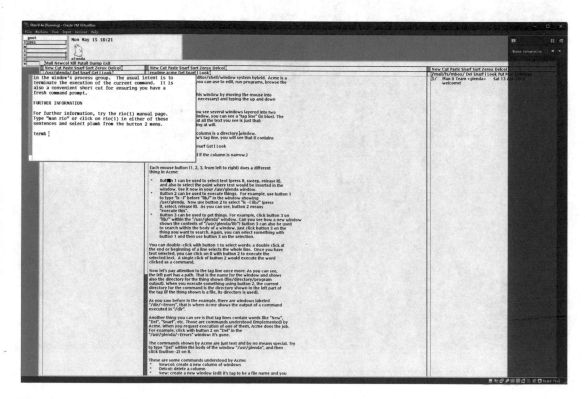

Figure 7-33. *Shutting down the VM*

a. It's safe to shut down the VM (see Figure 7-34).

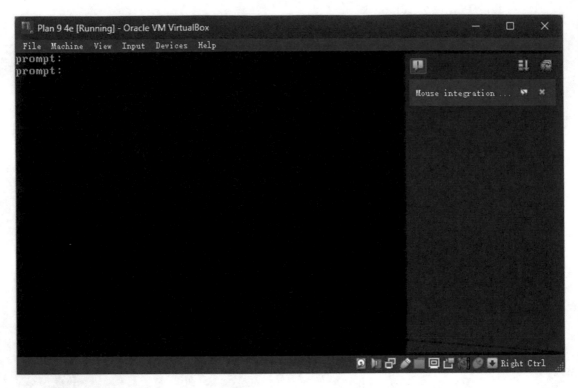

Figure 7-34. *Plan 9 is shut down*

Perhaps, on your way home, someone will pass you in the dark, and you will never know it... for they will be from outer space.

—Plan 9 from outer space

Index

R

S

T, U

V, W, X, Y, Z

Printed in the United States
by Baker & Taylor Publisher Services